"This is essential reading for those of us who care deeply about providing culturally relevant sex therapy to marginalized peoples. The collection of expert authors offer personal and professional reflections that give the reader insight, interventions and a road map for working with specific populations. If you are ready to incorporate fresh ideas into your therapy practice, an educator looking for a handy resource, or a graduate student looking for more nuance than traditional sexuality theory, this is the book you've been waiting for."

—**Juan Camarena,** *PhD, LMFT, LPCC; certified sex therapist and lecturer, San Diego State University, USA*

"What's captivating about this clinical compendium put together by BIPOC therapists is that it provides nuanced and focused therapeutic interventions that promotes healing and empowerment for people who have been traditionally marginalized or underserved. The case studies in each chapter provide excellent examples for how to effectively engage clients and their individual and systemic challenges that impact growth, happiness, and healthy sexual functioning. This is a must read for all mental and relational health professionals."

—**Monique S. Howard,** *Ed.D; executive director, Women Organized Against Rape (WOAR), Philadelphia, USA*

AN INTERSECTIONAL APPROACH TO SEX THERAPY

When a Black, Indigenous, or racialized individual or relationship works with a sex therapist, a host of cultural circumstances can contribute to intimacy discord and sexual dysfunction. This collection brings together clinicians and educators who share their approaches, bridging sex therapy with a client's relationship to their racial, cultural, and ethnic identity.

This essential book aims to enhance therapists' supervisory practices and clinical treatments when working with culturally diverse and marginalized populations, fostering greater understanding and awareness. Innovative tools that integrate the impacts of acculturation, minority status, intersectionality, and minority stress are discussed, with case studies, demonstrations, and critical questions included.

This collection is a necessary read for anyone who is training to be or who is an established sex therapist, marriage and family therapist, relationship counselor, or sexuality educator and consultant.

Reece M. Malone is a sexologist, sex therapist and sexuality educator. He is an associate professor at Antioch University Seattle and is a certified sexuality educator supervisor through the American Association of Sexuality Educators, Counselors and Therapists.

Marla Renee Stewart is a sexologist, sex coach, and educator at Velvet Lips. She is also a co-founder of the Sex Down South Conference, Faculty in the Department of Interdisciplinary Studies at Clayton State University, and co-wrote *The Ultimate Guide to Seduction and Foreplay.*

Mariotta Gary-Smith is a cultural sexologist and community-based sexuality educator. She's a Co-Foundress of the Women of Color Sexual Health Network and is a certified sexuality educator through the American Association of Sexuality Educators, Counselors, and Therapists.

James C. Wadley is a professor and chair of the Counseling and Human Services Master of Human Services department at Lincoln University. He is the founder and principal of the Association of Black Sexologists and Clinicians.

AN INTERSECTIONAL APPROACH TO SEX THERAPY

Centering the Lives of Black, Indigenous, Racialized, and People of Color

Edited by
Reece M. Malone, Marla Renee Stewart,
Mariotta Gary-Smith, and James C. Wadley

NEW YORK AND LONDON

Cover image: © Getty Images

First published 2022
by Routledge
605 Third Avenue, New York, NY 10158

and by Routledge
2 Park Square, Milton Park, Abingdon, Oxon, OX14 4RN

Routledge is an imprint of the Taylor & Francis Group, an informa business

Library of Congress Cataloging-in-Publication Data
A catalog record for this title has been requested

ISBN: 978-0-367-47194-1 (hbk)
ISBN: 978-0-367-47195-8 (pbk)
ISBN: 978-1-003-03406-3 (ebk)

DOI: 10.4324/9781003034063

Typeset in Minion
by Apex CoVantage, LLC

CONTENTS

ACKNOWLEDGEMENTS

Reece M. Malone: I wish to acknowledge several individuals who have provided encouragement, advice, and unwavering support that helped to bring forward this important contribution, specifically Linda Weiner, Katheryn Hall, Jessica O'Reilly, Corine Mason, Joe Kort, and Alycia Mann. I want to especially thank James C. Wadley for being my pillar throughout this project; and finally, my husband Daryl who after all these years stood by and anchored me throughout my professional development.

Mariotta Gary-Smith: I would like to acknowledge and appreciate my beloved community that was a well of support and encouragement. I'd like to thank Dr. Reece Malone for honoring me with this opportunity, to Dr. James Wadley, and Marla Renee Stewart for being unknown mentors to and for me and my passion work, to my mother Sharon Gary-Smith for her lifetime of agitation, and to Trina Scott, Cindy Lee Alves, and Triniece Rozier-Sheidun for loving me through this new experience.

Marla Renee Stewart: I wish to acknowledge my many clients who have helped me solidify my sexual strategy curriculum; Dr. Reece Malone who brought me on and provided inspiration and patience; Angelique Burke whom I admire and have learned so much in the realms of intersectional sex therapy; my parents, Ursula and Rodney Whitfield who have always supported me; my wife and child, Esther and Malakhi, who adore me, but keep me humbled and loved.

James Wadley: I wish to acknowledge Drs. Robert Staples and Reginald Jones. Dr. Staples was one of the pioneers who researched sexual health issues among persons of African descent. Dr. Reginald Jones edited the book *Black Psychology* which was influential to me on my journey to becoming a Black mental health practitioner and sexuality therapist/researcher. Finally, I would like to acknowledge my colleagues at Lincoln University and Council for Relationships (Philadelphia, USA).

EDITORS

Reece Malone

Dr. Reece Malone (he/him/siya) is a sex therapist, sexuality educator, and program and policy consultant based out of Winnipeg, Manitoba, Canada. He is an international trainer and speaker on diversity, equity, and inclusion specializing in human sexuality and is a certified sexuality educator supervisor through the American Association of Sexuality Educators, Counselors, and Therapists. He holds certifications in sexology and sex therapy and is an adjunct professor at Antioch University Seattle, Couples and Family Therapy Department. He maintains a private practice that centers the needs of marginalized populations while treating sexual health issues and concerns for individuals, couples, and diverse families.

Marla Renee Stewart

Marla Renee Stewart (she/her) is a sexologist and a sex coach who runs her own sexuality education company, Velvet Lips. She is also a co-founder of the Sex Down South Conference and faculty in the Department of Interdisciplinary Studies at Clayton State University. She has studied human sexuality for more than 20 years and has been featured on a variety of media outlets, including Netflix's "Trigger Warning with Killer Mike" and VH1's "Love & HipHop Atlanta." She co-wrote her first book, *The Ultimate Guide to Seduction & Foreplay* with Dr. Jessica O'Reilly, which debuted in April 2020. She is an innovator in the Sexual Liberation Movement and works towards destigmatizing sex, love, and seduction in her communities.

Mariotta Gary-Smith

Mariotta Gary-Smith (she/they) is a third-generation social justice agitator from the Pacific Northwest and alum of the Center of Excellence for Sexual

Health Scholars Fellowship Program at Morehouse School of Medicine, the Rollins School of Public Health and Agnes Scott College, respectively. She co-founded the Women of Color Sexual Health Network and is a certified sexuality educator through the American Association of Sexuality Educators, Counselors, and Therapists.

Mariotta has built a reputation for thoughtful, challenging, and honest exchanges about racial justice and equity, sexuality/sex education and social critique, and the impact of white supremacy/white nationalism on Black sexuality, reproductive rights/justice and liberation. She provides collaborative consultation with various organizations about racial justice in sexuality education, and she remains committed to curating spaces that support clear and accountable learning on the intersections of Black people, social justice, sexual health, health equity, and "actionable agitation."

James C. Wadley
Dr. James C. Wadley (he/him/his) is Professor and Chair of the Counseling and Human Services Master of Human Services department at Lincoln University and Director of the Sex Therapy program at Council for Relationships in Philadelphia. As a scholar-practitioner, he is a licensed professional counselor and maintains a private practice in the states of Pennsylvania and New Jersey. He is the founding editor of the scholarly, interdisciplinary journal, the *Journal of Black Sexuality and Relationships* (University of Nebraska Press). He is also the founder and principal of the Association of Black Sexologists and Clinicians, and his professional background in human sexuality education, educational leadership, and program development has enabled him to galvanize scholars and practitioners in the field of sexology around the world.

CONTRIBUTORS

Jaxx Alutalica
Jaxx Alutalica (they/them) is a transgender writer, researcher, educator, healer, and a connoisseur of pleasure's many expressions. Jaxx is a certified sex therapist and a licensed marriage and family therapist based out of San Francisco, CA, where they are currently completing their PhD in human sexuality from the California Institute for Integral Studies. Their research focus surrounds transgender folx practices of BDSM and their erotic embodiment of gender euphoria. Jaxx's approach to sexuality centers the dynamic experience of the body and becoming wholly present in desire while deepening understanding of the hows and whys behind intimacy and pleasure.

Arva Bensaheb
Dr. Arva Bensaheb is a clinical psychologist and sex therapist who works with individuals and couples struggling with difficulties surrounding sexuality, relationships, sexual dysfunction, and also mood disorders. She got her PhD in clinical psychology from the University of Nevada Las Vegas and currently practices in NYC. Her practice is inclusive, and she uses a combination of goal-oriented, existential, and dynamic modalities to address her clients' concerns.

De-Andrea Blaylock-Johnson
De-Andrea Blaylock-Johnson is licensed in the state of Missouri as a clinical social worker and LCSW supervisor and has worked in the field of behavioral health since 2004. She sees herself as a catalyst for positive change, serving as a collaborator and co-facilitator in healing and enjoys the journey

of working with her clients. As the owner of Sankofa Sex Therapy, LLC, she works with individuals and those in all types of relationships and also provides therapy from a Christian perspective when requested. She conducts workshops about sexuality and intimacy and is a member of the Leadership Collective of the Women of Color Sexual Health Network. She also serves as a facilitator with Theater of War Productions, completing two off-Broadway runs of the critically-acclaimed *Antigone in Ferguson*. In addition to being #YourFavoriteSexTherapist, she is a hunter of fabulous earrings and a baby sneakerhead.

Lexx Brown-James

Dr. Lexx Brown-James (she/her/Dr.) is an Amazon best-selling author, a licensed marriage and family therapist, and an AASECT-certified sexuality educator and supervisor. As CEO of The Institute for Intimacy & Sexuality, LLC, she works to support healing in couples, families, and individuals. Helping to ensure folks build and maintain fulfilling intimate relationships is integral. As the #couplesclinician, she works to take care of the relationship between lovers as opposed to the ego of lovers. She also merges education and therapy using her skillset training professionals within and outside of human sexuality.

Ericka Burns

Ericka Burns is a sex educator and the founder of Sacramento Peers on Prevention (SacPOP), a non-profit organization dedicated to educating youth about sexual health and reproductive justice. SacPOP utilizes social media, workshops, and community events to educate and empower youth and young adults to be advocates for their health as well as their community. As a doctoral candidate at the California Institute of Integral Studies, her goal is to incorporate the ways Black queer and non-queer identifying people use language to identify their sexuality through media analysis and capturing sexual histories.

Leyla Gulcur

Leyla Gulcur is a multicultural psychologist with a focus on culture, sexuality, and relationships. In addition to her research and clinical practice, she has taught psychology for over two decades as an adjunct associate professor at New York University. Dr. Gulcur has also worked for organizations involved in sexual health and rights worldwide, particularly in Asia and the Middle East. She co-founded the Turkish NGO Women for Women's Human Rights and has also headed research departments at organizations in New York City, conducting research on programs serving individuals with co-occurring mental health disorders and histories of homelessness.

Having lived or worked in over 25 countries spanning the Middle East, South Asia, North America, and Europe, Dr. Gulcur is multilingual and works with people who are often bicultural, multicultural, or expats. She is allied with LGBTQIA+ individuals and those in the poly, kink, and open relationship communities.

Laverne Gervais

Laverne Gervais (she/her) is a sexual health educator, living and working in Winnipeg, Manitoba, Canada. She has worked in the areas of sexual exploitation and HIV in Indigenous health for over ten years. She is a member of N'ISH: Niin Indigenous Sexual Health exploring Indigenous sex positivity and pleasure.

Shane´ J. Gill

Shane´ J. Gill is a native of Portland, Oregon. Her interest in counseling and mental health blossomed during her undergraduate career at George Fox University as she gained exposure to multicultural counseling and social justice. A graduate of the Clinical Mental Health Counseling program of Regent University and doctoral candidate in the Counselor Education and Supervision program at Capella University, she has dedicated her career to studying the plight of Blacks as it relates to social justice, inequality, and the intersection of counseling and criminal justice as a means of intergenerational trauma that has resulted from systemic oppression and discriminatory practices. Her research interests are in re-entry and recidivism, with the desire to explore culturally relevant practices and interventions that address systemic factors that contribute to the marginalization of ethnic minorities. With nearly ten years of experience and having served in various roles, she currently chairs the Restorative Justice Committee and the Re-Entry Committee of the International Association of Addictions and Offender Counselors. She is committed to education, service, and advocacy. She currently serves as a counselor and is the owner of HER Village Foundation, LLC, a counseling practice in Douglasville, Georgia, that offers a tribe-oriented, culturally informed, and comprehensive approach to treatment.

Roger J. Kuhn

Roger J. Kuhn is an enrolled member of the Poarch Band of Creek Indians. He is a PhD candidate in human sexuality, where his community-based participatory research is focused on Two-Spirit people and Indigenous understandings of love. His work is informed from a social and sexual justice perspective. Roger considers himself a soma-cultural sex therapist. He is interested in the body and its relation to culture which helps shape, challenge, and ultimately influence our experiences. In addition to his work as a sex therapist, Roger is also a professor of American Indian Studies and

Counseling Psychology at universities in the Bay Area of California. He is a board member of the Bay Area American Indian Two-Spirits and the American Indian Cultural Center of San Francisco, CA. He currently lives in Guerneville, CA (Pomo Territory), with this husband and two dogs.

Estefanía Simich Muñoz

Estefanía Simich Muñoz is a migrant Peruvian living in Baltimore, Maryland, and is a certified sex therapist and sex therapist supervisor in training. Her work is primarily focused on migrant populations who have experienced gender violence, domestic violence, and sexual violence, and is deeply passionate and dedicated to work with her community.

Estefanía has a private practice in Baltimore City, is a clinical director of a domestic violence/sexual assault center in Maryland, and has consulted in the Netherlands with Spot46 and in Peru with PROMSEX, CHS Alternativo, and Universidad de Lima. She is also a human sexuality PhD candidate at the California Institute of Integral Studies and is currently working on a study about the sexual citizenship of Peruvian migrant women in the United States. Estefanía plans on continuing her work in gender violence in migrant populations and becoming a professor at the completion of her PhD.

Anne Mauro

Anne Mauro (she/her/hers) was born in the Pacific Northwest in the Loving Generation. She is a licensed couples and family therapist; clinical sexologist; and American Association of Sexuality Educators, Counselors, and Therapists-certified sex therapist and certified sex educator. She has earned her M.A. from Antioch University Seattle and a doctorate of human sexuality from the Institute for the Advanced Study of Human Sexuality. Her private practice, Mending Connections, in Tacoma, Washington, specializes in couples counseling and sex therapy. In addition to her private practice, Anne is currently adjunct facility at Antioch University Seattle, where she teaches her favorite subject: human sexuality.

Midori

Originally from Japan, Midori (she/her) brings a multicultural approach to discussion of BDSM. The strength of her teaching style lay in her ability to deconstruct complex matters of desire into approachable lessons with humor and humanity. Midori emerged from the sex-positive movement in San Francisco in the 1990s. In 2003, she founded Rope Dojo. In 2004, she launched ForteFemme Women's Dominance Weekend. Midori is also the co-director of Education for Kink Informed Certification, as well as Advisor for Shibari Study and Subject Expert Educator for CoralApp. Her books include *Seductive Art of Japanese Bondage*, the first English instruction book on *Shibari, and Wild Side Sex, and Silk Threads*. When she's not teaching, she creates social practice art around memory and identity.

Ruth Neustifter
Ruth Neustifter (they/them) is the academic program director for the Couple and Family Therapy Program at the University of Guelph, Ontario, Canada. As a queer white settler, they continuously strive to deepen their dedication to anti-oppressive work. Their areas of focus include sex, pleasure for all bodies, resilience during and after trauma, and queer resilience.

Jomo M. Phillips
Jomo M. Phillips (he/his) holds a master's of science in social work—marriage and family therapy specialization from the University of Louisville, Kentucky. He is a clinical fellow and a supervisor candidate in the American Association for Marriage and Family Therapy who practices and supervises on the island of Barbados. As an Afro-Barbadian, cisgender, and straight man, Jomo is interested in identity and identity work in therapy and accounting for intersectionality in the lives of both his clients and supervisees.

Judy Tsing Ting Lui
Daughter to two immigrant parents from Hong Kong, China, Judy Tsing Ting Lui (she/her) is a first-generation Chinese-Canadian born and raised in the Greater Toronto Area. Judy is a registered psychotherapist and certified Canadian counselor. She is the clinical director of Your Story Counselling Services, a private practice in Vaughan, Ontario, Canada, that provides individual, couple, family, and sex therapy both online and in-person. Alongside her diverse team of associates, Judy provides culturally adaptive and sensitive psychotherapy to a wide range of clients seeking a variety of issues (anxiety, coming out process, depression, consensual non-monogamy, relational issues, sexual anxiety, sexual intimacy, sexual pain, trauma and post-trauma). As a passionate ally to the LGBTQ2+, Judy provides low-fee and sliding-scale sessions for clients who are part of the LGBTQ2+ community in the Greater Toronto Area.

Yan Wei (Andy) Mok
Andy Mok (he/him) is a first-generation Chinese-Canadian who immigrated to Canada from China when he was one year old. He is a community and mental-health registered nurse who is currently working as an HIV and primary care nurse. As a self-identified Chinese gay man, Andy is committed to making a positive impact in the Canadian healthcare system by advocating for equitable rights and the fair treatment of marginalized groups, such

as LGBTQ+, people living with mental illness, and people living with HIV/ AIDS. Working in the community setting, Andy proactively raises public awareness of the negative impact of stigma on the health of affected individuals and communities. He engages in stigma-reduction training with the goal of becoming a nursing leader and champion to address social stigma and health inequities.

INTRODUCTION

Role of Clinicians and Educators

When individuals, couples, or polycules within a diverse relationship dynamic extend their trust to the professional capacities of a sex therapist, sexuality counselor, sexuality educator or sex coach, there is a hope or expectation that they will be guided towards a path of healing, understanding, and awareness that facilitate a pathway to better intimate sex life. This hope emerges from a history of unresolved sexual or relational challenges that the client(s) feel that they need professional support with.

As clinicians and educators, we hope to help resolve sexual distress; within the therapeutic process, we identify and explore unforeseen circumstances and implicit contributing factors that impact sexual function and sexual expression. In addition, we promote sexual healing and wellness by advocating for healthy relationships. By working collaboratively with our clients, the intent is to create and maintain a safer container for them to disclose unfiltered aspects of their sexuality and to provide an environment that unburdens them from the rigors of cultural and social expectations, suspicion, and judgment.

In our work with clients who are navigating emotionally, psychologically, physically and spiritually difficult situations that have impacted their sexual health and sexual relationships, there is an unspoken expectation that our awareness and therapeutic approaches include broad and social ecological insight. The unspoken expectation may be related to assumptions made about our credentials and/or expertise related to serving as sexual health practitioners. As clinicians and educators, it is a privilege to witness our clients evolve and express feelings of enlightenment, empowerment, and hope

DOI: 10.4324/9781003034063-1

and leave better equipped with practical tools and strategies that promote sexual autonomy, authenticity, and self-determination.

Representation of Racialized and People of Color in the Field of Human Sexuality

The underrepresentation of diversity is well known in the counseling and therapy fields, with white clinicians being the face of leadership within the profession. In North America, the first 19 of 20 presidents of the American Counseling Association (ACA), founded in 1952, were White. Even the Society for the Scientific Study of Sexuality (SSSS), founded in 1957, has only had one president of color out of 45. For the Society of Sex Therapy and Research (SSTAR), founded in 1975, it is unknown how many racialized people served as president. The American Association of Sexuality Educators, Counselors, and Therapists (AASECT), the largest professional association for sexuality professions, does not carry demographic information of their membership. Since its 1967 inception, and from the recollection of previous executive leadership, there have been "maybe a few" to "none that I'm aware of" racialized or people of color serving as president and/or board members.

Alongside sex therapy leadership, and among current and emerging sex therapists and sexuality counselors, there remains an underrepresentation of diversity among clinicians. Despite slightly higher numbers of representation, many sexuality educators (including community-based education researchers) are based out of non-profit organizations where employment requirements often do not include a minimum graduate or post-graduate degree. Nonetheless, a parallel trend of disproportionate white sexuality educators and clinicians remains steadfast.

The legacies of whiteness within sex therapy and sexuality education fields is unsurprising given the well-documented historic wage disparities between white and non-white people, the cultural perceptions of sex therapy, intergenerational cultural taboos on human sexuality, and lack of accessible comprehensive sexuality education at home and in school systems.

Traditional Approaches and Interventions: Contemporary Approaches to Sex Therapy

Sex therapists, counselors, and educators obtain knowledge and training on sexual dysfunctions (low desire, erectile dysfunction, rapid ejaculation, painful intercourse, anorgasmia, delayed orgasm, out-of-control, impulsive and compulsive sexual behaviors), identity matters (sex, gender, sexual orientation and gender identity), and sexual relationship issues and concerns (body autonomy, consent as practice, ethical non-monogamy, infidelity, desire discrepancies, sexual communication, sexual quality, alternative and diverse sexual lifestyles).

Traditional treatment modalities and approaches include cognitive behavioral therapy, dialectical behavioral therapy, acceptance and commitment therapy, emotionally focused therapy, narrative therapy, sensate focus therapy, sexual coaching, solutions focused therapy, and psychoeducation. These, along with other approaches, have been proven effective for many clients. These and other modalities may contain treatment formats that include timed, successive, and sequenced exercises as well as specific scripting for therapist-client processing. These modalities are evidence-based and peer-reviewed for their effectiveness as well as to determine when their use may be contraindicated.

While success rates vary depending on a host of circumstances, there has not been enough clinical consideration on whether ethno-racial identity of the clinician correlates with treatment success. Moreover, research that explores the contextual histories and intersections of race, culture and ethnicity in a client's sexual health, sexual relationships, and overall sexual satisfaction are few and far between, and they are often led by researchers who are both professional and personal stakeholders.

Do Social Inequities Impact Sexual Functioning? The Maintenance of Colonial Systems of Governance and the Regulation of Sexuality

The histories of settler colonization around the world feature the regulation of Indigenous identities as a primary form of social control. As millions of inhabitants from Western Europe took custody of foreign lands, they eventually formed the large majority of the population. Canada and the United States were founded from this colonization. Even though many Indigenous populations had been living on this land and had thrived, the European settlers determined that this land—land that was not influenced by them—was uninhabited, which made it available to them for the development of colonies. Growth and maintenance of economic opportunities to benefit European settlers were regulated by and mandated through the establishments of Acts. For example, in Canada, the Indian Act of 1876 allowed the government to control most aspects of aboriginal life regulating Indian status, land rights, resources, and education. Regulations as a form of social control also included the regulation of sexuality. By then, the assimilation and acculturation from Indigenous identity by those in both political and social power included increasingly sexually restrictive legislation, defining the right and wrong essentialist expressions of sexuality and the consequence of deviance from such legislation. The pillar of the European standard of colonial sexuality was to center sexuality as discreet, held in a private domain, heterosexual in practice, monogamous in expression, and patriarchal in its organization.

Currently, our society is shifting in many ways due to the easy access of information and integration of various ideals within the sexuality realm. Mostly because of media exposure, we are seeing new ways of developing and maintaining relationships that are located in the domain of storytelling and storytellers who are willing to expose their authentic sexual realities. The move from private domain to public has been vital in the exposure around what types of identities and relationships are acceptable depending on the authorities of the major social institutions, such as family, schooling, religion, government, and the economy. The ability to question whether certain lifestyles are valid is being challenged more than ever; with that comes the stained (and old) ideals that pervade individuals who struggle with forming new traditions as they relate to their sexual health and satisfaction. Our goal is to highlight these stories to help therapists, counselors, and educators alike to see how we can move forward in this industry and produce new thought leaders of color in sexuality studies.

Intersectionality and Minority Stress

The term *intersectionality* was coined in 1989 by Black feminist scholar Kimberlé Williams Crenshaw. Intersectionality began as an exploration of the oppression of women of color within social cultures. The term has been expanded to include other diverse social identities including sexual orientation, class, disability, ethnicity, gender, and how social stratification impacts social determinants of health (income and social status, employment and working conditions, education and literacy, childhood experiences, physical environments, social supports and coping skills, healthy behaviors and access to health services).

Centering human sexuality with an intersectional lens acknowledges and illuminates the relationship of social oppressions and discrimination on sexual health and wellness. In a culture that privileges White, cisgender, heterosexual, monogamous, and non-kinky identities, those who straddle the boundaries of what is perceived as acceptable or those who altogether transcend or reject cultural normatives of sexuality are often in a position of negotiating authentic identity versus discrimination and stigmatization.

In an era that has witnessed the resurgence of white nationalism, racialized and people of color are burdened with the realities of the compounding effects of systemic racism, the continued impact of colonization and intergenerational trauma, and social and familial pressures of assimilation. With the stressors associated with "minority" status, it is with greater urgency that sexual and sexuality health professionals recognize the intersections of sexual identity, sexual expression, and minority status as well as the interwoven intergenerational legacies of colonialism that remain an undercurrent of social control.

Minority stress is a concept developed by Ilan Meyer (2003), who purports that the prevalence of negative mental health outcomes for minority populations is due to actual or perceived experiences of external and internal factors that include the accumulation of chronic stress from general stressors, cultural biases and dominant values, and systemic and internalized stressors. While Meyer's original research referred to sexual minorities, it has been expanded to include gender minorities i.e. transgender, non-binary, agender, and genderqueer individuals, as well as those who identify as Black, racialized, and people of color.

It's important for clinicians and educators to take into account the compounding effects of colonization, intersectionality, and minority stress by recognizing where these concepts converge throughout an individual's sexual and gender identity development, where they intersect in relationship formation, and how they may interlock and influence sexual encounters and decision making. By doing so, clinicians obtain a more idiosyncratic and thorough clinical portrait that helps to avoid a myopic treatment approach while at the same time appreciating the diversity of cultural experiences in the therapeutic milieu.

Why Is This Book Important, and What Does It Offer?

This collection offers therapists, counselors, and educators nuanced and complementary approaches while working with ethno-culturally diverse individuals and relationships that converge with current sex therapy treatment models and approaches. At the forefront, we ask clinicians and educators to introspectively consider the following:

- What ethno-cultural competencies are needed in order to be better equipped while working with diverse cultures?
- What is my knowledge of colonization, systemic, and internalized racism, and intersectionality? Furthermore, have these concepts woven into the field of human sexuality? If so, how; and if not, why?
- In what ways does social oppression impact self-concept? How about interpersonal and sexual self-concept?
- How does ethnocentrism impact relationship formation and sexual expression within the relationship?
- How can ethnocentrism intentionally and unintentionally emerge within the clinician (countertransference), and what are the checks and balances to preserve the integrity of the therapeutic alliance?

Given the lack of awareness and resources within sex therapy training that critically explore the impacts of colonization, racism, intersectionality, and minority stress in sexual health and sexual relationships, this collection will serve as a major contribution to the field of sex therapy and individual, marriage, relationship therapy. The collection will help clinicians broaden their attentiveness and build their professional capacity while also providing strategies, treatment, and therapy for individuals and relationships of diverse ethno-racial cultural backgrounds. It will also offer an opportunity for sexuality educators to determine how to better develop curricula and other educational and training materials that serve the needs of their communities as well as help them be accountable to the community members they are working with, by holding space for the narratives of the clients to be centered.

Chapters will center the lives of culturally diverse individuals, couples, and relationships in sex therapy and sexuality counseling, and the innovative tools and approaches that integrate the impacts of acculturation, minority status, intersectionality, and minority stress on sexual health and dysfunction. This book is a necessary read for anyone who seeks to become or is currently an established sex therapist, marriage and family therapist, relationship counselor, or sexuality educator and consultant.

This book is divided into two sections. The first section highlights the expansion of core knowledge and application competencies for the clinician. The second section constitutes the majority of the book and consists of contributors who are sexuality therapists, sexuality counselors, and sexuality educators. It was important for the co-editing team to prioritize that the contributing clinicians themselves are racialized or people of color so they could write directly from their lived personal and/or professional experiences. Each chapter author will highlight case examples sharing the following:

- Presenting issue or dilemma
- Considerations and impacts of colonization and intersectionality on identity
- Nuanced or complementary approaches and interventions
- Any personal, professional, and ethical dilemmas
- Conclusions as well as future considerations

Due to this book's purpose and organization, we do recommend that the first section be read to provide foundational knowledge while utilizing the second section as an example of how your peers integrate social ecological approaches when working with diverse clientele. We emphasize the importance of integrating systemic sex therapy approaches that explore the client's relationship to—and impacts of—colonization, racism, intersectionality, and minority stress on sexual and gender identity, sexual expression, sexual empowerment, and sexual wellness.

Whether clients present with a primary sexual health or sexual wellness matter or whether these matters surface through clinical assessment or later in therapy, our intention is to encourage and support all seasoned and new clinicians and educators to integrate an anti-oppression and social ecological lens as a core professional capacity. Especially while working with Black, Indigenous, racialized, and people of color, clinicians and educators cannot ignore the effects of intersectionality and systemic oppression on identity development, sexuality and sexual self-concept, sexual functioning, and intimacy and sexual relationship dynamics.

References

Crenshaw, K. W. (1989). Demarginalizing the intersection of race and sex: A Black feminist critique of antidiscrimination doctrine, feminist theory and antiracist politics. *University of Chicago Legal Forum, 1989,* 139–167.

Meyer, I. H. (2003). Prejudice, social stress, and mental health in lesbian, gay and bisexual populations: Conceptual issues and research evidence. *Psychological Bulletin, 129,* 674–697. doi: 10.1037/0033-2909.129.5.674.

1

INTERSECTIONAL AWARENESS IN TRAINING AND SUPERVISION

Jomo M. Phillips and Ruth Neustifter

Key Terms

There are several key terms we will utilize in exploring aspects of our clinical training and supervision processes; we begin this chapter by explaining these terms. These terms include *intersectionality, minority stress, clinical supervision, trans* and *cis*, and *sexuality*.

- The term *intersectionality* was first coined by legal scholar Kimberlé Crenshaw. Crenshaw (1989), in describing the experience of Black women who faced the legal system, noted that there was a "multidimensionality" in these women's experiences (p. 139). Crenshaw (1989) also argued that intersectionality challenges the idea that women of color are affected by single issues. Rather they are oppressed by multiple social forces. The term *intersectionality* has been widely appropriated by scholars concerned about various forms of oppression (Cho, Crenshaw, & McCall, 2013). Dhamoon (2011) points out that intersectionality is a "framework of analysis that is widely applicable to various relations of marginality and privilege" (p. 1).
- *Minority stress* accounts for the experiences of sexual minorities in a hetero supremacist (Kilhefner, 2017) culture and how the chronicity of stress, related to discrimination, ultimately affects our health status (Meyer, 1995).
- *Clinical supervision* refers to "the process of evaluating, training, and providing oversight to trainees using relational or systemic approaches for the purpose of helping them attain systemic clinical skills" (American Association for Marriage & Family Therapy, 2019, p. 8).

DOI: 10.4324/9781003034063-2

- *Trans* and *cis* are terms used to describe gender identities. *Cis*, in terms of gender, refers to a congruence between gender assignment at birth and individual identity (Schilt & Westbrook, 2009). In other words, a cis person may be born with a vagina and clitoris, and know they are a woman, while a trans person "lives a social gender that is not the gender [sic] they were assigned at birth" (Schilt & Westbrook, 2009, p. 441); so that person's internal sense of self and gender differs from the assumptions made at birth. They may or may not identify on a gender binary, and they may or may not pursue medical options.
- *Sexuality* is a broad term that has many possible definitions. Because of the variety of ways it can be defined, it can quickly become confusing. *Sexuality* can refer to the people, relationships, and activities that people are (or are not) erotically or romantically attracted to. It can also be used to talk about erotic behaviors, keeping in mind that what is erotic differs from person to person. However, none of these are innate phenomena that are separate from social influences. In other words a great deal about sexuality, no matter how you define it, is impacted by how, where, and when we live. Elements that may be largely biological and less social, like the genders to which we are attracted, are still impacted by political forces and other systemic considerations. Being able to recognize and express aspects of sexuality is a social complexity, for example.

Background

Couple and family therapy (CFT) is practiced across the globe, and the history of the profession reveals that it has developed across several continents and countries (Kaslow, 2000; Mason & Shuda, 1999; Retzlaff, 2013; Relvas, Alarcão, & Pereira, 2013; Sim, 2012; Stratton & Lask, 2013). Unfortunately, CFT as a profession in North America has traditionally been White and homogenous. As McGoldrick (2001) has noted, "The time is long overdue for us to become uncomfortable with the impact of white privilege on the economics of our field and our society and on the well being of the families we serve" (p. 17). CFT, in North America, has also been critiqued for its exclusion of LGBTQ+ people and its failure to systematically address heterosexism (Long, 1996; Long & Lindsey, 2004; Long & Serovich, 2003).

A key development tool for CFT professionals is clinical supervision; while there have been several explorations of clinical supervision across cultural differences (Killian, 2001; Weiling & Marshal, 1999; Wieling & Rastogi, 2003), there has not been a huge amount of exploration of clinical supervision across countries, much less supervision across the North-South global divide (Seponski & Jordan, 2018). A published exploration of supervision across the North-South divide that privileges intersections that include sex and gender is completely absent.

The authors of this chapter are both couple and family therapists (CFTs). Jomo Phillips is a straight, cisgender, Afro-Caribbean father. He lives and works in Barbados, an island in the Caribbean and part of the Global South, where he is in the process of becoming the first marriage and family therapy supervisor on the island to have been approved by the American Association for Marriage and Family Therapy (AAMFT). The AAMFT is currently the largest international professional association for the field of CFT (Nichols, 2004), and as a result it can be argued that it has an exaggerated influence on CFT and its development. Currently, Jomo's supervision of therapists in training and other mental health and outreach workers takes place within a variety of contexts, systems, and backgrounds that blend together to require a keen awareness of intersectional considerations.

Jomo and Ruth (Ruthie) Neustifer first met during their Masters of Social Work—Marriage and Family Therapy training program in Louisville, Kentucky, an area with a culture unfamiliar to both of them. Had Ruthie never met Jomo, Ruthie would never have decided to pursue their PhD. Ruthie is a sex- and gender-queer (they/them) White settler and Canadian immigrant living in a multi-partner family and working as a university professor with focuses on relational therapy, trauma, resilience, and sexual pleasure across diverse genders and sexualities.

Both Jomo and Ruthie, in their work and supervision of therapists in training, have privileged an inclusion of sex including sexual desire, pleasure, and identity. While the AAMFT (2004) has listed human sexuality as a necessary competence in the clinical diagnosis and assessment process, it is important to note that many therapists receive little training related to sex (Timm, 2009). Research indicates that of the human sexuality-related training that CFTs specifically receive while in training, it is often a one-off course from faculty who might not be specifically trained in human sexuality and marginalized issues related to sexual health (Zamboni & Zaid, 2017). In fact, personally, Jomo and Ruthie can remember very little related to sexuality in their CFT-related training; it was almost like there was a divorce of the carnal and pleasurable from the professional. Ruthie vividly recalls stepping in to unofficially co-teach the few opportunities for official sex and gender training that they received in their doctoral studies, as their instructors were uncomfortable and often poorly informed. Instead, they contracted with a different professor to receive additional training on the side, for a fee. Jomo's experience living and training therapists in Barbados, part of the larger Commonwealth Caribbean, is that the community is characterized by hetero supremacy (Kilhefner, 2017), reflected in laws that criminalize sodomy (Human Rights Watch, 2017; Itaborahy & Zhu, 2014), widespread negative public views of sexual minorities (Beck et al., 2017), and the real risk that LGBTQ+ people will experience discrimination, violence, and abuse (Human Rights Watch, 2017).

Over the last three years, Ruthie and Jomo have met regularly online for supervision-of-supervision consultations; in this chapter we collaborate to explore and share aspects of this clinical training and supervision across countries, cultures, ethnicities, sexualities, genders, and more. Using a systemic approach, we explore our own experiences as therapists and supervisors, as well as our relationships as supervisor-in-training and supervisor-of-supervision. The themes we explore specifically focus on intersectionality, minority stress, negotiating power imbalances, and best practices within clinical supervision, therapy for sexual issues, and sexuality education. As authors, we initially struggled with how to write about our experiences. We settled upon interviewing each other about the clinical training and supervision process that we have embarked upon together on over the last three years. We recognized the dialogical process inherent in interviewing each other and the way this dialogical process hopefully contributed to a rich description of both our social lives and personal narratives (Tanggaard, 2009).

Navigating Our Work Together Across Different Intersectional Identities

Jomo: Ruthie, I do want to talk about a case that one of my supervisees has brought to me. It involves one of her female clients who is in a heterosexual relationship and who is currently quite economically vulnerable. She has experienced several incidents of violence from her partner in the past; she wants to leave the relationship, but right now she has to stay put because she is not working and she has nowhere to go. She has talked about how threatened she often feels; this includes when she and her partner are sexually intimate. My supervisee's dilemma is how does she talk to this woman about trying to safeguard herself, including in the most intimate of moments when she is having sex with her partner. This is something that my supervisee has not experienced: talking to a woman about keeping safe when she is, in a way, completely exposed.

Ruthie: I'm so glad that she brought this up to her therapist, that the therapist brought it up to you, and you and I are now able to talk about it together. This takes a lot of courage, risk, self-awareness, and dedication to discuss at each of those times. Has the client or therapist brought up anything in specific that they hope we discuss, so we can make sure to do that and return our thoughts to them in a useful way? First off, I want to make sure that everyone is currently safe and ask about how safety has been assessed, to the best of your knowledge. I heard you saying that it is harmful to stay and would be harmful in different ways if she stayed. These things are so complex and hard! How is the therapist handling this, and how are you doing?

Jomo: I am concerned about the client. The therapist is cautious; she is aware of the client's vulnerability, and she is concerned about her client being safe and providing her with support as she makes choices in terms of the future of her relationship. We did discuss how my supervisee, as a woman, could create a sense of safety in the therapy room.

Ruthie: For this conversation I'm going to say *us* and *our*, even though I'm not a woman, because I've been raised as one and am usually mistaken for one, so some of the social contexts around gender might have limited similarities. This stuff is so hard for us to balance. I wish it were as easy, as I used to think it should be: if he's bad news, just leave as soon as you're safely able. Finances, families, fear, love, good times shared, religious commitments, and more are part of the equation in such big ways. Have there been any conversations about proactively acknowledging risks in order to minimize them? When I say that, I am thinking about research and personal stories that talk about how people who date sexually violent men sometimes use a variety of techniques to try to regulate and calm their violent partners, both when things are already calm and when they are escalating. This shouldn't be her job, but it may be a necessary safety strategy if leaving is not on the table (which we should also talk about). In what kinds of ways is she already doing this, sexually and otherwise?

Jomo: That is a very good question. No we haven't discussed how she could engage in this de-escalation process; that would be a useful discussion though, since so many of the clients my supervisees consult with are women who are confronting violence—particularly in a community where sometimes there is not a lot of protection for these women.

Ruthie: Sometimes it can reduce some risks to initiate less destructive "sex" acts. This might look like initiating oral or manual sex to avoid other penetrative types of sex, for example. Lots of people who date men use these tactics without even realizing it, and others are very aware. Either way, it can make it especially hard to ask for support and help because, on one hand, they initiated it, and yet they also didn't want it. Of course, these are aren't sex things, they're rape acts because the survivor doesn't want them, or doesn't want them in the ways and times that they sometimes happen. But she has been describing this as sex, so I'll both recognize that it is non-consensual and that this is the wording she wants to use for now. Has this language been discussed yet in session? Sometimes calling things "rape" is hurtful in session, even if it is true. There are other options like "forced" or "unwanted sex," a "bad night/date," and so on. What role does authentically consensual sex and unwanted sex (rape) play in her life and in their relationship? What role does pleasure? It's possible that both are existing within the same relationship. Who else knows, and how do they feel and respond when she tells them or they find out?

Jomo: The language she has used is "He is making me do things that I don't want to do;" she has never articulated her experience as rape, and I have been cautioning my supervisees to use language their clients use, even if sometimes it is language that can make them feel personally uncomfortable, especially when clients talk about sex and sexual intimacy. I am aware that different groups of people, including various groups on the island, have different words they use when they talk about sex. You have asked some really good questions in relation to the role of sex and sexual pleasure in her life, particularly consensual versus coercive. We are sexual beings, and even exploring the role of sex and pleasure in our lives can hopefully move people in an agentive direction with regards to what they might want in the future. As a man, I will be honest, I never gave much thought to the fact that women might need to use strategies to engage men in less destructive sex, and this could be a potential resource for my supervisee's client. I guess my lack of thought about this reflects my own intersectionality.

Ruthie: Wow, yes. That's all incredibly important to be considering in this situation; thank you for taking the time to explain it to me. How much of this is being discussed between you and the therapist, and between her and the client? Is this seen as just the way things everywhere are versus as something that is specific to the time, place, and context of their lives? I hear you saying that, where you live, there may be fewer sources of social and resource support at the community level, at least to support leaving or finding ways to make him stop. While there is a shortage of resources and support where I am, too, it sounds like our situations are also different from each other. Thank you for that perspective. Would it help to brainstorm a potential list of questions to discuss at all of the systemic levels here: you/me, you/therapist, and therapist/client?

- **Jomo:** How does the way we are currently having this conversation in supervision reflect some of the struggles you might be experiencing having these conversations with your client? How might those same struggles be reflective of the larger struggles we have in the Caribbean talking about sexual pleasure, consensual, and non-consensual sex?
- **Ruthie:** What would a realistic best-case balance be between risks, harms, joys, and values? How does it differ from now, the worst realistic possibilities, and the best but probably unrealistic possibilities?
- **Jomo:** What types of language would you want us to use, now that we are having this conversation about various types of sexual interaction and sexual pleasure to help inform this current discussion about consensual and non-consensual sex?

- **Ruthie:** What are our personal ideas of what it means to be a woman, a partner, a mother, a lover in our own lives? What do we navigate to avoid harm/risk, and what do we navigate to increase pleasure, connection, and intimacy? Jomo, for you that will probably involve some listening and imagining, but you'll also have unique perspectives that are less tainted by cultural silencing of femininity.
- **Jomo:** What are some of our differences as we talk about these things, and how do these differences, maybe coming from the multiple overlapping identities, influence or shape this current conversation? What ways would you want us to take account for these identities as we talk about sex and sexual pleasure?
- **Ruthie:** How do/can we find ways to hold onto our internal senses of selves (our core identities and values) so that we don't forget who we are in the face of oppressions and violence? In what ways are already good at this, and in what ways might we benefit from added skills and support? What would those skills and support look like?
- **Jomo:** What do sources of support for navigating harmful relationships, both socially and for needed resources, look like in each of our lives? Are there sources that could be further developed or explored? Are there sources to avoid?

What does it take to become a relational therapist, and then a supervisor? For the two of us it was, and still is, an ongoing challenge to be trained and to offer training within a field that was not founded with either of us in mind. However, just as our demographics differ, so have our experiences of oppression and privilege. In order to explore our experiences, we invited each other to journal our answers to questions that we each created for the other. We then read each other's answers and worked together to craft this chapter based on what we discovered about ourselves and each other through this exercise.

Jomo noted that we both trained together in the same cohort within the same program, one that combined both social work and family therapy training. For both of us, this program offered a unique opportunity to look at psychotherapy from two very different lenses. Because social work has a long tradition of highlighting and addressing issues related to social justice and social suffering, it became a way for both of us to find support in our disenchantment with CFT. Jomo noted that his introduction to family therapy began with learning canon, traditional family therapy theory—something that bothered him then and still bothers him today. The traditional family therapy theory, theories like structural and Bowenian family therapy, premised their assumptions on models of family that were white, nuclear, patriarchal, heterosexual, and monogamous. Families in the community where Jomo lives are usually Afro-Barbadian, multi-generational, and matriarchal. Ruthie quickly recognized that these families were not included in the foundations of the field either, except perhaps as the image of a troubled client bound for disaster. Being sex-queer, gender-queer, and polyamorous meant that few of the techniques could be used with members of their own cultural communities without some significant revisions for which there was little guidance. Additionally, it seemed that Ruthie would have to choose between keeping their queer and non-monogamous collectivist "fictive kin" (an offensive term at best) and social circles versus serving them as a therapist, due to the stringent individualistic expectations around professionalism and ethics. Jomo faced a similar concern around dual roles, being based in a smaller community that thrives more collectively than the founders of field ever seemed to live. For Jomo, clients often prefer to already know their therapists. For Ruthie, it is almost impossible to not run into queer clients in the limited queer-focused spaces that do exist. For both of us, the more social justice-oriented family therapy models grounded in social constructionism and postmodernism were obtuse and wordy. Using those techniques as they were presented in our textbooks would have meant failing to connect with many clients who shared our own backgrounds. Both of us wanted to serve our own home communities, and to speak to most members of our home communities in that way would have been taken as offensive, elitist, and ultimately harmful and ineffective.

At the same time, we both graduated with the goal of claiming CFT as our home field. Some of our educators supported our critical thinking in essential ways. We both wanted to bring something better to the field and to also bring the potential we saw in the better parts of the field to our own home communities. We continue to face the task of unlearning and adapting our training in order to better serve and advocate for our "diverse" communities and others. Part of that unlearning and adapting has come from working with each other.

Insights and Guiding Principles

Comparing and contrasting our experiences is a daunting idea. Ruthie knows that it is undeniable that they benefit from the single most powerful privilege they have ever witnessed: being white. At the same time, Ruthie is also aware that there is no country in the world where they could experience being surrounded by others who share their minority statuses or consistently govern in ways that respect their queerness and family structure. All the same, their whiteness ensures that it is a privileged experience of being a sex, gender, and familial minority. Jomo recognizes that his experience is very influenced by his identity as a Black man who has experienced discrimination in white spaces but who in his home territory has some more privilege being male, middle class, educated, and having power as a clinical supervisor. Together, we recognized a list of guiding principles and insights that have been the underpinnings of our work together:

- We each hold unique areas of expertise, academically and through life experience. We humbly recognize each other's areas of expertise, especially through life experience. What we think we know from purely academic learning takes a distant backseat to what the other knows through life experience and areas in which experience is intertwined with formal education. We work together to reject the allure of unfounded certainty with each other.
- Supervision must be approached as a collaboration with the goal of liberation and healing. It is a process of mutual collaboration, and never one-directional teaching and assessment. We are honest, kind, gentle, generous, and direct in helping each other learn.
- Ongoing and overt exploration and acknowledgement of our differences is vital.
- We trust each other to honor each other. Errors and offenses are unintentional and can be addressed promptly, directly, and lovingly without shame, anger, or self-protection.
- We value healthy, nonviolent relationships of all types—however they happen. That means valuing collectivist thinking and resisting individualistic ideals at the expense of interpersonal well-being. That's why we decided to stick with this field instead of to opt for more individualistic approaches to psychotherapy.
- The most widely taught approaches to family therapy are harmful to the communities we are closest to, if we do not constantly question, critique, resist, and improve them in our own work with each other and our clients and supervisees.
- White supremacy has to be acknowledged, particularly for the part it has played in developing family therapy theory and practices. As we start to acknowledge its influence, we begin to recognize what experiences those theories and practices actually de-center. We must then work to return those experiences in relation to significance and importance.
- We are not just in this to nurture healing and connection. We are also in it to actively resist the immense potential for oppression that was an essential (and insidiously unrecognized) to the founding and growth of our field.
- While Ruthie and Jomo are both doing important work, Jomo's professional role in his country must be supported as a priority. Ruthie's career aspirations are important, but they also will continue to benefit greatly from White colonist privilege. Whenever there is a need to prioritize benefiting one of us over the other, the decision is clear.

Therapeutic and Educative Approach

Ruthie is most strongly influenced by the underpinnings of narrative therapy, which was taught to them primarily through the work of Michael White and David Epston and the generations of therapists who they trained to be trainers of others. The history of narrative therapy is as problematic as any other mainstream family therapy model, and perhaps worse than some when proponents of narrative claim that it is less problematic. Appropriation is rampant, and recognized founders of the field are mostly white cis-men who did not appear to be publicly queer. The language used in some prominently narrative training is frequently so complex and convoluted as to be inaccessible to practitioners, and thus it is inaccessible when repeated to clients through various techniques. At the same time, Ruthie feels energized by the ways in which narrative therapy has been claimed, explored, adapted, and applied within oppressed communities for their own benefit. They strive to use the resources and training created by these communities with their clients, students, supervisees, and themself. These approaches to narrative therapy are the biggest influence on Ruthie's goals for how they offer clinical training, supervision, and supervision of supervisors in training.

One example is potential for narrative therapy to utilize witnessing, deconstruction, and other key concepts to actively resist and dismantle white supremacy, hetero supremacy, cis-supremacy, patriarchy, and monogamy supremacy. In order to do this, Ruthie recognizes that they must bring their own lived experiences to conversations with both pride and humility. This is the nature of being a member of multiple oppressed minority groups while also benefiting unduly from membership in the largest oppressive demographic. Listening is more important than talking, a concept that is consistently promoted in psychotherapy training and supervision but less frequently practiced. How can I be most helpful here? When can I be most helpful by stepping forward, and when are others best served by my stepping back and/or trying to reduce factors that prohibit others from stepping forward or being appropriately recognized? Ruthie does not know whether Jomo thinks of narrative underpinnings when he is in conversation with Ruthie, but Ruthie constantly sees those beloved qualities in how Jomo interacts with them.

Jomo is particularly influenced by solution-focused brief therapy (SFBT), as developed by Steve de Shazer and Insoo Kim Berg (Berg & de Shazer, 1993; de Shazer, 1985). He was first attracted to SFBT because of its accessibility, systemic roots, non-pathologizing focus, and its belief in the discovery and the utilization of client strengths. Jomo believes that a SFBT approach can be quite liberating for clients who have experienced a pathologizing gaze; this is particularly so for clients who have experienced multiple forms of oppression because of their identities. Jomo has also witnessed the transformational nature of SFBT ideas for supervisees, particularly in terms of how the approach challenges their preconceptions about clients who experience oppression. Jomo has had many dialogues with his supervisees about seeing and hearing with solution-focused eyes and ears. He is also conscious of how the eyes and ears of his supervisees (many of them middle-class, female, cisgender, and straight) might have been affected by hetero-supremacy, cis-supremacy, patriarchy, and monogamy supremacy.

Jomo is very aware of the critiques of SFBT, particularly the critique of its apolitical nature. But he is also enlivened by the fact that the approach has been adopted by queer, Black, and other minority therapists who have stressed the value and strengths inherent in being queer, non-gender conforming, Black, and Brown. Jomo, living in the Global South, is concerned about the vulnerability of many of the clients that his supervisees serve. He has made a conscious effort to make things political and to have political conversations with his supervisee—particularly conversations about the larger contextual and social justice issues that affect client systems. He is very appreciative of the many contextual and social justice issues that Ruthie has brought to supervision of supervision conversations, helping him to account for and address certain things he may missed as a cisgender straight man, with some privilege, in Barbados.

Systemic and Intersectional Issues for Consideration

Jomo and Ruthie both live within contexts that can feel like different worlds. Both of them embody strengths and weaknesses unique to their contexts and identities. Jomo is aware of the strengths and disparities that come with his context as an Afro-Caribbean man who will be the first Barbadian-approved clinical supervisor in this field. Ruthie recognizes implications of binary and non-binary genders uniquely as a non-binary trans person, as well as those of sexual and relationship structure minorities. Ruthie also benefits unfairly as a member of the demographics that continue to violently colonize at every opportunity, while Jomo benefits from being a cisgender man in a straight, monogamous family structure. Jomo approached Ruthie for supervision that would be necessary to achieving goals around his career as well as larger social justice efforts. There is an inherent power imbalance in that; Jomo would be immensely harmed and betrayed if Ruthie withheld things like signatures, while Ruthie would only miss out on learning opportunities that their career can flourish without, due in part to white colonizer supremacy.

Conclusion

Our two-way dialogue captured earlier in this chapter indicated that conversations about sex, sexual pleasure, and consensual versus coercive sex are nuanced and influenced by multiple things including power, access to resources, and the intersectionality that is experienced by all who are involved in the conversation—client, clinician, and supervisor. We are sexual beings, and ignoring this part of a client's identity is not only naïve, but it is a form of silencing, violence, and oppression. To avoid this triple threat the carnal and pleasurable have to be accounted for in significant and meta ways, including in conversations between client and clinician and clinician and supervisor.

Supervisory relationships, as well as therapist/client relationships, are impacted and influenced by a large number of systemic factors. Working with topics and contexts that include increased awareness of sex, gender, sexuality, and sexual intimacy are no less influenced by these systemic factors. It is essential for therapists to continue to strive to increase our awareness of these intersections throughout our lives—and that includes within supervisory relationships, too. Dynamics between therapists and clients are sometimes discussed in training, with varying amounts of usefulness and accuracy. Since the main governing bodies and many of the main figures that receive wide recognition in our field are founded in, and continue to serve, supremacist ideologies around ethnicity, nationality, sexuality, gender, relationship types, and more, it is all the more important that our supervision training address and explore these areas. Without authenticity grounded in safety and respect, supervisory relationships will reinforce these same forms of oppression and subjugation no matter how positive the intentions may be.

Often times it is not possible for minority clients to be able to access therapists of their desired demographics—people who are more likely to share some cultural and historical subtext and who do not embody so many attributes of oppression. The shortage of affordable and otherwise accessible mental health services and the failure of political systems to prioritize funding to help therapists become more accessible, combined with the White, cis, masculine and heterosexual supremacist foundations of the field, make it unnecessarily challenging to find any services, much less preferred services. Furthermore, these areas of privilege allow therapists who embody one or more those demographics to remain blissfully unaware of their own acts of oppression. It is not possible to adequately address the context and therapeutic foci with minority clients when therapists continue to inflict this oppression, whether intentionally or through ignorance.

It is essential to mindfully co-construct more aware, liberationist, and ever-evolving therapeutic relationships grounded in ongoing accountability and anti-oppressive learning. The same is true for supervisory relationships, which also involve tremendous power dynamics. When intimate topics such as sex, gender, sexuality, relationship types, and so on are present in therapy and supervision, those with less power may feel protective of themselves and the topics being shared. This is especially likely with unaddressed power dynamics, or a lack of mutually beneficial structure for handling them. It is possible to build stronger, healthier, safer, and more mutually beneficial relationships in all areas of our lives, including in supervision for especially sensitive therapy topics. All involved must carefully consider and authentically discuss the implications of the power and oppression across demographics.

This is an ongoing process requiring humility, sitting with discomfort, and the risk of expecting accountability for oneself and each other. In a field that claims to prize interpersonal connection and self-insight, we can hold ourselves and each other to no less.

Lessons Learned by the Authors

We have come to recognize some important steps in creating supervision relationships grounded in a dedication to anti-oppression that, in turn, can nurture a more anti-oppressive approach to therapy involving sex, gender, and relationship diversities. Since we approach our work from a systemic lens, we recognize that it is necessary to engage in such ethics in every aspect of psychotherapeutic practice and training.

1. Recognize the inherent value and expertise of all present in the conversation, both physically and symbolically.

    a. While this sounds simple, obvious, and common, our experiences of training, supervision, and practice have found that it is all too rare. In order to do this we are called to constant humility in the face of the knowledge of others and constant vigilance that our own knowledges are not subdued or silenced. How can we reach out to each other to ensure the co-creation of a context that encourages this stance? In what ways are our knowledges similar and different? Mental health professionals are trained to determine what is and isn't healthy; this is a challenging privilege to set aside.

    b. For example, when discussing the work of Jomo's supervisees who are seeing clients living with HIV, many factors are at play. It would be easy for either of us to assume that our perspectives are likely to hold more value because they are what we know, and what we think about. However, we will lose sight of these clients, the supervisee, and each other if we do not first listen and then strive to recognize the many strengths, needs, and questions vital to the consultation.

2. Engage in ongoing, direct conversations about power and privilege.

    a. In our cultures it is sometimes considered rude or confrontational to address and discuss imbalances of power and privilege. This is a useful tactic of oppression and does not serve our best interests, nor those of our clients. Conversations about power and privilege can and do belong in all contexts, including psychotherapy training, practice, and supervision. If we cannot recognize and discuss these things with each other, then there is little hope that we can do so with clients.

b. For example, when considering strength and risk factors around abuse and violence within a sexual relationship, it is first necessary to examine where power is held and withheld at every level from the microsystem, mesosystem, and macrosystem as well as across time. How does Ruthie's whiteness limit their ability to see important factors? White North American culture is often individualistic and heavily reliant on non-profit organizations and para-militaristic police services to step in and direct next steps in situations of intimate violence. Jomo's experience as a cis-man may make him less aware of the ways in which feminine people are vigilant and protect themselves. If we do not discuss the implications of power in clients' lives as well as our own conversations, we will fail to do our best work

3. Resist settings in which clients and trainees have no useful choice of the professionals with which they work.

> This is much more easily said than done. In our training, as well as in the supervision we sometimes offer, there is typically little choice as to who will train and supervise us. Our clients and students may both be assigned to us, as well. How can we co-create settings in which clients and trainees are both able to exercise their own agency in setting up services that best suit their needs? We were able to choose each other for this professional relationship, which meant not choosing people we feared would continue the legacies of harm and trauma that have been an ongoing part of our training and practice in our field.

Critical Questions for Readers to Consider

Critical questions must be asked in order to do better supervisory work across minority cultures in our field, in hopes of also yielding better work with clients.

1. What questions cannot be asked or answered here?

a. Words that cannot be said contain incredible power in their silence. We must work together to keep on identifying these unspeakable questions and answers so that we can normalize them as part of ongoing conversations.

2. Who is seen as the most trustworthy, and when?

a. We don't like to admit when we are not the person who should be trusted to have the best potential answers in a given moment. However, humility around the limits of our experience and experience-supported knowledge is necessary. We must recognize our clients, supervisees, trainees, and other reputable, honest, and dynamic experts. Similarly there are times when we are these experts. However, we live within a world where certain demographics and life experiences are seen as most knowledgeable and trustworthy. We must actively resist these oppressive traps.

3. How is intersectionality impacting things, and are we both aware and recognizing its impact?

    a. Jomo may consider resource shortages, communal support, or racism as the aspects that have been prioritized. Meanwhile, Ruthie may be more strongly considering the impact of queerness, sexism, or erotic pleasure on situations. We both hold important knowledge, but our ideas on what takes precedence is shaped by our differing intersectional identities.

Suggested Readings and Resources

Barker, M. J. (2016). *Queer: A graphic history*. London: Icon Books. Pages TBA.

Black, C., Frederico, M., & Bamblett, M. (2019). Healing through connection: An aboriginal community designed, developed and delivered cultural healing program for aboriginal survivors of institutional child sexual abuse. *The British Journal of Social Work, 49*(4), 1059–1080. www.stitcher.com/podcast/diamondstylzgmailcom/marshas-plate

Burnes, T. R., Singh, A. A., & Witherspoon, R. G. (2017). Sex positivity and counseling psychology: An introduction to the major contribution. *The Counseling Psychologist, 45*(4), 470–486. (Ares)

Cho, S., Crenshaw, K. W., & McCall, L. (2013). Toward a field of intersectionality studies: Theory, applications, and praxis. *Signs: Journal of Women in Culture and Society, 38*(4), 785–810

Cyrus, K. (2017). Multiple minorities as multiply marginalized: Applying the minority stress theory to LGBTQ people of color. *Journal of Gay & Lesbian Mental Health, 21*(3), 194–202

Ivanski, C., & Kohut, T. (2017). Exploring definitions of sex positivity through thematic analysis. *The Canadian Journal of Human Sexuality, 26*(3), 216–225.

Sexual orientation microaggressions: "Death by a thousand cuts" for lesbian, gay, and bisexual youth

Suicide risk in trans populations: An application of minority stress theory

Linklater, R. (2014). *Decolonizing trauma work: Indigenous stories and strategies*. Black Point, NS: Fernwood.

Mona, L. R., Syme, M. L., & Cameron, R. P. (2014). Sexuality and disability: A disability-affirmative approach to sex therapy. In Y. M. Binik & K. S. K. Hall (Eds.), *Principles and practice of sex therapy* (5th ed., pp. 457–481). New York: Guilford.

Mosher, C. M. (2017). Historical perspectives of sex positivity: Contributing to a new paradigm within counseling psychology. *The Counseling Psychologist, 45*(4), 487–503. (Ares)

Tambling, R. B., Neustifter, R., Muska, C., Reckert, A., & Rua, S. (2012). Pleasure-centered educational program: A comprehensive approach to pleasure-oriented sexuality education in domestic violence shelters. *International Journal of Sexual Health, 24*(4), 267–289.

References

American Association for Marriage & Family Therapy. (2004). *Marriage and family therapy core competencies.* Alexandra, VA: Author. Retrieved from www.coamfte. org/Documents/COAMFTE/Accreditation%20Resources/MFT%20Core%20 Competencies%20(December%202004).pdf

American Association for Marriage & Family Therapy. (2019). *Approved supervision designation: Standards handbook.* Alexandra, VA: Author. Retrieved from www.aamft. org/documents/Supervision/AS%20Handbook%20March%202019%20version.pdf

Beck, E. J., Espinosa, K., Ash, T., Wickham, P., Barrow, C., Massiah, E., . . . Nunez, C. (2017). Attitudes towards homosexuals in seven Caribbean countries: Implications for an effective HIV response. *AIDS Care, 29*(12), 1557–1566. doi: 10.1080/ 09540121.2017.1316355

Berg, I. K., & de Shazer, S. (1993). Making numbers talk: Language in therapy. In S. Friedman (Ed.), *The new language of change: Constructive collaboration in psychotherapy* (pp. 5–24). New York: Guilford Press.

Cho, S., Crenshaw, K. W., & McCall, L. (2013). Toward a field of intersectionality studies: Theory, applications, and praxis. *Signs: Journal of Women in Culture and Society, 38*(4), 785–810. doi: 10.1086/669608

Crenshaw, K. W. (1989). Demarginalizing the intersection of race and sex: A Black feminist critique of antidiscrimination doctrine, feminist theory and antiracist politics. *University of Chicago Legal Forum, 1989*, 139–167.

de Shazer, S. (1985). *Keys to solution in brief therapy.* New York: W. W. Norton.

Dhamoon, R. K. (2011). Considerations on mainstreaming intersectionality. *Political Research Quarterly, 64*(1), 230–243. doi: 10.1177/1065912910379227

Human Rights Watch. (2017). *"I have to leave to be me".* Discriminatory Laws against LGBT People in the Eastern Caribbean. New York: Author. Retrieved from www.hrw. org/sites/default/files/report_pdf/easterncaribbean0318_web_0.pdf

Itaborahy, L. P., & Zhu, J. (2014). *State-sponsored homophobia. A world survey of laws: Criminalisation, protection and recognition of same-sex love* (9th ed.). Geneva, Switzerland: ILGA—The International Lesbian, Gay, Bisexual, Trans and Intersex Association.

Kaslow, F. W. (2000). History of family therapy: Evolution outside of the USA. *Journal of Family Psychotherapy, 11*(4), 1–35. doi: 10.1300/J085v11n04_01

Kilhefner, D. (2017). It's time to retire the word 'Homophobia'. *The Gay & Lesbian Review Worldwide.* Retrieved from https://glreview.org/article/its-time-to-retire-the-word-homophobia/

Killian, K. D. (2001). Differences making a difference: Cross-cultural interactions in supervisory relationships. *Journal of Feminist Family Therapy, 12*(2–3), 61–103. doi: 10.1300/J086v12n02_03

Long, J. K. (1996). Working with lesbians, gays, and bisexuals: Addressing heterosexism in supervision. *Family Process, 35*(3), 377–388. doi: 10.1111/j.1545-5300.1996.00377.x

Long, J. K., & Lindsey, E. (2004). The sexual orientation matrix for supervision: A tool for training therapists to work with same-sex couples. In J. J. Bigner & J. L. Wetchler (Eds.), *Relationship therapy with same-sex couples* (pp. 123–135). Binghamton, NY: Haworth Press.

Long, J. K., & Serovich, J. M. (2003). Incorporating sexual orientation into MFT training programs: Infusion and inclusion. *Journal of Marital & Family Therapy, 29*(1), 59–67.

Mason, J., & Shuda, S. (1999). The history of family therapy in South Africa. *Contemporary Family Therapy, 21*(2), 155–172. doi: 10.1023/A:1021691308349

McGoldrick, M. (2001). Response to "family therapy saves the planet". *Journal of Marital & Family Therapy, 27*(1), 17. doi: 10.1111/j.1752-0606.2001.tb01134.x

Meyer, I. H. (1995). Minority stress and mental health in gay men. *Journal of Health & Social Behavior, 36*, 38–56.

Nichols, W. C. (2004). Continuing professional development. In R. H. Coombs (Ed.), *Family therapy review: Preparing for comprehensive and licensing exams* (pp. 569–588). Mahwah, NJ: Lawrence Erlbaum.

Relvas, A. P., Alarcão, M., & Pereira, M. G. (2013). Family and systems therapy and training in Portugal. *Contemporary Family Therapy, 35*(2), 296–307. doi: 10.1007/s10591-013-9255-5

Retzlaff, R. (2013). Development of family therapy and systemic therapy in Germany. *Contemporary Family Therapy, 35*(2), 349–363. doi: 10.1007/s10591-013-9267-1

Schilt, K., & Westbrook, L. (2009). Doing gender, doing heteronormativity: "Gender normals," transgender people, and the social maintenance of heterosexuality. *Gender & Society, 23*(4), 440–464. doi: 10.1177/0891243209340034

Seponski, D. M., & Jordan, L. S. (2018). Cross-cultural supervision in international settings: Experiences of foreign supervisors and native supervisees in Cambodia. *Journal of Family Therapy, 40*(2), 247–264. doi: 10.1111/1467-6427.12157

Sim, T. (2012). The growing pains of family therapy in Singapore. *Journal of Family Therapy, 34*(2), 204–224. doi: 10.1111/j.1467-6427.2010.00519.x

Stratton, P., & Lask, J. (2013). The development of systemic family therapy for changing times in the United Kingdom. *Contemporary Family Therapy, 35*(2), 257–274. doi: 10.1007/s10591-013-9252-8

Tanggaard, L. (2009). The research interview as a dialogical context for the production of social life and personal narratives. *Qualitative Inquiry, 15*(9), 1498–1515. doi: 10.1177/1077800409343063

Timm, T. M. (2009). "Do I really have to talk about sex?" Encouraging beginning therapists to integrate sexuality into couples therapy. *Journal of Couple & Relationship Therapy, 8*(1), 15–33. doi: 10.1080/15332690802626692

Wieling, E., & Marshal, J. P. (1999). Cross-cultural supervision in marriage and family therapy. *Contemporary Family Therapy, 2*, 317–329.

Wieling, E., & Rastogi, M. (2004). Voices of marriage and family therapists of color: An exploratory survey. *Journal of Feminist Family Therapy, 15*(1), 1–20. doi: 10.1300/J086v15n01_01

Zamboni, B. D., & Zaid, S. J. (2017). Human sexuality education in marriage and family therapy graduate programs. *Journal of Marital & Family Therapy, 43*(4), 605–616. doi: 10.1111/jmft.12214

2

BLACK LIKE ME

Reflections from a
Black Male Sex Therapist and Supervisor

James C. Wadley

With support from colleagues near and far, I am fortunate and privileged to hold professional space as an AASECT certified sex therapist and supervisor. There have been any number of positive and negative experiences in my academic and professional training that have enabled me to be supported as well as to offer some clinical and mentoring support to those around me. As a Black male-identifying clinician, one of the challenges that I faced along the way to becoming a sex therapist clinical supervisor was the sometimes intentional and possibly unintentional conversation about race and how it may play itself out in supervision as well as with my clients. In some patient-therapist interactions, there may be experiences of implicit racism and less obvious forms of racism among some white therapists (Khazan, 2016; Kugelmass, 2016). Even Black and Brown racially identified therapists may hold feelings of White supremacy, internalized racism, and/or bias (Williams & Wyatt, 2015). In a field that is predominantly White and has foundations that seemingly neglect the historical and contemporary contributions of Black and people of color (POC) professionals, sometimes it was been difficult to find or create space that takes into account the unique experiences as a racial minority practitioner and supervisor. The goal of this chapter is to share some reflections about serving as a Black sex therapist as well to offer some insight into my experience as a supervisor.

Sex Therapy

There is no single academic or professional path to becoming a sex therapist. Professionals enter into the field from the disciplines of counselor education, psychology, social work, human services, and marriage and family

DOI: 10.4324/9781003034063-3

therapy. All of these areas contribute to the growing field of sexology and sex therapy. When I first started my journey into the field through psychology (undergraduate education) and school psychology (graduate school), I had no idea how my career would unfold to become a sex therapist. My interest and understanding of gender roles and fluidity never really integrated into becoming a clinician until after I learned about sexuality education. Once I started my postgraduate training and learned how to practice as a couple, family, and sexuality therapist, I was curious about why some of my supervisors and I rarely (if ever) talked about race. Aesthetically, I am bronzed complexioned, 6'4", male, slender/athletic build who has remained curious about being the only person of color or of African descent in supervision or in class. In my training, I was always the only person of color, and it felt as if I needed to represent myself and my undergrad institution (Hampton University) well and also any other African American who might come after me. In individual and group supervision, most of my supervisors were white, and there seemed to be an implicit understanding that race would not be addressed unless I brought it up. The few times I mentioned race in supervision, it was addressed at a surface level and rarely processed in a way that allowed for professional growth. The only time that race may have been mentioned, it was to identify a couple or individual who may have been "non-white." Race was never tied into the etiology of the presenting issue or into any other relational or systemic factor that may have enabled the client to come in. I do not hold any contempt towards my supervisors for not addressing this sensitive issue, and there were several moments where I was unsure whether I should have shared more about my own experiences as a Black clinician. I did not have any role models or mentors at the time, and there were few professional representations of persons who maintained the same identities as me (e.g., cisgender, heterosexual, Black, able bodied, middle class, etc.). It feels like there were scores of opportunities along the way that were missed out of concern, anxiety, or fear of saying the wrong thing by my supervisor(s) *and* me.

Schen and Greenlee (2018) contend that sometimes supervisors are reluctant to raise issues of race during supervision because of fear of illuminating racial differences at the expense of highlighting common factors. There may be a fear of saying something in supervision that could be harmful or traumatic with a potential outcome of being seen as racist by some supervisors and supervisees. Sometimes, supervisors (and supervisees) feel inexperienced, unprepared, and without necessary tools to address sensitive issues around race. This interaction may serve as a microcosm of American society where professionals create or hold few spaces to talk honestly and candidly about race. Given the painful history of slavery, segregation, Jim Crow laws, health disparities, stereotypes and myths, and racist rhetoric, there are a myriad of trauma-related challenges that may be obstructions to talking and listening about racial-related issues in non-professional and professional spaces. When race is tied with the taboo subject of sexuality, it seems even more difficult to address how it may be woven into supervisor and supervisee identities in therapeutic decision making.

There were times that I questioned my own place in the field but continued to evolve over the years, feeling more and more comfortable talking about being a Black man in a predominantly white field. Because I am one of a few (Black men) in the field of sexology, I work hard at trying to remain mindful about my privilege (e.g., gender, socioeconomic status, ability, and sexual identities) in this space and cognizant of the need to invite and support others to be in some of the spaces that I occupy.

With my Black and POC clients, I am intentional about discussing race because I am aware of how identities are fluid and have to be negotiated in friendship, romantic, and familial relationships. To not have a conversation about one's skin tone and how some people must remain self-aware as well as vigilant of external perceptions would feel short-sighted on my part and possibly become an obstruction for my client(s) to trust me with engaging in sensitive dialogue. Hamer (2001) offers:

> *The rush to get past race seems to me misguided and rather unpsychoanalytic. In fact, the complexity of racial material in the mind suggest how eager both patient and therapist may be to avoid its discussion, and to make use of other material for discussion that is perhaps more comfortable.*
>
> (p. 1224)

In a similar vein, Peoples and Dell (1975) found support for the assumption and proposition that counselor-client racial similarity increases the likelihood of success in counseling for Black clients, but they also reported other studies in which white counselors were demonstrated to be as effective and as highly rated as Black counselors in dealing with Black clientele.

In clinical sessions, we routinely have conversations about politics, navigating oneself or relationship, parenting, and other systemic substrates that may be negatively (or positively) impacting the relationship or one's sense of self or intimacy. The assumption between my Black clients and I is that we may have experienced systemic oppression in some form or another and sometimes have an unspoken understanding that the other "gets it." Obviously, this is an assumption that is usually confirmed as the conversation unfolds. When I take my clients' sexual history, a few questions that I may ask about race include:

- What did you learn about race, racial identity, and race relations growing up? How does what you learned about race relate to your sexuality?

- What did your family, friends, coworkers, and media (e.g., television, radio, internet) share with you about race?
- What role has your race played in your understanding of sex, sexual behavior, fantasy, and desire?

If I am meeting a Black or POC client, I may also ask about colorism:

- Please share about colorism in your family of origin.
- What role does colorism play in your relational decision making? Your sexual decision making?
- Please share how colorism may influence your erotic attraction and desire for someone.
- Please share your interpretation and experience with texturism in your family of origin.

With my white-identifying clients, depending upon the presenting issue, I am more likely to invite a conversation about the current national landscape of systemic unrest, protest, or anti-POC sentiment. Given the number of therapist locator platforms (e.g., PsychologyToday.com) that exist, clients have an opportunity to view my picture as well as see my academic and professional background, and so I am frequently curious about how white folx may have decided to see a Black therapist. In session, when I've asked a specific question about race, I have not had a client who opted to shift the conversation to something else or decline sharing. If the presenting issue does not have anything to do with race, I am always mindful of setting a time boundary to allow for a few moments of reflection and then possibly move on to the presenting issue. Sometimes, white clients will ask me to share my thoughts or sentiments about larger social events (e.g., political ideas, elections, and activism) and will even ask me how I am doing in relationship to these events. After acknowledging their transference, I will share my honest sentiments and make sure that my clients have an opportunity to respond with their understanding and experience of relative events. The process allows for grounding, as it allows for my client and myself to take into account larger external factors that may be impacting relational or sexual functioning. There is vulnerability in this exchange, as it invites clients to consider racial as well other identities that may or may not be complicit in oppressive conditions within and external to the relationship.

I typically don't ask about colorism with my white-identifying clients based upon the assumption that they may not be familiar or have had conversations about some of these cultural phenomena. My experience as a therapist has impacted my role as a sex therapist supervisor in that I try to create and hold space for the conversations that I rarely had when I was a supervisee.

Sex Therapy Supervision

In one study, Tummala-Narra (2004) provides an analysis of race and culture in supervision (2004). The researcher contends that in supervision, supervisees miss opportunities to actively engage supervisors (who may be unaware or possibly resistant) to discuss issues of race. Leary (2000) suggests that when supervisors and supervisees fail to discuss critical issues regarding race in supervision, they may be complicit in enabling oppression. Hamer contends:

> *The simple fact that the therapist is of a particular race introduces race into the therapeutic situation whether or not it is made explicit. We may resist talking about race because race is not simply a difference, but one freighted with particular social and psychological history.*
>
> (2001, p. 1224)

This intentional or unintentional omission about discussing race may also hold true during sex therapy supervision. In this setting, there may be challenges that exist between supervisor and supervisee to address race related issues in supervision as well as with clients.

The field of sexology and sex therapy supervision is relatively new in the landscape of mental health and wellness. There are approximately 200 sex therapist supervisors around the world with varying degrees of competency and skill. Sex therapy supervision can be a complex process that involves a clinician and a supervisor engaged in conversation that unpacks some of the social, familial, affective, cognitive, and spiritual substrates that may exist between the therapist and his/her/their client. Mead describes supervision as a mentoring relationship that allows for the supervisee to be guided by a supervisor to help make sound clinical decisions (1990). What's unique about sex therapy supervision is that supervisors are positioned to help foster professional and personal change for the supervisee (Wadley & Siegel, 2018). While the number of sex therapists and supervisors has increased over the years, there still remain relatively few supervisors of color.

Similar to the experience that I had as a supervisee, some sexuality supervisors may remain reluctant to have nuanced and deeper conversations with their supervisees about perceptions of race in supervision. Moreover, when Black or POC supervisees enter into supervision with white supervisors, they may be reluctant to create and hold space to have conversations about race.

Conversations about race take center in any individual or group supervision that I host. I make the assumption that because the fields of sexology and sex therapy are predominantly white, my Black, POC, and white supervisees have had relatively few opportunities to talk about race in supervision as well as in their academic and professional training. In supervision, some of my supervisees have contended that the issue of race can be the "elephant in the room" that no one addresses in previous supervision experiences. Thus, I am very intentional about inviting my supervisees to share why they selected a Black supervisor and what they would like to get out of supervision. What's unique about individual and group supervision is that we take the opportunity to examine race, racism, systemic and economic oppression, white supremacy, notions of privilege, intersectionality, colorism, texturism, bias, and other sociocultural phenomena that may impact clients' capacity to form, maintain, or sever intimate and familial relationships. I suggest to my supervisees that they may, at times, feel uncomfortable and possibly anxious over having frank dialogue about the confluence of race, gender, and sexual expression, and I encourage them to reflect and share their own history (which may be parallel with their clients).

Here are a few general questions that I ask my supervisees during any supervisory session:

- Please share your thoughts or feelings about how systemic unrest regarding race has impacted you and how you position yourself with your clients. What are you willing and capable of talking about, and what conversations do you tend to shy away from?
- When sharing your case, please offer a narrative that takes into account how race is positioned in your clients' lives.
- Considering race, please share your sentiments and experience with transference and countertransference with your client(s).
- How do race and sexuality overlap with your clients, and what is their experience?
- How do race and sexuality overlap for you, and how you relate to your clients?

Even though some of my supervisees enter into supervision with a willingness to discuss race-related issues, when the moments arise, they are sometimes unsure about how to share their clinical insights, what they are thinking, how they are feeling, and how they might address this sensitive issue with their clients.

The American Association of Sex Educators, Counselors, and Therapists (AASECT) offers one path for professional certification that acknowledges the need for training and processing issues around diversity. A few years ago, the organization formed a diversity, equity, and inclusion (DEI) committee to address sensitive issues around the needs of traditionally marginalized and/or underrepresented communities. As a part of the certification process, members must have several hours of training devoted to working with individuals, couples, and families who may be culturally different. There were a number of challenges that emerged both within and external to the field of sexology that enabled the leadership to create this opportunity for its members to be more attuned with working with BIPOC (Black, indigenous, people of color) communities. In a short amount of time, the committee has done extraordinary work with pushing the organization to proactively respond to the needs of BIPOC professionals.

Case Study 1

John is a 37-year-old African American cisgender, heterosexual, male. He is married to Patricia, who identifies as a cisgender, heterosexual, Black woman. The couple has three children ages 5 (Sarah), 7 (Paul), and 12 (Simon) years of age. I saw John and his wife four years ago to help them address discordant parental expectations and roles as well as struggles around creating time for intimacy. When John re-entered therapy two months ago, we spent time talking about his challenges of managing the rigors of his job as an electrician and union president, in that he receives a lot of opposition towards doing his work, as well as managing disgruntled union workers. He indicated that he had been feeling angry and "short" with his wife and that his patience wasn't what it used to be. John shared that his job and his relationship were "manageable" but that he was really having difficulty trying to control his anxiety over a recent killing of a Black man in West Philadelphia.

During the fall of 2020, a Black man who struggled with mental health issues was confronted by law enforcement outside of his home. When he came out of a house, he was carrying a knife and was asked to drop it several times by the police. He did not drop the knife and continued to walk towards the police. He was shot several times, and chaos ensued in the streets of West Philadelphia. Protests and subsequent rioting and looting occurred over the next two days until a city-wide curfew occurred and the National Guard was brought in by state officials.

At the conclusion of the first individual session with John, here are the goals we established:

1. Discuss history of managing systemic oppression and racism and its impact on romantic and parental relationships.
2. Discuss successful anger management and healthy conflict resolution with wife.
3. Discuss the role of racialized trauma and its influence over family of origin.
4. Discuss the interpretation and intersection of masculinity and expectations/experiences with law enforcement.
5. Discuss feelings of anxiety and how it affects intimacy.

Over several sessions, we continued to talk about his experiences as a professional Black man and the need for him to regain control over his emotions and the possibility of sharing his feelings with his wife. John indicated that he sometimes struggles to agree with his wife's interpretation of events but finds her to be a source of comfort any time he holds a discussion about race-related issues. We also talked about his capacity to code switch and compartmentalize some of his experiences in order to survive microaggressions experienced at work. Alvarez, Liang, and Neville (2016) assert that people of color and Indigenous individuals experience racism, discrimination, and microaggressions, and these constructs affect their mental health and well-being. Because of this, racial trauma is a product of real or vicarious race-based events that are dangerous (Comas-Díaz, Hall, & Neville, 2019). For John, it was prudent for us to discuss his job-related trauma as well as the tragedy that happened to the man killed by law enforcement officials in West Philadelphia.

Case Study 2

During the fall of 2020, a Black man who struggled with mental health issues was confronted by law enforcement outside of his home. When he came out of a house, he was carrying a knife and was asked to drop it several times by the police. He did not drop the knife and continued to walk towards the police. He was shot several times, and chaos ensued in the streets of West Philadelphia. Protests and subsequent rioting and looting occurred over the next two days until a city-wide curfew occurred and the National Guard was brought in by state officials.

In sex therapy supervision with four White women the following week, I opened the discussion inviting my supervisees to share their thoughts about the events that unfolded in Philadelphia and how those events may have impacted their clients over the past few days. One person shared that she was "stunned and saddened" about the incident and could not understand why a less-lethal intervention method was not used (e.g., use of stun gun, police dogs, or conflict negotiator). Another supervisee indicated that she spent time with a client who reported that he was traumatized by the event because the media continued to play the event many times over the past several days. A third supervisee asserted that the police were well within their rights to shoot the man because of his refusal to drop the knife and comply with the officers' demands.

As we processed the tragic events as well as their relevance to clients' needs, we talked about the need for therapists to inquire and understand larger systemic issues that may impact clients' functioning. We discussed the influence that race, socioeconomic status, and gender roles have on public and private relational decision making. We also took time to process the impact of white supremacy in society and how it may filter into clinical discussions that do not honor cultural differences of people of color.

Discussion

Some of the literature regarding supervision seems to intentionally/unintentionally circumvent, minimize, or negate the affect that race has on supervisor selection, case consultation, and professional development (Schen & Green-lee, 2018). While there is a body of literature that addresses the supervisory needs of people of color (POC) as trainees, there is a lack of research or clinical recommendations for sex therapist supervisors of color who supervise clinicians using social justice frameworks and specifically discuss race. The existing supervisory literature fails to address issues of white privilege and supremacy and the relevant clinical strategies to hold safe and honest dialogue about supervision. It seems important that supervisors be competent and skilled about how the notion of race may play itself out in a supervisory or clinical setting. This is crucial for two reasons. First, there is a need to address the confluence of race, sexuality, and supervisory models as the field of sexuality professionals and clientele become increasingly racially diverse. Second, it may be assumed that supervisors may have little to no experience addressing race and racism and may be unprepared to examine the nuances of inherent power hierarchies within supervision.

Critical Questions for Readers to Consider

1. Please share your thoughts about factors that may enable or prohibit supervisees from choosing a person of color as their sex therapist supervisor.
2. Why might it be important for race and other identities (e.g., ability, socioeconomic status, religion, gender, and sexual identity) to be considered and discussed while meeting with clients?
3. Share your thoughts and experiences about what you may have learned about race in your academic and professional training. How do you use this training in sex therapy?

References

Alvarez, A. N., Liang, C. T. H., & Neville, H. A. (Eds.). (2016). *The cost of racism for people of color: Contextualizing experiences of discrimination.* Washington, DC: American Psychological Association.

Comas-Díaz, L., Hall, G., & Neville, H. (2019). Racial trauma: Theory, research, and healing: Introduction to the special issue. *American Psychologist, 74*(1), 1–5.

Hamer, F. M. (2001). Guards at the gate: Race, resistance, and psychic reality. *Journal of the American Psychoanalytic Association, 50*(4), 1219–1236.

Khazan, O. (2016, June 1). *Not white, not rich, and seeking therapy.* Retrieved September 8, 2020, from www.theatlantic.com/health/archive/2016/06/the-struggle-of-seeking-therapy-while-poor/484970/

Kugelmass, H. (2016). "Sorry, I'm not accepting new patients." An audit study of access of mental health care. *Journal of Health and Social Behavior, 57*(2), 168–183.

Leary, K. (2000). Racial enactments in dynamic treatment. *Psychoanalytic Dialogues, 10*(4), 639-653. doi: 10.1080/10481881009348573.

Mead, D. E. (1990). *Effective supervision: A task oriented model for the mental health profession.* New York: Brunner/Mazel.

Peoples, V. Y., & Dell, D. M. (1975). Black and white student preferences for counselor roles. *Journal of Counseling Psychology, 22*(6), 529–531.

Schen, C. R., & Greenlee, A. (2018). Race in supervision: Let's talk about it. *Psychodynamic Psychiatry, 46*(1), 1–21.

Tummala-Narra, P. (2004). Dynamics of race and culture in the supervisory encounter. *Psychoanalytic Psychology, 21*(2), 300–311.

Wadley, J. C., & Siegel, R. (Eds.). (2018). *The art of sex therapy supervision.* London: Routledge.

Williams, D., & Wyatt, R. (2015). Racial bias in health care and health. *JAMA, 314*(6), 555–556.

3

WORKING WITH INDIGENOUS PEOPLES IN CANADA

The Legacies of Colonization on Sexuality

Reece Malone and Laverne Gervais

Key Terms

cultural humility: In the document *Creating a Climate for Change*, cultural humility is defined as "a process of self-reflection to understand personal and systemic biases and to develop and maintain respectful processes and relationships based on mutual trust. Cultural humility involves humbly acknowledging oneself as a learner when it comes to understanding another's experience."

2SLGBTQQIA: A broad acronym that stands for Two-Spirit, lesbian, gay, bisexual, transgender, queer, questioning, intersex, and asexual.

Introduction

The following chapter is a reflection and collaboration of the work of two allies committed to addressing the sexual health needs within their community. Opening the chapter, Laverne Gervais introduces the geographic historical context of her work. While working with Indigenous clients, Reece Malone shares five guiding principles and counseling strategies to incorporating cultural contexts and humility in sex therapy and psychodynamic practice, both collaborated on the backgrounder section of this chapter.

Laverne Gervais

When Reece asked me to collaborate on a chapter that would touch on Indigenous sexual health, I was intrigued and excited. I identify as an Anishnabe/Dakota-French Canadian. English is my first and primary language, and I have always preferred the pronouns *she* and *her*. Within the gender binary,

DOI: 10.4324/9781003034063-4

I am a cisgender woman, and I have had mostly heterosexual, monogamous experiences. I live with white skin amid a beautiful array of Brown faces. In my work as a sexual health educator I see the day-to-day realities of inequitable health services for Indigenous people.

I have the privilege of working in Treaty One Territory within the Indigenous community of Winnipeg, Manitoba, Canada. Winnipeg is home to one of the largest urban populations of Indigenous people—it is my birthplace. It is the land on which the foundation of my own sexual identity and health started. The more I understand this land, and my ancestral relationships to it, the more I understand what is needed to live and heal within the colonial violence still invading it.

As an Indigenous sexual health educator, I see the need for culturally safe(r), trauma-informed, anti-oppressive, sex-positive, and decolonizing ethical spaces for Indigenous people to explore the healing tools they could use to care for their own sexual health and well-being. There are multiple generations still healing from the sexualized violence experienced by Indigenous children through the Canadian residential school system. At the same time, these same generations continue to confront ongoing violence and a disproportionate rate of missing and murdered women, girls, and 2SLGBTQQIA people (National Inquiry into Missing and Murdered Indigenous Women and Girls, 2019). While there is a growing body of Indigenous-led sexual health initiatives—formally and informally exploring the legacies of colonization on sexual identity, sexual relationships, and sexual decision making—there remains inequitable access to health care.

Both Reece and I agree that it's imperative for clinicians and educators to practice cultural humility and incorporate intersectionality and the minority stress model (Meyer, 2003) as foundational while working with Indigenous clients. By doing so, this helps to identify unconscious cultural and racial biases, and strengthens a therapeutic relationship.

The following two case examples illustrate how Reece embeds cultural humility when working with Indigenous clients in sex therapy practice that centers self-determination, sexual agency, and social justice.

Case 1: Linda

Sitting on the edge of my couch, Linda explains that she came to sex therapy to better understand her history of infidelity and her inability to maintain a monogamous relationship.

Linda: "I just don't understand why I can't seem to stay still. Like, there's a barrier or something why when something is so good I just seem to end things or start something new when he's not even doing anything wrong. . . . I dunno."

As I reviewed her intake form and goals for therapy, Linda concludes, "I want to be able to give respect and have healthy sexual connections. I think my history of child abuse has something to do with it."

Linda is a 44-year-old heterosexual cisgender Cree woman from a First Nations community in southern Manitoba. Linda works for a social services organization as a case manager who provides programming for Indigenous women at risk. She is the mother of a 19-year-old daughter and a 23-year-old son. She has been separated from their father, her ex-husband, for eight years. While she doesn't currently have a steady partner, she has been dating casually for the past year.

As a child, she was raised by her mother, grandparents, great grandparents, and several aunts and uncles. Her grandparents were survivors of the residential school system where they met. They had nine children, the eldest three of whom also suffered through residential schools. Linda's mother and her remaining five siblings attended public schools.

In our first few sessions, Linda shared many stories of generational and intergenerational trauma. As early as 4 years old, Linda recalls being sexually exploited by her uncle—events that continued until her early teens. Her brother, with whom she was close, died while drinking and driving, and her grandfather died of a drug overdose. Although Linda was originally told that her grandmother's death was caused by accidental drowning, rumors suggested her grandfather had been directly responsible for her grandmother's death.

Case 2: Graham

When Graham rose from a slumped, seated posture to greet me, I could see he was a surprisingly tall, broad man. Standing 6'4", his stature resembled that of a professional rugby player. His black, wavy, shoulder-length hair was slicked back, and his chiseled goatee amplified his masculine appearance. I greeted him with a handshake and immediately noticed a barely assertive grip. "Hi, my name is Reece Malone." He smiled back, and with a single nod he replied with a barrelsounding, "Hello."

At 37 years old, Graham is a social worker at an agency that provides grief counseling for individuals and families. His clients are mostly underemployed, on social assistance, living in subsidized housing complexes, and Indigenous. Many of his clients are living with addictions, are associated with gangs, and have had a history of violence. His deeply compassionate desire to help his community is rooted in his own family's lived trauma and survival within residential schools, as well as his experiences living in several foster homes throughout his childhood and adolescence.

As I conducted his intake, he didn't answer directly. Instead, Graham would be expansive and verbose, telling a story before circling back and summarizing the original question and finally answering in earnest. He spoke slowly, intentionally, and methodically.

As we concluded our first session, Graham shared that he wanted to understand why he selects sexual partners whose relationships end in high conflict while activating self-loathing spiraling patterns within himself. His goals for therapy were to help him be better equipped to select healthier sexual partners, as well as to learn how to better respect women by honoring his monogamy agreements. Graham also shared that he experienced occasional erectile dysfunction and, though he didn't find it distressing at current, he would eventually like to address it.

Graham: I feel that the sex is good, like we would be having a good time, then something happens and we end up in a big conflict.
Malone: Something happens?
Graham: Yeah. Like things would be going good; then she would want to spend more time together even though . . . like we would be intimate, and she would fall for me. I would tell her where I was at with things and the next thing you know, there would be an explosion and I would just walk away. Then I would feel really badly about myself.
Malone: Is this dynamic a pattern that you've noticed within your previous sexual relationships?
Graham: Yes, ever since my ex-wife. My ex-partner.
Malone: When did the relationship with your ex-partner dissolve?
Graham: Well it never really did. She went missing. She's been missing in our community for over two years. So it's just been my son and me ever since. I'm assuming she's most likely dead.

Linda and Graham each have unique interpersonal characteristics, genetic temperaments, and social dispositions. Both have fulfilling career paths and rich family histories that—despite their individualism—converge upon parallel histories of grief and loss rooted in legacies of colonization, familial histories with residential school systems, struggles with addictions, and experiences of violence.

Background

The history of colonization and the residential school systems have had a profound and denigrating effect on every aspect of Indigenous culture and identity (Ross, 2014). On June 11, 2008, the Canadian federal government acknowledged and made formal apologies to Indigenous Canadians for the atrocities and forced assimilation of Indigenous people. Regardless, the systemic, intergenerational, and developmental trauma resulting from the horrors of cultural genocide has profoundly intersected sexual decision making, sexual agency and autonomy, gender identity and expression, as well as sexual relationships and dynamics.

Indigenous women, girls, and 2SLGBTQQIA have been especially affected. Ongoingly they are epidemically subjected to violence and are disproportionately missing and murdered. Indigenous leadership groups and communities have advocated for a national inquiry to explore the "underlying social, economic, cultural, institutional, and historical causes that contribute to the ongoing violence and vulnerabilities" as well as to identify culturally informed policies and practices that address violence and increase safety (National Inquiry into Missing and Murdered Indigenous Women and Girls, 2019).

While working with Indigenous populations, it is imperative for clinicians and educators to reflect on their own unresolved traumas and inflictions and acquire more than a working knowledge of the history of colonization's effect on Indigenous people or we risk overt and covert bias, projection, and conjecture known as transference (Jung, 1954). We must recognize that modern medicine and mental health treatment approaches have been built upon the over pathologizing of a minority status, racist ideologies, and social control (Foucault, 1967; Gould, 1981). This knowledge emphasizes an undercurrent that sexuality education, sexuality counseling, and sex therapy approaches are inherently designed to be compliant with a colonialist, top-down framework antecedent to Indigenous learning and healing principles, traditions, and rituals. By bridging historical contexts with Western frameworks and incorporating Indigenous cultural worldviews, we begin the process of decolonizing human sexuality and support an inclusive and collaborative narrative of healing.

When I work with Indigenous populations, I apply an approach that incorporates this historical understanding and a socio-sexual ecological lens that includes developmental patterns of attachment, self-regulation, and self-perspective (Gil, 1996; Siegel, 2012; van der Kolk, 2014). I also consider how these developmental patterns cascade intimate and sexual relationship dynamics, influence the formation of sexual health principles and decision making, and effect romantic and erotic expressions with self and with others.

Recognizing the therapist-client power dynamic, I pay close attention to both overt and covert messages and implications within my physical space as a healing environment. As spirituality is a core part of the Indigenous identity, it's important for me to create an authentic metaphorical and spiritual boundary so that Indigenous clients feel safer as their healing process emerges. The task of creating such a space infers that therapy and healing is a ceremony (Duran, 2006). In my physical space I clearly make visible certain items gifted by elders, or purchased from Indigenous creators and knowledge keepers—items known within traditional contexts to have significant meaning, power, and energy. Indigenous clients often notice and remark on how they relate to these sacred objects. It's commonplace for me to invite Indigenous clients to reflect and share how sacred objects have or can support sexual health and healing.

Cultural connections through items and objects can help build a stronger connection or relatability to the clinician either consciously or subconsciously (Duran, 2006).

Guiding Principles for Clinicians Working with Indigenous Peoples

To my current knowledge, there are no Indigenous identified sex therapists within the region where I live and practice. This poses unique challenges in delivering culturally competent sex therapy with Indigenous clients. While intentional effort goes into curating the healing space, over time I have developed guiding principles that shape my approach when working with Indigenous populations. As these are foundational, they are not exempt from interrogation and must be frequently revisited to ensure that I do not lose sight of how evolving knowledge, beliefs, and values maintain a relationship with these principles.

1. Adopt a Cultural Humility Lens

As educators, counselors, and therapists, it is important to reflect on what it means to be a settler on land that was colonized and the implications of colonization on Indigenous identities. Self-reflection questions include:

- Who am I, and what does my identity as (sex, gender, sexual orientation, ethnicity, caregiver, etc.) mean to me? What cultural factors helped shape this or influence my identity?
- What does it mean for me to be a settler on Indigenous land? What social power and privileges do I hold as a non-Indigenous person that I may take for granted?
- What prejudices, assumptions, and biases do I hold when I reflect on the sexual development and experiences of Indigenous clients?
- (Indigenous clinicians and educators) As an Indigenous person, what power do I hold? What are the implications of such power when working with Indigenous individuals and relationships?

Case Applications

Linda noticed the jar of sage that is kept in my office and remarked how unexpected it was to see in a sex therapy office. In building a stronger connection with Linda, I briefly shared my experiences working with Indigenous Elders, what draws me to Inuit art (I currently have several art pieces hanging in both my waiting room and in my office), my gifted spiritual name, and my understandings of colonization paralleling my own ancestry and the colonization of the Philippines.

Malone: I was gifted this sage by a Métis client who felt it was important to incorporate spirituality and ritual as part of her healing journey. This is a similar practice that Aboriginal and Indigenous people of the Philippines practice. We can include smudging and traditional prayers as a part of our sessions if that is something you would find beneficial.

We also discussed our client-therapist relationship and what approaches would facilitate safety and comfort.

Knowing that sharing historical contexts is often through storytelling, I find it important that Indigenous clients know that an authentic voice—rather than a medicalized or psychoanalytic approach—is welcomed. Graham second guessed how he responded to intake questions believing it was taking up too much time and I explained that it was important that he be able to speak with an unvarnished reflection of himself without fear or judgment.

Malone: Graham, from my experience, I appreciate getting to learn about someone's history in ways that are truly authentic. Please don't worry about how you think you need to sound. For instance, using medical terms about body parts or sexual references. Some people are direct while others share through storytelling. I may synthesize your reply to make sure I got it right but please, just be yourself.

Counseling Strategies

When conducting a sexual history intake, include questions that draw upon the generational oral history teachings that help guide sexual developmental and relationship formation. This can include questions like:

- Were there any teachings by Elders, knowledge keepers, your family, or those in your community about sex? What stood out for you from these teachings? Did you feel you were missing out? What have you passed along to your children or community?
- What traditional teachings, rituals, and ceremonies were you aware of that had to do with:
  - Sexual development including puberty and adolescence?
  - Gender and gender expression?

- Sexual orientation or attraction?
- Monogamy, non-monogamy, or polyamory?

- What can it mean for you to be sexually empowered as an Indigenous person?

Case Applications

Linda shares that inappropriate sexual activity within her community was a common "secret."

She first learned about sex at 5 years old. This included an older cousin exposing her to a pornographic magazine. She was then exploited by this person and coerced to mirror the different positions of the women seen in the magazine.

Malone: Who knew about what happened to you?
Linda: I told my sister.
Malone: Anyone else?
Linda: Yes, my mother.
Malone: How did your mother respond?
Linda: Well, she didn't really do anything. Our relationship has been strained over the years. We're kind to each other, but when it came to this, I would go to my sister for comfort, and she would tell me stories to help calm me. I remember a prayer by my grandmother that I would say. It was in Cree.
Malone: Would you be open to sharing your grandmother's prayer with me?
Linda: *Kehcimantou,*
Nintahthentin tawahpamisawan
Tahpetahman, tahkiskethtahman, tamahmahtaickiskethimisewan.
It means, "Creator,
I want to see myself, hear, know myself in a most wondrous magical way you that you created me."
It would bring me so much comfort. . . . I even catch myself reciting it without thinking about it. My prayer helps me to connect and see myself from a place of love and compassion. Even though I barely remember the Cree language, I'm taking classes to learn.
Malone: What you just said is an important reminder of the consequences of the genocide of the Indigenous languages and identity.
Linda: *My* language is my identity and it's been lost with us having to speak English and all the shame that was brought on to us [by those who ran residential schools].

I was cognizant of my own verbal pacing and followed Linda's lead when the topic of sexual trauma was discussed. We reviewed inner resourcing, coping tools, and the strategies of resilience she acquired while seeing a trauma therapist several years back.

Drawing upon the theme of "lost identity," several of our sessions focused on legacies of colonization and residential schools, on sexuality, and sexual decision making.

2. Reflect on One's Own Relationship with Spirituality

As spirituality is foundational to Indigenous identity and tradition, it's important for the therapist to self-reflect on their relationship with spirituality, even if spirituality is not a part of the therapist's own identity or practices. Without such self-reflection, discussions can be inauthentic, risk unconscious microaggressions and countertransference, and compromise the therapeutic relationship.

Self-reflective can questions include:

- What is my understanding of spirituality?
- Who am I as a spiritual being?
- What is my own relationship with spirituality, and how can it impact my relationship with Indigenous clients?
- What are the differences and intersections of religion and spirituality?
- Do I hold any biases or judgments when a client discloses they are either spiritual or have a critical or negative view of spirituality?

Counseling Strategies

Explore the topic of spirituality as a potential source of wisdom, insight, and resilience.

Reflective questions can include:

- What is your relationship with spirituality?
- How has your spirituality strengthened you?
- When have I drawn on spirituality and under what circumstances?
- Has spirituality informed parts your identity (example, gender)? If so, how?

3. Bridge Western Approaches and Traditional Worldview Perspectives

The principle of bridging diverse perspectives and approaches supports therapeutic collaboration, helps to identify sources of generational resilience and personal pride, and strengthens the overall process and journey of healing.

The territory where I currently live is the original land of Anishinaabe, Cree, Oji-Cree, Dakota, Dene, and Métis peoples. While many values and principles are shared, each tribal community holds unique beliefs passed generationally through traditional oral teachings—these stories include ways in which people and communities are to make decisions. When working with Indigenous clients, encouraging and inviting traditional teachings that can serve as a foundational approach to discussing sexual principles and ethics, sexual decision making, and relationship dynamics.

I consulted with an Anishinaabe Elder who shared Seven Sacred Teachings (*Niizhwaaswi gagiikwewin*), otherwise known as Seven Grandfather Teachings, that include honesty, wisdom, respect, humility, courage, love, and truth. While working with Indigenous clients, if appropriate and with permission by the client, I invite a reflection and critique of whether and how these teachings can interweave with Doug Harvey-Braun's Six Sexual Health Principles that include consent, non-exploitation, protected from STIs and unintended pregnancy, honesty, shared values, and mutual pleasure.

Case Applications

Malone: An elder shared with me the Seven Sacred Teachings that I understand serve as traditional guiding principles. Do you think they can be applied to mapping out your sexual health values?

Linda: Honesty, wisdom, respect, humility, courage, love and truth—they absolutely parallel sexual health. I think the more that I can frame my principles that way, the more I can stay true and be in truth with myself. Sex was all about them. I was always taking care of them and now I need to take care of myself.

I can ask myself am I being honest, wise, respectful, courageous, loving, and truthful when I'm wanting to hook up? It's not going to necessarily stop me from doing it, but I know that if I do, I won't feel so guilty after.

Malone: My colleagues, Doug Harvey-Braun and Michael Vigorito, introduced the six principles of sexual health which include honesty, consent, pleasure, non-exploitation, protection, shared values, as well as the prevention of pregnancy and sexually transmitted and blood-borne infections. What are your thoughts about collaborating the seven teachings with the six principles?

Linda: That really sounds good. They both resonate and it's a solid way that I can pass along to the clients I work with too.

4. Include Aspects of Culture and Traditions that Foster Sexual Empowerment

Not only can inviting and including aspects of culture and tradition be empowering, it can help broaden the depth and breadth of the therapeutic process and help to identify other fundamental aspects of identity that intersect sexual health and well-being.

For both Linda and Graham—as well as other Indigenous and racialized clients—a clinician inquiring about traditional healing was unheard of but was very welcomed and appreciated, and it strengthened the therapeutic process.

Counseling Strategies

Offer clients the opportunity to incorporate Indigenous rituals including smudging, prayers, and meditations.

- Smudging is a traditional ceremony or ritual used to connect individuals and places to the Creator. It serves several purposes including inviting clarity, purifying, calming, or dispelling the soul from negativity, and it is incorporated in spiritual ceremony.
- It's important that clinicians become aware of the impact of acculturation where unconscious bias may impact the therapeutic paradigm. By exploring the client's cultural and traditional teachings on sexuality, it can help broaden the clinician's understanding of the client's identity while simultaneously offering opportunities for a client to deeply and meaningfully reflect on straddling traditional and European or Western worldviews.

"What cultural traditions and rituals honor and celebrate _____:

- Gender, gender identity, and gender expression?
- Sexual orientation and diverse attractions?
- Sexual expression and sexual freedom?"

Case Applications

For Linda, being part of the Sun Dance ceremony is a fundamental part of her Spirit and spiritual practices. Sun Dance ceremonies are considered the most sacred of traditional ceremonies, where communities gather for prayer, take part in ceremonies and paths of healing, and find a way to connect with spirituality and culture (*The Sun Dance Ceremony Part 1* [video file]. (2013, August 14). Retrieved from *www.aptnnews.ca/featured/the-sun-dance-ceremony/*).

In one of my discussions with Linda, we unpacked and explored her relationship to her own gender and the connection between spirituality and gender identity. For Linda, this was a centerpiece that anchored her identity and nurtured her self-value.

Malone: What has Sun Dance meant for you?
Linda: What comes to mind is my Spirit. It's such an individual experiential journey.

To be part of my Ceremonial Family* is a gift that I earned because of physical, emotional, spiritual, and mental suffering. This is the extreme opposite of the euphoric joy I get during the time of Sun Dance. One of the many traditions of my Ceremonial Family includes my earning the right to call myself a Sun Dancer. I fulfilled the commitment of fasting and dancing for four years, and I have continued as a Helper—a role that brings much responsibility and honor.

Our Ceremonial Family has very specific traditions, protocols, and values. Racism, sexism, and gender inequality is not tolerated in the Ceremonial Family Sun Dance Family. This is respected and applauded, but these values are unfortunately not an absolute for all Sun Dance Ceremonies. All nations, creeds, and sexual identifications are all welcomed, respected, and treated equally. I love this aspect of our Sun Dance and am very proud of this fact; I could not have it any other way.

This is a part of me, bearing witness to a human being at a raw and vulnerable state and supporting each person in the manner they need to be supported in this time of the Sun Dance Ceremony. Sundance to me is the great equalizer. Sun Dance has no criticism or prejudice. It has no bias. Sun Dance is the journey of the human Spirit and of the soul of the human participant: personal, intimate, unique, and connected.

Sun Dance to me is not something that I do every summer; it is a way of life for the rest of my life. The Sun Dance Ceremony again reminds me that I am Spirit having a human Experience.

Last year my role of taking care of the women was a huge responsibility, but this year, I'm dancing on behalf of someone who can't dance because she's very pregnant.

* For confidentiality, the name of the client's Ceremonial Family has been redacted and replaced with "Ceremonial Family."

Malone: To dance on her behalf . . . how incredibly meaningful.
Linda: Yes, you know she has a same-sex partner, and this is their first baby. (Name omitted) and (name omitted), I think you know them.
Malone: (nodding)
Linda: (starts to tear) To dance for her—to dance for them—it's truly an honor to be asked. It gives me so much hope for the future.
Malone: So you're a surrogate dancing for, and on behalf of (names omitted). At the same time, you're a part of that spiritual healing bridge, the journey with them . . .
Linda: (nodding)
Malone: Does it feel affirming to your gender and healing journey?

Linda: As a woman, it nurtures me. When I reflect back on my history and how the women in my life have been treated and exploited . . . addicted, how I've been treated and exploited by my ex-husband . . . being a part of Sun Dance is sacred to my identity . . . to being a woman. And it's a part of my healing journey with addictions and the traumas I've lived.

5. Incorporate Intersectionality and Minority Stress Model to Explore the Intersections of Identity, Mental and Sexual Health, and Wellness

The availability of courses, programs, and educational opportunities on colonization, intersectionality, and minority stress are either inconsistent in sex therapy learning institutes or—at best—offered as an optional workshop or taught within another interdisciplinary field.

Both systemic oppression and identity-based discrimination are culturally overt, casual, and insidious. Because of the pervasiveness of both these themes it is important to be intentional and explore the manifestations of external and internalized oppression and marginalization.

As traditional sex therapy treatments for erectile dysfunction, delayed or anorgasmia, delayed or rapid ejaculation, and lowered desire may have evidence-based protocols, contributing factors to mental health cannot be ignored.

Counseling Strategies

- Help identify facets of a client's identity that inform their worldview and sexual worldview:

  - Have you experienced discrimination and prejudice growing up? How has it affected you?
  - What are the traditional cultural messages about sexuality and relationships that you've received? How do you feel about them? Do they align with your values?

- Unpack and process the impact of systemic racism and microaggressions on relationship formation, intimacy, and sexual encounters.

  - Discrimination and prejudice can be hard to identify. They can be casual or come in forms of microaggression such as (clinician to insert examples relative to gender, sexuality, and relationships). Have you experienced something similar to these examples?

- Acknowledge the impact of stereotypes, prejudice, and marginalization on sexual functioning.

Case Application

For Graham, a significant part of his identity was in women's acknowledgement and affirmation of his physical attractiveness. As we unpacked his social relationships in childhood and adolescence, Graham realized that his external appearance was a source of stress, especially because the majority of his adolescent friends were white. To fit in, it meant that Graham needed to conduct himself in parallel with his "white guy" friends and censor his feelings when faced with racism himself or racism against Indigenous people. Being "white passing" was paramount, constantly surveilling and being a spectator to his own sexuality.

Malone: When we experience cumulative racism and prejudice, how can it not erode our sense of self and well-being? When we internalize these messages, we may start to feel unattractive and undesired. If we don't feel good about ourselves, it can affect how we "are" in relationships and how we "do" relationships.

Graham: That totally makes sense. I'm constantly thinking, thinking, thinking, and it's really hard to stay present with my partner, even when we're having sex. Sometimes that's when I lose my erection. I realize now that I'm sabotaging the relationship, but I think there's a part that I still feel so much shame.

Malone: If you could give a voice to that part, what would it say?

Graham: It would say, "It's time to get out because she's going to know you're not good enough and she can do better. She'd be better off."

Malone: With . . .?

Graham: A white guy.

Concluding Remarks

Over the course of several months, both Linda and Graham worked on developing their own sexual health values and principles and putting them into practice in their dating and sexual encounters. Both leveraged wisdom from Elders and the strength of their traditional cultures to foster a greater sense of pride in their own Indigenous identity. We incorporated ceremonial traditions like smudging and prayer in their own dialect to help self-regulate and to self-soothe. We also used complimentary modalities including psychoeducation, cognitive behavior exercises, mindfulness, and inner-child approaches.

It is imperative that Indigenous people are agents of their own health and are recognized for their continuing efforts to work through the impacts of colonization. By doing so, they are bringing the intersection of identity, sex, sexuality, and intimate relationship into *mino-pimatisiwin*, which translates to "the good life" in Cree.

Lessons Learned

The most important lesson I learned is the importance of acknowledging and recognizing the intergenerational developmental impact of settler colonization and residential schools on all aspects of Indigenous identity.

While there is a lack of comprehensive sexual health and wellness education available in public and private schools, as well as for caregivers and families, what cannot be ignored are the intersections of culture, traditions, and social ecological factors on identity and sexual health value formation.

How can clinicians effectively "treat" sexual dysfunctions or address sexual wellness when the foundational framework in which treatment was developed, prescribed, or facilitated is rooted in European and Western ways of thinking? The following points offer concluding insights that can help conceptualize a clinician's approach to working with Indigenous clients:

- Colonization's legacy percolates through all aspects of identity. Decolonizing sexuality is recognizing the generational and intergenerational effects of Western-Euro values on Indigenous sovereignty, cultures, and traditions relative to sexual health and well-being.
- Cultural humility identifies unconscious bias and countertransference. The practice of cultural humility is a lifelong process.
- Identifying salient parts of the client's identity and the relationship of those parts with culture and traditions can strengthen the therapeutic process.
- Inviting practices of traditional healing while incorporating appropriate sex therapy modalities amplifies the quality and delivery of care while working with Indigenous clients.

Suggested Readings

Braun-Harvey, D., & Vigorito, A. M. (2016). *Treating out of control sexual behavior: Rethinking sex addiction.* New York: Springer Publishing Company.

Bouchard, D., & Martin, J. (2016). *Seven sacred teachings.* Vancouver, Canada: Crow Cottage Publishing.

Duran, E. (2006). *Healing the soul wound. Counseling with American Indians and other native peoples.* Multicultural Foundations of Psychology and Counseling Series. New York: Teachers College Press. Columbia University.

National Inquiry into Missing and Murdered Indigenous Women and Girls. (2019). *Reclaiming power and place. The final report of the national inquiry into missing and murdered indigenous women and girls* (V 1a). Retrieved from www.mmiwg-ffada. ca/wp-content/uploads/2019/06/Final_Report_Vol_1a-1.pdf

Truth and Reconciliation Commission of Canada. (2015). *Truth and reconciliation commission of Canada: Calls to action.* Retrieved from http://trc.ca/assets/pdf/Calls_to_Action_English2.pdf

References

Duran, E. (2006). *Healing the soul wound. Counseling with American Indians and other native peoples.* Multicultural Foundations of Psychology and Counseling Series. New York: Teachers College Press. Columbia University.

Foucault, M. (1967). *Madness and civilization.* London: Tavistock.

Gil, E. (1996). *Treating abused adolescents.* New York: Guildford Press.

Gould, S. J. (1981). *The mismeasure of a man.* New York: W. W. Norton.

Jung, C. G. (1954). *The practice of psychotherapy.* Princeton: Bollingen Press.

Meyer, I. H. (2003). Prejudice, social stress, and mental health in lesbian, gay and bisexual populations: Conceptual issues and research evidence. *Psychological Bulletin, 129,* 674–697. doi:10.1037/0033-2909.129.5.674

National Inquiry into Missing and Murdered Indigenous Women and Girls. (2019). Retrieved from www.mmiwg-ffada.ca/mandate/

Ross, R. (2014). *Indigenous healing. Exploring traditional paths.* Toronto: Penguin Group.

Siegel, D. J. (2012). *The development mind: How relationships and the brain interact to shape who we are* (2nd ed.). New York: Guildford Press.

Van der Kolk, B. A. (2014). *The body keeps score: Brain, mind, and the body in the healing of trauma.* New York: Penguin Random House.

4

REAL MEN DON'T CRY

The Effects of Racism and Oppression on Masculinity, Emotionality, and Intimacy in Black Men

Shane´ J. Gill

Introduction

Hypermasculinity: A term frequently used to describe the process of socialization of men. For Black men, hypermasculinity is defined as overtly sexual, aggressive, and having relations with multiple sexual partners (Ward, 2005).

Invisibility Syndrome: A term used to describe the outcome of the failed grueling task of negotiating one's identity, which poses even more of a threat to their well-being and self-perception, as they are often not accepted by the dominant culture, and due to systemic oppression, frequently unable to access the same opportunities afforded to their White counterparts (Franklin & Boyd-Franklin, 2000).

Emotionality: Historically this has been defined as a feminine quality, attitude, belief, and behavior that poses a significant threat to one's manhood.

Trauma-Informed Approach: An approach that attends to social and cultural factors that contribute to self-perception and identity development in persons of color (Garo & Lawson, 2019).

Post-Traumatic Growth: An assumption that individuals are resilient and have the ability to create meaning and to evolve from traumatic experiences (Triplett, Tedeschi, Cann, Calhoun, and Reeve (2012).

Masculinity

Identity development in males has been studied extensively (Ferber, 2007; Franklin & Boyd-Franklin, 2000; Hammond, Banks, & Mattis, 2006). The

DOI: 10.4324/9781003034063-5

stages of development are consistently observed cross-culturally. There appears to be a dichotomy that remains salient in our society, separating men and women according to the presence of masculine and feminine character-istics. One might assume that definitions of masculinity and femininity vary by culture and are, in fact, culture-specific. There are implications of history in our current perceptions, characterizations, and portrayals of masculinity and femininity. One such factor is racism, which has historically created a perception of the Black man as being similar to a caricature. Black men have been categorized and portrayed as being violent, threatening, incapable of higher-order functioning such as logic and reason, and overtly sexual (Curry, 2018). For example, the historical literature indicates that White men feared the sexuality of Black men, often dehumanizing them and reducing them to their physical attributes, likened to animals and barbarians (Ferber, 2007). In essence, these individuals may be perceived as lacking higher-order func-tioning such as logic, reason, and awareness of the impact they have on other individuals, perhaps, even careless about the impact of these actions. Degruy (2017) indicated that racism and discrimination are inherent in our litera-ture, research, and current or modern practices. Separatism by skin color and associated mental capacities of Blacks reverberates in history (Degruy, 2017). The beliefs mentioned here have resulted in our development of trauma due to historical and trans-generational trauma.

Perhaps we should consider the trauma of racism and marginalization and the intersection between gender and race. Feminist theory has long con-tended as a theory by which we come to understand the intersection of the factors mentioned earlier, among others, such as class, socioeconomic sta-tus, sexual orientation, and a plethora of others. The feminist theory ignores the effects of systemic oppression, emasculation, and deprivation of power (Curry, 2018). Furthermore, this theory suggests that Black men endure due to societal endorsement of separatism and race (Curry, 2018). Power and privilege appear to coincide and are the birthright of the elite, a birthright not afforded to Blacks. One may question how Black men cope with and respond to the oppression of this magnitude. Psychological and emotional stunting in the growth and development of Blacks and men, in particular, could be a manifestation of racism, discrimination, and oppression. When one experiences microaggressions, it influences his/her self-perception, appraisal, and perspective of the world (Franklin & Boyd-Franklin, 2000). Microaggressions are subtle acts that occur in various components of the system and are exhibited through behavior and policies that are aligned with racist and discriminatory practices. According to Franklin and Boyd-Franklin (2000), Black males must negotiate their sense of self and identity influenced by cultural expectations and requirements while attempting to adjust to the dominant culture's expectations. Failure to be socialized and forced assimilation contribute to a sense of invisibility.

Identity development, therefore, for Black men must be understood from a different perspective. One staple of the Black community that has been well researched is the Black church. The Black church continues to serve as a beacon of fellowship, restoration, tradition, and liberation from the plight of Blacks. The church is also a source of value-laden information regarding what is acceptable in the Black community and aids in socializing Black men and women. Hypermasculinity in Black men has often been attributed to the messages preached in the church and reinforced in the community. In church related spaces, some Black men are encouraged to present as hypermasculine or overtly and overly sexual, aggressive, and engaging with multiple sexual partners (Ward, 2005). Consistent with this assertion is the risk Black males take in overcoming Black women's defenses to engage in intercourse and achieve a sense of masculinity (Wolfe, 2003). The author contends that these behaviors are an example of overcompensation, consistent with being overly aggressive as they attempt to gain stature and recognition and to reduce their invisibility. Curry (2018) indicates that Black men's contemporary theories are polarized and consistent with the notion of the good versus bad Black man, further feeding into the inherent racism and discrimination that has plagued the Black community. Also, despite these compensatory behaviors, Black men will never achieve the White man's status concerning power and privilege despite being in a patriarchal society (Wolfe, 2003). Hypermasculinity has been linked to a lack of intimacy and poor relationships. This chapter will explore masculinity in Black men and discuss the emergence of trauma as a result of systemic oppression, racism, and the process of socialization on Black men. The expression of Black mens' emotions will be examined.

Evolution of Masculinity in Black Males

Identity development of Blacks has consistently evolved. Modern-day perceptions of Blacks and the construction of masculine and feminine identities are deeply rooted in racist and discriminatory acts that continue to reverberate throughout history. In the era of slavery, Blacks were considered property, with owners being able to trade, sell, and exchange them. The value of Blacks was attributed to their physical appearance and the quality of their labor. Ferber (2007) explored the construction of gender-specific imagery of Blacks during the slave era. Black men were considered the primary source of manual labor and considered large, durable, and incompetent. Black men, perceived as beast-like, posed a threat to White masculinity and created a pervasive fear of White women being affected if the beasts were unable to be controlled.

Slavery can be credited with the construction of the dual identity observed in Black men. Distinguishing the house and field Negro, for example, was a strategy implemented to demonstrate separation effectively.

One must consider the psychological implications of this separation from persons enslaved based on color and perceived inferiority by Whites. Separation served to assert power, control, and influence and to reduce the likelihood of rebellion. Two figures evolved from the separation of Black men—the bad Black man and the good Black man. This dichotomy was reserved for heterosexual Black men and stemmed from theories of evolution and animalism that were rampant among Europeans and the colonial period. The image of the bad Black man was based on the assumption that Black men were animal-like, criminal by nature, and lacked sexual restraint (Cooper, 2005).

On the contrary, the good Black man was defined as one that separates himself from other Blacks and is more aligned with White norms. Present-day perceptions of Black male identity maintain the notions of value being associated with a physical presence, appearance, and innate skill. The ideology of Black men as beasts, untamable, brute, and incompetent reduces them to being inhuman and unworthy of a fundamental right to exist. These images create stark contrasts with current practices (primarily, control of the media), perpetuating the risks, volatility, and fear of Black men.

Negotiating Black Identity-Invisibility

With racism and slavery continuing to be the beacon of America's alleged great past, color-blindness has become an alternative coping and adaptive mechanism, with proponents seeking to ignore the implications and effects of color. The color-blind ideology is based on the assumption that inequality is not due to racism but can be attributed to differences in culture (Ferber, 2007). Blacks have the grueling task of negotiating their identity to assimilate into White or the dominant culture while maintaining a connection to the Black culture. Racism and discrimination create conditions of comfort and the norm for what is socially acceptable and who is desirable (Franklin & Boyd-Franklin, 2000). While fighting for equality, recognition, and success that is comparable to their counterparts, Black men often fall victim to an overwhelming sense of powerlessness, creating internalized anger, rage, anxiety, and depression, among other symptoms, as the effects of racism exceed their ability to cope (Franklin & Boyd-Franklin, 2000). The majority's normative identity to create conditions of comfort requires Blacks and, more specifically, Black men, to assimilate and risk losing recognition, rewards, validation, respect, dignity, legitimacy, and ultimately, their identity (Franklin & Boyd-Franklin, 2000). Loss of identity can be a traumatic experience contributing to emotional and mental dysfunction with long-term consequences, including a threat to one's self-esteem (Courtois & Gold, 2009; Franklin, 1999; Olff, 2012). Emotional well-being and the ability to remain resilient despite these difficulties are necessary for the survival of Black men (Franklin & Boyd-Franklin, 2000). However, one must consider the perceived consequences of Black men's vulnerability in a society where emotional expression is a threat to masculinity, and for Black men may cause increased susceptibility to racial insults and emotional wounds.

Emotionality and Black Males

Racism and discrimination are two factors that have shaped masculinity and, consequently, the emotionality of Black men. Perceived inadequacy and the fight to be seen and heard has contributed to emotional abuse and psychological trauma that has manifested in many generations (Franklin, Boyd-Franklin, & Kelly, 2006). Historically, aggressive behavior and limiting emotional expression have been considered manhood hallmarks, with anything on the contrary being perceived as feminine (Hammond et al., 2006). For Black men, the portrayal of feminine qualities, characteristics, attitudes, and beliefs poses an even more significant threat—being disowned by persons in the Black community. The portrayal of stereotypical masculinity has contributed to Black men. Feared but revered, Black men have the burden of being protectors and providers in their homes, neighborhoods, and communities. How do Black men compensate when faced with difficulty in reconciling their identity in America? How do they cope with invisibility? What are their alternatives when faced with inferiority? How do they compensate for areas in which, based on societal standards, they are lacking? Some scholars speculate that Black men resort to controlling their sexuality, using the number of female partners as a symbol of power (Malebranche, Fields, Bryant, & Harper, 2009). To further exercise power and control, women have reported that men will control their emotional expressiveness, often withholding their emotions and intimacy to exert control (Pease, 2012). There are several consequences of men accepting social norms. These consequences include but are not limited to loneliness, isolation, lack of satisfaction in relationships, challenges in attachment, poor intimacy, and the possibility of rejection. Examples of social norms in the Black community may include phrases such as *suck it up, man up, boys/men do not cry, let him go, he will be OK, stop babying him,* and *stop crying, or I'll give you something to cry about.* These norms reinforce the traditional ideology of masculinity. For Black men, failure to challenge traditional ideology and separation from collectivism and intimacy, characteristics of the Black community, exacerbate symptoms of psychological trauma. The next section of this chapter will introduce two case studies that address traditional masculinity and barriers to emotional expressiveness, attachment, and intimacy in relationships using a trauma-informed approach.

Case Studies: Emotionality, Trauma, and Therapeutic Approaches

Case Study: Andrew

Andrew is a 25-year-old single, heterosexual Black male. He identifies as upper-middle-class. Andrew is a recent graduate of a local community college and is pursuing a career in law and criminal justice. Andrew had been receiving counseling for six months before his most recent session in which he had been absent for nearly five months. Andrew stated, "I have no idea what I am doing here. I was thinking about that when I pulled up. Well, yes I do. I am still having problems with people not being genuine with me. I feel like they're fake." Andrew has an extensive history of tumultuous relationships with his parents, often conflicted with meeting their expectations and pursuing his internal desires and interests. Andrew reported that he is involved with a woman but that it is "unsatisfactory." During his most recent session, he was challenged to explore patterns in his relationships and attraction to women. He stated, "I guess that roughneck side. I mean, I hate to say it, I am talking about that hood shit even though they are so good at masking it." He would repeatedly state, "I feel sorry for them. One of them even disrespected and I'm like 'who the fuck are you talking to, after I did all of this for you?'", and was uncomfortable when confronted about the incongruence in his response to the context of the topic. He reported feeling "hurt" due to a prior partner being in a sexual relationship with another man and the possibility of his current "potential girlfriend" having multiple partners. He expressed discomfort with being "hurt" and "played," stating that men are "savage," and he is attempting to transition more fully into manhood. Andrew expresses that he desires a woman who is "only for him" but acknowledges reservations about closeness and connectedness with women.

Case Study: Mark

Mark is a 44-year-old single, heterosexual Puerto Rican and Black male. He identifies as upper-middle-class. He possesses a high school diploma and certification in a trade. He is currently employed as a construction manager and reports that he frequently travels for work. He is divorced and has three children, two of whom he raises while the third child resides with the mother. Mark presented for the session, expressing that he "just feels depressed." He reports being unsatisfied with his romantic relationships stating, "I do everything. I am a provider, a protector, and a giver. I do not see what more someone could want." He reported that his wife "cheated" during their marriage, and he was "devastated. [They] tried to work it out, but that was not enough." He became dysregulated in session when exploring the relationship with his biological mother, who abandoned him when he was 3 years old due to substance abuse. He reported being raised by his father, who was "poor but did his very best and raised [him] to be the hardworking man that [he] is." Mark reports that he is romantically involved with a "younger woman" and "just does not know." He expressed fear of being vulnerable and "not wanting someone to take advantage of [him] because of that."

Trauma-Informed Practice and Application of Interventions

Inherent in Andrew and Mark's dialogue are cultural narratives of masculinity in Black males. Consistent with previous assertions of masculine expression, both clients have defined their manhood by physical ability, financial contributions, and providing to meet their partners' needs in romantic relationships. Both clients alluded to gender norms ingrained in Black males, including hypersexuality of Black men, degradation of women, involvement with multiple partners, invulnerability, and being emotionally unavailable. Power and control were exercised through providing tangible or material items while being negligent of emotional needs, the desire for connectedness and attachment, and fulfillment beyond sexual satisfaction in romantic relationships. Like Andrew and Mark, Black men suffer silently, continually being conflicted with whether to express their emotions or risk the consequences of vulnerability (Pease, 2012). Often, Black men will opt to withhold their emotions as they are reminded of the consequences of vulnerability. As a result of assimilating to protect oneself, devastation, rage, loneliness and isolation, depression, and assaults to one's sense of value and self-esteem often occur as emotional restraint becomes a protective mechanism (Franklin & Boyd-Franklin, 2000).

For Blacks, historical narratives that are derived from transgenerational trauma must be prioritized in treatment. To explore Black men's narratives and the effects on emotionality and intimacy, an adept counselor would implement a trauma-informed approach that attends to social and cultural factors contributing to self-perception and identity development (Garo & Lawson, 2019). The following techniques and interventions would be appropriate in treating Black males who experience race-related trauma that impacts emotionality and intimacy: (1) identify the internalized story(ies), (2) identify expectations of the dominant culture from the client's perspective, (3) identify and explore the client's cultural identity, (4) explore the effects of conflict between the expectations of the dominant culture and one's identity, (5) deliberate rumination, and (6) implement post-traumatic growth strategies (Evans, Hemmings, Burkhalter, & Lacy, 2016; Garo & Lawson, 2019; Triplett et al., 2012). Post-traumatic growth assumes that, in this case, Black males are resilient and possess the ability to create meaning and evolve from a traumatic experience (Triplett et al., 2012).

I begin the succeeding session by engaging both clients in exploring their internalized perception of manhood. For example, Andrew described men as "savage." His statement, "Who the fuck are you talking to, after I did all of this for you?" suggests that he has internalized providing or offering material and tangible items as a strategy for exerting control and influence over women. In the session, I would engage Andrew to define further "savage." Given that Andrew has frequently referenced the slave mentality in session, I would engage Andrew in exploring how savagery can be perceived as primitive and relates to Black men's earlier perceptions. Exploring the social and cultural context of identity is important in understanding individuals' identities (Franklin & Boyd-Franklin, 2000).

Similarly, I would explore Andrew and Mark's perceptions of manhood. Exploring their perceptions of manhood would include having an in-depth dialogue that seeks to understand the roles and tasks assigned to men and, more importantly, similarities and differences based on race and ethnicity. Character traits such as being a "provider, protector, and forgiver" suggests that both clients have internalized these traits and experience dissonance when their female counterparts fail to reciprocate in the manner expected of them. Dominant cultural norms and expectations perpetuate harmful stereotypes that have been internalized and adopted by minority groups (Garo & Lawson, 2019). To identify these stereotypes, I engage both clients in storytelling, a process in which they freely express experiences and encounters that have constructed their perception of self. For example, in the following session, Mark stated, "When my dad left my mom, he just kept going. He didn't cry about it. He was stern, strong, and would whoop my behind, but he loved me." Mark reported that this experience taught him "not to cry. Get your shit together and move on. It ain't no sense in crying over spilled milk." I encouraged Mark to elaborate on this analogy and how it relates to his thoughts and behavior. Mark reported that he believes "Black men are supposed to be strong and fearless. It's a sign of weakness to cry even though we want to." Andrew reflected these sentiments but went further to suggest, "That's what the White people want from us. They want to see us broken. Crying and acting crazy. So we have to hold it together." I engaged both clients in exploring the dominant culture's expectations from their perspectives, expectations of the Black community and the culture both clients identified with. Both clients reported that Black men are expected to be "strong, unafraid, blunt, and aggressive. That's the only way to make it."

Interestingly, both men reported that Black women "love that shit." Andrew expressed that despite his attraction to "ghetto females and the ones that act like they don't care," he desired to have a woman that he could call his own and a woman he can be vulnerable with. Due to both fear of vulnerability and expressing their emotions in an intimate setting, I would engage both clients in deliberate rumination. Deliberate rumination is an intervention in which the clients reflect on unpleasant experiences that contribute to negative perceptions (Garo & Lawson, 2019). From a trauma-informed approach, this intervention is comparable to in-vivo exposure. For example, I explored with Andrew an incident in which an unknown individual robbed him. Andrew stated, "Whew, this shit is all coming back to me now. I remember him saying, 'Shut the fuck up shaking and sweating. You're a grown ass man.'" Andrew became nostalgic during the session and appeared to be in a trance. I implemented grounding techniques (e.g., the five senses) to bring Andrew into the present. I explored with Andrew what was occurring in his body to create awareness of how the body stores traumatic events. Andrew was able to identify thoughts and feelings related to the incident and how this encounter shaped his response to fellow Black men.

Black men are likely to experience great anguish as they cope with conflicting expectations (Franklin & Boyd-Franklin, 2000). In their plight to become visible and accepted, these men often overcompensate, and even more often, it is to their disadvantage (Wolfe, 2003). Due to systemic racism and inequality, Black men are more likely to experience powerlessness. The powerlessness Black men experience occurs as the result of them attempting to cope with the lack of opportunity, underachievement, and invisibility, all of which summate to emotional torture (Franklin & Boyd-Franklin, 2000; Franklin et al., 2006). For Black men to evolve and flourish despite these experiences, counselors must create a strengths-based environment that is solution-focused and explores self-efficacy (Hoge, Austin, & Pollack, 2007).

I engaged both clients in challenging maladaptive thoughts that are associated with feelings of anger, frustration, sadness, and inadequacy. Both clients identified the accuracy and helpfulness of these thoughts associated with negative experiences. Clients were then encouraged to separate themselves from the problem and identify alternative thoughts that are accurate and helpful. For example, Mark's statement, "I do everything. I'm a provider, protector, and a giver. I don't see what more someone could want" was reframed to "I am more than enough. I'm a provider, protector, and a giver. There is someone that will appreciate that if they are for me." This statement empowers Mark and aids in increasing his self-esteem as he recognizes positive attributes in himself.

Reconstructing narratives allows clients to create meaning from their experiences. For example, Mark expressed fear of vulnerability as his previous wife took advantage of him. I engaged Mark in exploring how vulnerability does not equate to naivety and to consider strategies to gradually become vulnerable with individuals who he is safe with and able to trust.

Mark was able to identify examples of individuals with whom he has a close relationship and who have not manipulated or abused him. Mark was able to reconstruct his wife's negative interaction and identify what he learned from the relationship to strengthen further romantic relationships. Both clients were able to identify how being invulnerable, although beneficial, was counterproductive to their goal of companionship. Both clients engaged in redefining vulnerability in the context of romantic relationships and safe environments that encourage and support vulnerability as a positive character trait in men.

Clinical Expertise and Insights

For Black males, the grueling task of negotiating one's identity poses even more of a threat to their well-being and self-perception, as they are often not accepted by the dominant culture, and due to systemic oppression, are frequently unable to access the same opportunities afforded to their White counterparts. Invisibility becomes an inevitable consequence, with Black males developing maladaptive coping and compensatory strategies to manage trauma. An adept counselor uses a trauma-informed approach when counseling ethnic minorities and, in particular, those significantly affected by racism. A culturally relevant assessment (e.g., biopsychosocial and spiritual assessment) that seeks to obtain information about the client's personal and family history, social interactions and environment, and culture is valuable in creating an environment that fosters safety and trust. Exploring perceptions of manhood and experiences that have contributed to Black men's assumptions about their role and tasks allows for the construction of the narrative that shapes thoughts, feelings, and behaviors. It is beneficial to identify and label maladaptive thoughts about traditional roles and tasks of manhood as defined by the dominant culture and those specific to the individual's culture. It is important to explore how Black men define emotionality and social and cultural constructions of these beliefs, as this influences intimacy and satisfaction in relationships. For example, Mark's fear of being vulnerable because he "does not want anyone to take advantage of that" indicates that Black men may associate vulnerability with femininity. This association contributes to an internal conflict that becomes increasingly difficult to cope with. Deliberate rumination and in-vivo exposure to intimate environments that evoke strong emotional reactions allow Black men to gradually identify with their emotions and observe intimacy outside of sexual relationships. Challenging and replacing maladaptive thoughts identified through deliberate rumination is the beginning of reconstructing the trauma and identifying alternative thoughts to bring a new meaning to these experiences. Black men require recognition, validation, and empowerment to become visible to themselves and begin the healing process.

Critical Clinical Questions

In counseling Black men who present with these challenges, the adept counselor may pose the following four questions:

1. How does the power and control dynamic inherent in the counseling relationship perpetuate feelings of powerlessness?
2. How can a counselor's presence in the relationship serve as a reference for secure attachment and foster belonging?
3. How do the counselor's beliefs and assumptions reinforce the oppression and invisibility experienced by Black men?
4. How does failure to explore the social and cultural context of racism and narratives of manhood reinforce Black men's trauma?

Readings and Additional Resources

Curry, T. J. (2017). *Man-not: Race, class, genre, and the dilemmas of black manhood*. Philadelphia, PA: Temple University Press.

Majors, R., & Mancini, J. (1993). *Cool pose: The dilemmas of black manhood in America*. New York: Touchstone.

Muhammad, W. (2016). *Understanding the assault on the Black man, Black manhood, and Black masculinity*. Atlanta, GA: A-Team Publishing.

Wilson, J. (2019). *Like a man: Fighting for freedom from emotional incarceration*. Colorado Springs, CO: David C. Cook.

References

Cooper, F. R. (2005). Against bipolar black masculinity: Intersectionality, assimilation, identity performance, and hierarchy. *UC Davis Law Review, 39*, 853. Retrieved from https://scholars.law.unlv.edu/cgi/viewcontent.cgi?article=2151&context=facpub

Courtois, C. A., & Gold, S. N. (2009). The need for inclusion of psychological trauma in the professional curriculum: A call to action. *Psychological Trauma: Theory, Research, Practice, and Policy, 1*(1), 3–23.doi: 10.1037/aa0015244

Curry, T. J. (2018). Killing boogeymen: Phallicism and the misandric mischaracterizations of Black males in theory. *Res Philosophica*. doi: 10.11612/ resphil.1612

Degruy-Leary, J. (2017). *Post-traumatic Slave Syndrome: America's legacy of enduring injury*. Portland, OR: Joy DeGruy Publications Inc.

Evans, A. M., Hemmings, C., Burkhalter, C., & Lacy, V. (2016). Responding to race related trauma: Counseling and research recommendations to promote post-traumatic growth when counseling African American males. *The Journal of Counselor Preparation and Supervision, 8*(1), 1–20.

Ferber, A. L. (2007). The construction of Black masculinity: White supremacy now and then. *Journal of Sport and Social Issues, 31*(1), 11–24. doi: 10.1177/0193723506296829

Franklin, A. J. (1999). Invisibility syndrome and racial identity development in psychotherapy and counseling African American men. *The Counseling Psychologist, 27*(6), 761–793. doi: 10.1177/0011000099276002

Franklin, A. J., & Boyd-Franklin, N. (2000). Invisibility syndrome: A clinical model of the effects of racism on African-American males. *American Journal of Orthopsychiatry*, *70*(1), 33–41. doi: 10.1037/h0087691

Franklin, A. J., Boyd-Franklin, N., & Kelly, S. (2006). Racism and invisibility: Race-related stress, emotional abuse and psychological trauma for people of color. *Journal of Emotional Abuse*, *6*(2–3), 9–30. doi: 10.1300/J135v06n02_02

Garo, L. A., & Lawson, T. (2019). My story, my way: Conceptualization of narrative therapy with trauma-exposed Black male youth. *Urban Education Research & Policy Annuals*, *6*(1). Retrieved from https://journals.uncc.edu/urbaned/article/view/914

Hammond, W. P., Banks, H., & Mattis, J. S. (2006). Masculinity ideology and forgiveness of racial discrimination among African American men: Direct and interactive relationships. *Sex Roles*, *55*(9), 679–690.

Hoge, E. A., Austin, E. D., & Pollack, M. H. (2007). Resilience: Research evidence and conceptual considerations for posttraumatic stress disorder. *Depression and Anxiety*, *24*(2), 139–152. doi: 10.1002/da.20175

Malebranche, D. J., Fields, E. L., Bryant, L. O., & Harper, S. R. (2009). Masculine socialization and sexual risk behaviors among Black men who have sex with men: A qualitative exploration. *Men and Masculinities*, *12*(1), 90–112. doi: 10.1177/1097184X07309504

Olff, M. (2012). Bonding after trauma: On the role of social support and the oxytocin system in traumatic stress. *European Journal of Psychotraumatology*, *3*(1), 18597. doi: 10.3402/ejpt.v3i0.18597

Pease, B. (2012). The politics of gendered emotions: Disrupting men's emotional investment in privilege. *Australian Journal of Social Issues*, *47*(1), 125–142. doi: 10.1002/j.1839-4655.2012.tb00238.x

Triplett, K. N., Tedeschi, R. G., Cann, A., Calhoun, L. G., & Reeve, C. L. (2012). Posttraumatic growth, meaning in life, and life satisfaction in response to trauma. *Psychological Trauma: Theory, Research, Practice, and Policy*, *4*(4), 400. doi: 10.1037/a0024204

Ward, E. G. (2005). Homophobia, hypermasculinity and the US black church. *Culture, Health & Sexuality*, *7*(5), 493–504. doi: 10.1080/13691050500151248

Wolfe, W. A. (2003). Overlooked role of African-American males' hypermasculinity in the epidemic of unintended pregnancies and HIV/AIDS cases with young African-American women. *Journal of the National Medical Association*, *95*(9), 846. Retrieved from www.ncbi.nlm.nih.gov/pmc/articles/PMC2594477/pdf/jnma00313-0083.pdf

5

HONOR AND VIRGINITY

The Role of Honor and Virginity in the Sexual Acculturation of Women from the Middle East to the United States

Leyla Gulcur

Key Terms

sexual narrative: Sexual scripts, stories, and beliefs that are internalized based on cultural, familial, and relational experiences. Often these sexual narratives are unconscious, and part of the work of sex therapy is to make them conscious (Iasenza, 2010).

sexual acculturation: Sexual acculturation may look different from cultural acculturation, in that sexual migrants may pick and choose among whichever sexual narratives best fit their newly re-defined gender and sexual identities, regardless of whether they come from their culture of origin or host country (Fuks, Smith, Peláez, De Stefano, & Brown, 2018).

Background

In this chapter I explore the impact of narratives surrounding honor and virginity on the sexual lives of women from the Middle East living in the United States. I also discuss the challenges that women from these cultures face in reconciling a potential culture clash between sexual narratives that they may have internalized from their countries of origin with narratives they may be exposed to in their host country, the United States. I present case histories of women from two Middle Eastern countries—Turkey and Jordan—and discuss the competencies and counseling strategies that are needed in order to create effective therapeutic interventions with this population.

Although sexuality-related challenges such as vaginismus, dyspareunia, arousal, and orgasmic difficulties are common in women from Middle Eastern countries (Sungur, 2012), sex and relationship therapy services are

DOI: 10.4324/9781003034063-6

underutilized by Middle Eastern women in the United States (Rahman, 2018). This is likely influenced by the fact that Middle Eastern women's premarital sexualities are often regulated by their families and communities, through cultural and religious discourses and practices, and include norms on premarital virginity, norms on modesty and sexual passivity, lack of knowledge about sexuality, restrictions on mobility and pre-marital dating, and the regulation of marriage through forced or arranged marriages (Hawkey, Ussher, & Perz, 2018).

Cultural narratives that control women's sexualities exist in all regions of the world, but the form that specific narratives take varies according to local context, in regions as far flung as South Asia, Latin America, Europe, and even the United States (Olsen & García-Moreno, 2017; Noor, 2019). Nonetheless, these narratives are highly salient in the Middle East; additionally, an aspect that distinguishes the Middle East from other regions is the pervasiveness and monolithic nature of honor/virginity narratives, with little room for women to be exposed to alternative discourses (e.g. those encouraging sexual choice and pleasure).

There is thus a strong cultural imperative in the region that women must be virgins before marriage (Tuğrul & Kabakçı, 1997). Virginity is seen as a pre-requisite to sexual honor, and virginity tests can be performed on young girls and women who are unmarried to ensure that their hymen is intact, despite the fact that virginity tests are not an accurate measure of whether one has had intercourse or not (Olsen & García-Moreno, 2017). When a woman or young girl is perceived to be involved in any conduct that carries an implication of pre-marital sexual relations (thereby calling her "virgin" status into question), she may be sanctioned and ostracized as having "damaged" her family and community's honor; in extreme cases this can even take the form of "honor killings" (Abu-Odeh, 2011). These messages can be internalized to such an extent that they become both embodied (i.e. "My hymen needs to be intact until marriage") as well as "disembodied" ("I, as a woman, carry the honor for my family and community") (Abboud, Jemmott, & Sommers, 2015).

In addition, women from the Middle East who have immigrated may have to contend with constructions of sexuality from at least two cultures that may be at conflict with each other, therefore creating an internal "sexual culture clash" with which women may have to contend while living in the host country (Dune, Perz, Mengesha, & Ayika, 2017). This is a tension that many immigrants—not just Middle Eastern women—experience (Meston & Ahrold, 2010); however, in the case of women from the region, reconciling these competing sexual narratives to achieve sexual acculturation may hold challenges, especially in cases where the family and community of origin have had an excessive impact on sexual socialization. For example, often, on the wedding night, the extended family expects to be shown a bloodstained sheet following intercourse, as proof of the bride's virginity. It is no surprise that such pressures can create fear of sex in general and of penetration in particular for women.

Successful acculturation is defined as one in which the individual is able to integrate both the culture of their country of origin as well as that of their new host country, and most research has shown this type of acculturation to be the most adaptive response for bicultural individuals (Berry, 1997). However, successful *sexual acculturation* for women from the Middle East may not fit Berry (1997) model adequately, especially when sexual norms and narratives from the country of origin clash with the host country's narratives. In this chapter, I will also explore, through case histories, the limits to the acculturation model as it stands and suggest an alternative to Berry's acculturation model—one in which the individual gets to pick and discard aspects of sexual narratives that clash with each other.

The impact of such pressures on honor and virginity can explain why many women from the Middle East experience painful intercourse and vaginismus, often along with trauma symptoms, sexual inhibition, and low desire (Sungur, 2012). It is with this cultural background in mind that the therapist is encouraged to address the impact of these internalized social constructions of sexuality on possible sexual dysfunctions, while also working at the behavioral level to facilitate a change in the way clients have sex through culturally appropriate sex therapy interventions. For example, asking the client(s) to incorporate sensate focus (e.g. for painful intercourse or vaginismus)—or internal pelvic massage—without addressing the fear of penetration due to the cultural norm of virginity will most likely result in a failed therapeutic intervention.

Finally, this chapter specifically addresses situations faced by cis-women from the Middle East who are heterosexual. LGBTQIA+ individuals from the Middle East will have their own particular set of challenges that is beyond the scope of this chapter.

Case Presentations

A question to keep in mind when doing sex therapy with women from the Middle East is to ask oneself: "What are the culturally competent foundations that are important for me to know?" Within this context, there are some guiding principles to keep in mind. First, it is important for the therapist to work collaboratively with the client, and especially when it comes to creating take-home sex therapy exercises, it is important to co-create treatment approaches such that the exercises themselves take into account cultural sensibilities and even contradictions (e.g. shame or fear of losing one's virginity through penetration, coupled with the desire to experience sexual freedom and pleasure). Second, it is important to use a multi-modal approach (body-mind-emotions), which takes into account the impact of any cultural practices that are associated with fear, shame, or guilt. And finally, it is important during therapy to allow for, normalize, and hold space for competing and contradictory sexual narratives that may create cognitive dissonance for the client (e.g. "I must act demure and be a virgin to protect my family's honor" and "I want to feel free to experience pleasure in whatever way I want").

Case 1: Arzu

In her late 30s and originally from the southeastern region of Turkey, Arzu immigrated to the United States four years ago when she escaped her abusive husband, who remained in Turkey, and started divorce proceedings from afar. Originally a nurse, she now works as a physician's assistant at a large hospital in the northeastern United States.

Arzu's presenting problem when she came to see me for therapy was that she was having difficulty adjusting to life as a single woman in the US, and that even though she was trying to be open to a new relationship and was currently dating, she was under constant fear that her ex-husband and family would find her and kill her because she was "sullying" her family's honor. In addition, she was experiencing difficulties with her dating life because sexual intercourse was painful (dyspareunia) and penetration was often impossible due to chronic tension in her vaginal muscles (vaginismus); these sexual problems had started with her marriage and were made worse by the fact that her husband had forced her to have intercourse on their wedding night even though it was very painful and that the family had to be shown a bloodied sheet afterwards. "Immediately after he came, he pulled out of me and started to hit my back to try to get the blood to come out on the sheets so that he could prove that I was a virgin. I was hysterical, but he did not care."

Early on, beginning in our third session, I undertook an extensive sexual history assessing Arzu's socialization around sexuality and relationships. While space limitations prevent me from listing all components of the sexual history (Iasenza, 2010 for the full questionnaire), I asked her about her earliest childhood memories about sex and relationships, such as what messages about sexuality and gender roles she received from her family members, peers, books and the media, how affection was shown in the family, how nudity/body issues were handled, what she was told about dating and premarital sex, and her first sexual feelings and masturbation.

As we talked, Arzu told me that her childhood socialization was extremely restrictive, with her family background from a conservative religious rural area. Yet, as we talked further, it became clear that Arzu was struggling with integrating two competing sexual narratives (Iasenza, 2020): an honor/virginity narrative and a resistance narrative. Thus, much of our early work during early sessions together was to identify and unpack these two competing narratives and to deal with the cognitive dissonance that arose out of their seeming contradictions. In doing so, an important guiding principle was for me to help create a safe holding environment (Winnicott, 1987) where Arzu was able to explore these two narratives safely and without fear of judgment. To create this holding environment, I asked non-judgmental clarifying questions but also remained silent for long stretches of time and listened as Arzu unfolded her story, which allowed for the holding space:

> *M*y family was very strict with me when I was growing up. Women who go out by themselves are the subject of scandal and abuse by the rest of the community, which assumes automatically that she is loose and having illicit sex. I was not even allowed to go to the grocery store without my father or some approved male chaperone. My family took me to the doctor for virginity checks at least once a week from about the age of 6 years old until I was about 13 years old. They were very concerned that I needed to learn how to obey men so that when I got married I would be a good wife.
>
> But, even though I had to submit to my family's wishes and had a lot of fear, inside me I was seething and angry and yearned to feel free and not under pressure. When I came to the US I saw that the women here are able to date and love more freely. After a while, I knew this was the right way to live for me. So even though it is not part of my culture, and even though it was difficult for me at first, I started online dating.

At the same time, we also started addressing the vaginismus and painful intercourse experiences that Arzu was having. In general, treatment for vaginismus and painful intercourse follows a multi-modal medical approach that involves pelvic floor physical therapy, vaginal dilators, CBT, and even Botox injections (Pacik & Geletta, 2017). However, Arzu was very clear in stating that this approach would not work for her and that any penetrative techniques would in fact make her feel worse.

At this point, it seemed appropriate to drill down further into these fears that came up when she thought about intercourse. Thus I used the Downward Arrow Technique (Beck, Rush, Shaw & Emery, 1979) to drill down into core beliefs that fueled Arzu's fear of penetration. For this technique to work, I have found it important to ask the client to "communicate" with her "irrational self" in answering these questions, as core beliefs are very often covered up by more "rational" beliefs such as "There's nothing wrong with sex and sexual pleasure, especially when you're married." Unsurprisingly, these fears were fueled by the virginity/honor narrative. The following dialogue is an excerpt from a session in which we drilled down into a core belief.

Arzu: I worry that I won't ever be able to have a good relationship.
Me: And what would it mean if you couldn't?
Arzu: It would mean that I am damaged because I'm no longer a virgin and can't satisfy my partner if I can't have sex with him.
Me: And what would it mean if you couldn't?
Arzu: It would mean that I messed it up; it's my fault.
Me: What does it mean for it to be your fault?
Arzu: It means I'm damaged; I lost my honor.
Me: What would it mean to you if you lost your honor?
Arzu: It would mean that now I will be ostracized—or worse.
Me: What would it mean to you if you were ostracized?
Arzu: It would mean I'm completely alone and isolated in this world.

As you can see here, Arzu drilled down to a core belief that she will end up alone and isolated if she is unable to have sex; although the virginity narrative did not come up in this particular dialogue, during subsequent sessions Arzu also linked her fears and avoidance of sex/penetration to her family's expectation that she had to be a virgin and act like one even if she were married. Thus, the extreme emphasis on protecting virginity until marriage led Arzu to associate penetration with being loose/non-virginal, even when it was socially and culturally sanctioned after marriage.

The identification of this and other related core beliefs helped us move to the next stage of the therapy, which was to explore the contradictions between her (unconscious) core belief that pleasure equaled lack of honor with her desire to date, enter a new relationship, and experience pleasurable sex. This allowed us to further explore what pleasure might feel like in her body through somatic techniques and mindful sexuality exercises that she could do on her own (Brotto, 2018). Thus, rather than choosing treatments such as pelvic floor massage and dilators, which would possibly have re-traumatized and re-triggered feelings of fear around insertion and penetration, focusing instead on enhancing access to pleasure through non-penetrative means, paired with relaxation and mindfulness, allowed Arzu to start having more sex-positive experiences in addition to letting go of the core beliefs that prevented her from accessing her pleasure.

Later on, as Arzu started to feel more comfortable unpacking and examining her sexual narratives, we began to talk about how to integrate these two competing sexual narratives. This was the beginning of a sexual acculturation process that took several months, in which Arzu continued to navigate the challenges stemming from her internalization of patriarchal honor and virginity norms and to reconcile these values with a more pleasure-oriented approach to sexuality that she wanted to embrace as an immigrant and bicultural person. It is important to note that, unlike Berry's (1997) model of acculturation, this was not a linear process and what worked for Arzu's sexual acculturation was to pick and choose aspects of her culture or origin as well as her host country to create her own individualized sexual acculturation.

Case 2: Noor

Currently in her mid 40s and originally from an educated urban middle-class family, Noor was sent by her father from Jordan to the United States around 20 years ago to receive an MBA. While she was a graduate student, Noor was subsequently pressured by her family to get married so that she wouldn't "get into trouble" as a single woman living by herself with no one to monitor her behavior. Noor initially resisted, loving the feeling of freedom that she experienced living as a single woman in a large city. Nevertheless, when her family found out she was dating a fellow grad student, they threatened to cut off her tuition and living expenses and force her to return to Jordan if she didn't get married immediately, emphasizing how her behavior could negatively affect the honor of the family and their community back home if anyone found out.

Noor, afraid of losing her opportunity to be educated (which would provide her with some autonomy and self-actualization), married the man she was dating in a hastily arranged civil ceremony in the US. This was made even more complicated by the fact that her then-boyfriend told her that if she did not marry him, he would tell her family that she had sex with him and was no longer a virgin. In Noor's words: "I got married in order to save my honor."

Nevertheless, although she acquiesced to her family's wishes, Noor also had a resistance narrative. She told me that early on when she was living in Amman she really wanted to get married and divorced so that she could be free from people talking about whether or not she was a virgin. She told me she had dated boys secretly, often telling her parents that she was meeting a girlfriend, when in fact she was meeting her boyfriend. Noor told me that this resistance strategy felt empowering and shameful at same time: "It was the only time I was able to feel free, but at the same time it made me feel like I was a 'girl of loose morals.'"

When she came to see me, Noor's presenting problem was that she was unable to experience sexual pleasure and had difficulty having orgasms. She expressed that she wasn't able to ask her husband for what she wanted in sex, didn't even know what she liked or didn't like, and that she felt a lot of guilt and shame during sex with him.

A complicating factor was that Noor had experienced sexual abuse by an uncle when she was 8 years old. Her younger sister witnessed it and—playing into the narrative that the sex abuse was somehow her sister's fault— "tattled" to their mother. When Noor's mother found out about the sexual abuse, she was devastated—and promptly pressured Noor to keep it a secret from the rest of the family, fearing the "damage to the family honor" that might ensue. Noor had to carry the secret for the family and, through her mother, internalized her shame and guilt and responsibility for caring the honor of the family.

A large part of the reason Noor wanted to come to the US was to escape and have her sexual freedom. Even though she ostensibly came to the US to get an MBA, she confessed to me that the real reason was so that she could get away from the societal stigma and pressure around sexuality and dating.

A large portion of our work, after identifying her narratives, was to work with feelings of shame and guilt. As corroborated by other research (Ozyegin, 2009), sexual secretiveness in the form of lying about dating boys created feelings of guilt in Noor, but these feelings were overshadowed by guilt's more insidious cousin, shame. It is important to note here the distinction between the two; guilt comprised a feeling about something that Noor *did* (her behavior), whereas shame embodied a feeling about something that Noor *was* (her identity). In particular, Noor's sexual shame emerged as a combination of her internalized sexual narrative of her being responsible to maintain her virginity and thus her family's honor, and yet being unable to do so due to her uncle's sexual abuse. This became internalized by her telling me "I was now damaged (not a virgin) so I might as well be a slut and be with lots of guys" but "I can't experience pleasure because it reminds me of the pleasure my body felt when my uncle touched me."

Shame for Noor was a difficult emotion to process because it had both cognitive and somatic components. In order to address shame's cognitive components, I asked Noor to write down all the negative thoughts she had about herself as a sexual being ("I was abused, it's my fault, I'm damaged").

In addition, to address shame's somatic components, we used Gendlin's book *Focusing* (Gendlin, 1981) to help Noor slowly identify where shame resided in her body ("in my cheeks and stomach"), its texture ("it burns, it's hollow"), its color ("red"), and finally, whether it had a message or a statement ("this is unfair"). The final message shows how, by going *into* the feeling, rather than avoiding it, the shame eventually shifted and transformed into something else: a nascent recognition that having to carry the shame was unfair, creating room for a possible alternative narrative that rejected the idea that she was responsible for her sexual honor.

Later on, we used the Downward Arrow Technique (Beck et al., 1979) to drill down into core beliefs around sexual pleasure. Through this process, Noor arrived at a core belief that she was a "bad, damaged person of low worth" if she focused on her sexual pleasure. Thus, the extreme emphasis on protecting virginity until marriage led Noor to associate loss of control and pleasurable sex with being damaged/non-virgin, even when it was socially and culturally sanctioned after marriage. Yet, her being able to unearth and unpack these beliefs also opened Noor up to the idea that it was possible to think about having the right to feel sexual pleasure.

The desire to experience pleasure, coupled with sexual anhedonia can be seen as a symptom of clashing sexual narratives. I asked Noor, "What about pleasure and desire with even your husband, then? Can you express desire to your husband? Can you ask him to do things to you sexually that give you pleasure?" Noor's answer was conflicted. She told me: "No, you cannot show sexual desire to your husband. If you show sexual desire to your husband, then that means you have the capacity to go and have sex with someone else for pleasure. So I would be seen as a 'loose woman' even in the context of marriage."

However, at the same time, Noor said, "I know that there are women who can have pleasure. I have talked to my American friends here in the US, and they tell me things like how they have such great orgasms and how it makes them feel so good and so fulfilled. I want that for myself. I want to feel this thing that is so mysterious and scary and yet so good."

Thus in subsequent sessions, we were able to co-create homework that focused on "pleasure research." We created an exercise in which Noor touched herself sensually while simultaneously using objects around her that activated all of her sensory functions: a candle for seeing, music for hearing, a soft blanket for touching, chocolates for tasting, and thyme oil for smelling. This and other similar exercises, done repeatedly over several months, was based on the principles of mindfulness and sensate focus, but co-created by me and Noor, to accommodate both her personal tastes (e.g. chocolates) and cultural tastes (e.g. music by Jordanian bands). By the end of three months, Noor was able to experience sexual pleasure on her own.

Counseling Strategies

Counseling strategies as they pertain to women from the Middle East would ideally be multi-modal and address the mind (identify, process, and reframe the impact of sexual narratives, scripts, and core beliefs), emotions (feel and process guilt, fear, shame, etc.), and the body (somatic and mindfulness exercises):

- *Identify* competing and/or multiple sexual narratives via undertaking a thorough sexual history. The sexual history can also double as a therapeutic intervention to become aware of and process internalized scripts around sexuality, gender roles, and relationships (Iasenza, 2010).
- *Create* a holding space for and normalize the client's exploration of competing sexual narratives (e.g. "I'm damaged because I had sex before marriage," versus "I want the freedom to choose when and whom I have sex with").
- *Facilitate the processing of emotions/feelings* of fear, guilt, and shame associated with honor and virginity narratives via somatic techniques such as focusing.

- *Facilitate the identification and reframing of cognitions/core beliefs* regarding sexuality and relationships using CBT techniques such as the Downward Arrow Technique and reframing/restructuring (Beck et al., 1979).
- *Educate* clients on the availability of expanded sexual models that move beyond arousal, penetrative sex, and orgasms (Iasenza, 2010).
- *Educate* clients on mindfulness, mindful sexuality techniques, and the role of pleasure *before* suggesting "standard" sex therapy treatments such as vaginal dilators (Brotto, 2018).
- *Co-create* sex therapy exercises in collaboration with the client, rather than being prescriptive.
- *Facilitate sexual acculturation* by helping the client identify and investigate the wanted and unwanted aspects of competing sexual narratives to arrive at an integrated and re-defined sexual identity/sexual narrative.

Lessons Learned

An important consideration for the reader is that while the sex negativity and inequality that Middle Eastern women face in their own countries has primarily led local activists and practitioners to fight for sexual rights at the national level—often facing resistance from their own communities as well as governments—the context in the United States is more complicated. On the one hand, immigrant women are faced with culturally sanctioned forms of inequality in their own communities. On the other hand, the current political climate of hate in the United States, in which Asians and Middle Easterners—especially those of Muslim origin—are openly vilified and worse, creates a double bind for those of us who have to now deal with not only one source of inequality (from within our own communities/families) but also with the open hatred from many right-wing individuals and groups in our host country, the United States. This double bind creates an insidious trap—if we fight for our rights within our own communities, we are then seen by many in the majority as examples of "backwards Muslims." If, on the other hand, we fight against racism from the majority, we are then forced into the unenviable position of defending everything in our communities as part of our cultural heritage (even the sex-negative practices). Thus the reader is encouraged to balance being culturally sensitive within the larger context of an understanding of gender inequality and patriarchal sexual norms. Within this context, some lessons learned are the following:

1. A thorough assessment of sexual history forms an important cornerstone of identifying cultural factors that impact one's sexual narratives.

2. Especially in cases where there are complex emotions such as shame, guilt, and fear, the ability of the therapist to hold space in a non-judgmental way will allow for the client to explore these difficult emotions and to process them.

3. Sex therapy techniques and exercises developed in the West may need to be modified or sequenced differently for Middle East populations; homework needs to be co-created together with the client.

4. Sexual acculturation does not follow a linear path, and any changes in sexual narratives stemming from experiences in the heritage culture and in the host country culture may or may not contradict each other. The take-way is that it is important to let acculturation unfold at its own pace, where clients decide which cultural bits and pieces to keep and which to throw out.

5. For the therapist, there is a balancing act between being respectful of culture and taking a stance against gender inequities and practices that oppress women. This may pose some dissonance in therapists who believe that it is wrong to impose one's own worldview on clients and that the client must be met where they are culturally; however, while this stance is commendable, it must be balanced within the larger context of social justice and human rights principles.

6. Relatedly, it is important to be aware of and address how the therapist's values and own cultural background and experiences impact the therapeutic relationship and course of therapy, and to be aware of and acknowledge the match or mismatch between client and therapist.

7. Space limitations did not allow for a discussion of how other socioeconomic variables such as class, sexual orientation, gender identity and gender expression, can influence the path and outcomes of culturally sensitive therapy; however I encourage the reader to take these into account as well.

Questions for the Reader to Consider

1. How do I become aware of and identify my own values, ideologies, and cultural narratives around the notions of virginity, honor, pre-marital sex, and gender roles that could either facilitate or act as a barrier to developing a productive therapeutic relationship with my clients?

2. What steps do I need to take to ensure that I take cultural background into account as I work with so-called sexual dysfunctions? How do I take into account that sex therapy techniques developed in the US may sometimes do more harm than good (e.g. vaginal dilators to treat vaginismus may re-traumatize a client who is afraid of penetration) and may need to be modified?

Suggested Readings

Abboud, S., Jemmott, L. S., & Sommers, M. S. (2015). "We are Arabs": The embodiment of virginity through Arab and Arab American women's lived experiences. *Sexuality & Culture*, *19*(4), 715–736.

Ilkkaracan, P. (Ed.). (2016). *Deconstructing sexuality in the Middle East: Challenges and discourses*. New York: Routledge.

Sungur, M. (2012). The role of cultural factors in the course and treatment of sexual problems: failures, pitfalls, and successes in a complicated case from Turkey. In K. S. Hall & C. A. Graham (Eds.), *The cultural context of sexual pleasure and problems* (pp. 308–329). New York: Routledge.

Ussher, J. M., Perz, J., Metusela, C., Hawkey, A. J., Morrow, M., Narchal, R., & Estoesta, J. (2017). Negotiating discourses of shame, secrecy, and silence: Migrant and refugee women's experiences of sexual embodiment. *Archives of Sexual Behavior*, *46*(7), 1901–1921.

References

Abboud, S., Jemmott, L. S., & Sommers, M. S. (2015). "We are Arabs:" The embodiment of virginity through Arab and Arab American women's lived experiences. *Sexuality & Culture*, *19*(4), 715–736.

Abu-Odeh, L. (2011). Crimes of honor and the construction of gender in Arab societies. *Computational Law Review*, *2*, 1.

Beck, A. T., Rush, A. J., Shaw, B. F., & Emery, G. (1979). *Cognitive therapy of depression*. New York: Guilford Press.

Berry, J. W. (1997). Immigration, acculturation, and adaptation. *Applied psychology*, *46*(1), 5–34.

Brotto, L. A. (2018). *Better sex through mindfulness: How women can cultivate desire*. Vancouver, BC: Greystone Books Ltd.

Dune, T., Perz, J., Mengesha, Z., & Ayika, D. (2017). Culture Clash? Investigating constructions of sexual and reproductive health from the perspective of 1.5 generation migrants in Australia using Q methodology. *Reproductive Health*, *14*(1), 50.

Fuks, N., Smith, N. G., Peláez, S., De Stefano, J., & Brown, T. L. (2018). Acculturation experiences among lesbian, gay, bisexual, and transgender immigrants in Canada. *The Counseling Psychologist*, *46*(3), 296–332.

Gendlin, E. T. (1981). *Focusing*. New York: Bantam Dell.

Hawkey, A. J., Ussher, J. M., & Perz, J. (2018). Regulation and resistance: Negotiation of premarital sexuality in the context of migrant and refugee women. *The Journal of Sex Research*, *55*(9), 1116–1133.

Iasenza, S. (2010). What is queer about sex? Expanding sexual frames in theory and practice. *Family Process*, *49*(3), 291–308.

Iasenza, S. (2020). *Transforming sexual narratives: A relational approach to sex therapy*. New York: Routledge.

Meston, C. M., & Ahrold, T. (2010). Ethnic, gender, and acculturation influences on sexual behaviors. *Archives of Sexual Behavior*, *39*(1), 179–189.

Noor, P. (2019, December 9). 'Now I have to check your hymen': The shocking persistence of virginity tests. *The Guardian*. Retrieved from www.theguardian.com/lifeandstyle/2019/dec/09/hymen-virginity-tests-us-ti

Olson, R. M., & García-Moreno, C. (2017). Virginity testing: A systematic review. *Reproductive Health, 14*(1), 61.

Ozyegin, G. (2009). Virginal facades: Sexual freedom and guilt among young Turkish women. *European Journal of Women's Studies, 16*(2), 103–123.

Pacik, P. T., & Geletta, S. (2017). Vaginismus treatment: Clinical trials follow up 241 patients. *Sexual Medicine, 5*(2), e114–e123.

Rahman, S. (2018). Female sexual dysfunction among Muslim women: Increasing awareness to improve overall evaluation and treatment. *Sexual Medicine Reviews, 6*(4), 535–547.

Sungur, M. (2012). The role of cultural factors in the course and treatment of sexual problems: Failures, pitfalls, and successes in a complicated case from Turkey. In K. S. Hall & C. A. Graham (Eds.), *The cultural context of sexual pleasure and problems* (pp. 308–329). New York: Routledge.

Tuğrul, C., & Kabakçı, E. (1997). Vaginismus and its correlates. *Journal of Sex & Marital Therapy, 12*, 23–34.

Ussher, J. M., Perz, J., Metusela, C., Hawkey, A. J., Morrow, M., Narchal, R., & Estoesta, J. (2017). Negotiating discourses of shame, secrecy, and silence: Migrant and refugee women's experiences of sexual embodiment. *Archives of Sexual Behavior, 46*(7), 1901–1921.

Winnicott, D. W. (1987). *The child, the family, and the outside world.* Boston: Da Capo Press.

6

WHO AM I? AN INTERSECTIONAL APPROACH ON WORKING WITH GAY AND LESBIAN CHINESE YOUTHS IN CANADA

Judy Tsing Ting Lui and Yan Wei (Andy) Mok

Key Terms

dual minority status: Refers to individuals who hold more than one minority status and may experience discrimination not just for one status, but both identified statuses.

individualist culture: Recognizes the needs of an individual within a group or culture.

collectivist culture: Recognizes the needs as a group rather than the needs of an individual.

cultural humility: A process of active self-reflection recognizing power imbalances and to develop relationships based on mutual trust.

therapeutic alliance: Describes the interaction or connection between the clinician and the client.

Asian MSM: Refers to Asian-identified men who have sex with men.

coming out process: A lifelong process in which an individual discloses their sexual and/or gender identity.

Topic Introduction/Background

While all clients bring their own unique needs to therapy, people of marginalized identities and backgrounds are grossly underserved and misunderstood in the therapeutic context. In Westernized societies, Chinese clients not only underuse mental health services, but when they do seek help, they may find

DOI: 10.4324/9781003034063-7

that therapy does not meet their needs (Jim & Pistrang, 2007). Research from the Canadian Community Health Survey found that Caucasians were more likely to use mental health services than those of East Asian, South Asian, and South East Asian descent (Tiwari & Wang, 2008). In particular, Chinese individuals were least likely to use mental health services among other ethnic minority groups (Tiwari & Wang, 2008).

As a diverse multicultural society, it is important to understand the barriers that clients of Chinese descent and other ethnic minority groups face in seeking mental health services. Mental health clinicians must be cognizant of the disconnect between the Westernized services that are offered and the Eastern beliefs and values that Chinese LGBTQ+ clients hold. The elimination of such barriers can improve therapeutic outcomes and enhance the therapeutic experiences of clients currently accessing mental health services. This chapter is intended to aid mental health clinicians' knowledge in working with Chinese gay and lesbian (GL) youths by addressing the various systemic barriers that impact their mental and physical health.

Case Study: Ella

Ella is a 27-year-old female residing in the suburbs of Toronto. She identifies culturally as Chinese-Canadian, with her parents immigrating from Hong Kong to Canada in their late 20s. Ella was born in Canada and considers herself a C.B.C. or C.B.A. (Chinese-born Canadian/Chinese-born Asian). Ella feels fairly "Canadian" and "Whitewashed" but still identifies strongly with her Chinese roots. Ella currently resides at home, where she is expected to reside until she gets married.

Ella identifies as a lesbian and is out to her friends and some trusted colleagues. She is currently casually dating. Recently, Ella's friend, Natalie, came out to her family as bisexual. Receiving positive reactions and acceptance, Natalie shares with Ella and their friends about her positive experience of being "fully out." Natalie expresses that she feels free and can openly acknowledge her sexuality now that her family knows. Natalie has been encouraging Ella to also come out to her family. Since then, Ella has felt increasingly anxious and stressed about having to come out. Ella feels unsure about whether or not coming out to her parents is the right decision for her at this time. Feeling conflicted and uncertain, Ella sought out therapy.

Case Study: Kevin

Kevin is a 21-year-old male who was born in Canada after his parents immigrated from China back in the 1980s. Kevin self-identifies as Chinese-Canadian even though he cannot speak Mandarin, but having grown up in a "traditional" household, Kevin feels a strong connection to his Chinese heritage and cultural practices. He shares that there have been times where he felt conflicted between his Canadian and Chinese cultural identity, which has impacted his self-esteem and self-concept. Kevin avoids bringing home friends and partners that his parents consider "too White" in an attempt to appease his family.

Kevin identifies as a gay man and has been hiding in the closet as a result of his family's homophobic beliefs. After Kevin was caught having sex with another male friend, his father immediately packed his clothes and kicked him out while yelling, "You're a disgrace to our family! Don't ever show your face here again because you are going to hell after you die of AIDS!" With a limited group of friends who can accommodate him, Kevin had to put his post-secondary education on hold and has been moving between his friends' couches for the past four weeks. Kevin states that there have been weekends where he's been forced to meet strangers online and exchange sex for food and a place to stay. Kevin uses crystal meth and GHB to numb his experiences from having sex with strangers. Kevin states that he is scared, lonely, and depressed with no place to go and has very limited funds to financially support himself. Kevin has considered committing suicide but has no active plans. He doesn't know what to do or who to turn to for help, but he wants to finish his university degree and become self-dependent in the future.

Insights and Guiding Principles for Counseling

As clinicians, our role involves walking alongside individuals as they learn different coping strategies and skills to make decisions that help them move towards an authentic way of being and living. The following guiding elements and principles stem from our clinical experiences working with Chinese GL clients to help them develop a deeper awareness of their intersecting identities and the oppressions that they experience on a daily basis. While these principles may be applicable when working with *any* racialized individuals from a minority group, clinicians need to acknowledge the influence of individualized context, environmental factors, and other social determinants of health that can impact the approach used to provide a holistic and person-centered approach.

1. Obtaining Cultural Knowledge: Understanding the Tangible Relationship Between Individualism and Collectivism

To understand the experiences of Chinese individuals, clinicians should understand what it means to abide by collectivist rules within the context of North American society. Influenced by a mixture of philosophies in Taoism, Buddhism, and Confucianism, Chinese collectivistic culture is guided by a strong emphasis on social harmony and the collective good (Dias, Chan,

Ungvarsky, Oraker, & Cleare-Hoffman, 2011; Epstein et al., 2012). The key principle of Chinese collectivism emphasizes sacrificing personal interests and individual rights for the well-being of the collective (Epstein et al., 2012). People are taught to live with consideration first to others before the self (Epstein et al., 2012). This value extends beyond family circles and into relationships with friends, neighbors, and the larger overall community (Epstein et al., 2012). Personal sacrifice for the greater good in order to achieve harmony and balance for the self, family, and society is the driving principle behind Chinese collectivistic culture (Epstein et al., 2012).

The widespread migration of Chinese immigrants across the world has shifted and changed the levels of adherence to such collectivistic cultural expectations (Epstein et al., 2012). Even so, there are universal collectivist values and norms that exist across almost all Chinese communities (Epstein et al., 2012). Collectivist ideals and values have varying levels of connection and application for Chinese individuals living in North America as they need to co-exist with the wider North American ideals and values associated with individualism, which refers to the general principle and belief that individuals should prioritize independence and self-reliance over one's community (Epstein et al., 2012). By validating the unique experiences of Chinese individuals living within two different cultural ideologies, clinicians are promoting an open, holistic, and person-centered approach that can improve the therapeutic relationship, in addition to supporting the client's sexual identity.

2. Coming Out Process

The process of "coming out" is commonly used to describe the development of a gay, bisexual, lesbian, or other non-heterosexual identity that falls under the queer spectrum (Newman & Muzzonigro, 1993). It is an ongoing and dynamic process whereby LGBTQ+ individuals discover, acknowledge, and choose to disclose their sexual orientation and/or gender identity to themselves and others (Ritter & Terndrup, 2002). There is a common misconception that the coming out process is linear whereby once an individual chooses to come out, they are considered "fully out." In reality, the coming out process is dynamic and moves between stages; it is neither a single event nor a single declaration (Ritter & Terndrup, 2002). According to Cass (1979), there are six stages of the coming out process for sexual orientation:

1. **Identity confusion:** Feelings of being disconnected and/or feeling that one is not "normal" compared to their peers.
2. **Identity comparison:** The "bargaining" or "rationalization" stage where one admits to having non-heteronormative feelings and/or attractions but is reluctant to acknowledge a specific identity or label.

3. **Identity tolerance:** Starting to acknowledge a specific identity and label, but not fully accepting of this new identity. One may seek out other non-heterosexual and/or non-cisgender people to connect with.
4. **Identity acceptance:** Formation of friendships with other LGBTQ+ individuals and a more accepting view of one's own sexual orientation. Disclosure of sexual orientation may or may not be revealed to everyone (i.e. disclose to friends, but not to family).
5. **Identity pride:** Increased engagement with the LGBTQ+ community through exploring and learning about different queer subcultures. One might experience anger or resentment towards mainstream society and develop an "us versus them" mentality.
6. **Identity synthesis:** Individuals at this stage are willing to accept that there are trustworthy cisgender heterosexuals who are allies and that their preconceived "us versus them" mentality is not an accurate representation of the world.

It is important to recognize that not all clients going through the coming out process need to follow the stages in a prescribed linear order. Individuals may choose to remain "in the closet" with certain individuals and groups while coming out to others; they may even choose to not come out at all. Every individual's coming out process is unique and varies depending on their personal, cultural, and environmental circumstances. When supporting LGBTQ+ clients, it is essential to respect their individual coming out process and to meet them where they are. Respecting their decisions helps validate their lived experiences, further strengthening the therapeutic relationship.

Case Application: Ella

In the second session with Ella, the decision-making process around whether or not to disclose her sexual identity to her parents was discussed:

Clinician: Did you ever think about coming out to your parents before?

Ella: Believe me, it was a conscious decision to not tell them.

Clinician: Are you comfortable telling me about it?

Ella: I came to recognizing and accepting the fact that I was gay at around 12. A family friend who was a little older than me came out to his parents during that time. He was such a smart, well-behaved kid and my parents felt like his sexuality "ruined" his potential and his family's future. I wasn't allowed to play with him after that, and we just kind of stopped hanging out with his family. I remember then and there making the decision to not tell my parents about my sexuality.

Clinician: I'm sorry to hear that. I can't imagine how it must have been to see how they treated your family friend while you were coming to terms with your own sexuality.

Ella: Well, my family has always seemed "picture perfect;" we had to make sure we looked like a "good" family you know? Seeing how they treated him, I always knew I needed to keep my sexual identity a secret. I learned to build a life separate from them . . . one where I could be myself . . . not that I'm not myself with my family; this part is just for me.

Clinician: How has that been for you so far?

Ella: To be honest, it's worked pretty well. You know, they sometimes ask if I'm dating or not, but they don't ask specifically if I have a boyfriend . . . in some ways I think they might have a suspicion that I am gay. My uncle Frank on my mother's side . . . he's gay; he brings his partner to our family dinners, and everyone just calls his partner his "friend." He's never formally come out. There's just an understanding that we don't talk about it; I've kind of just followed along.

Clinician: I wonder if that's how you envisioned your future with dating too? Or had you thought about it before?

Ella: (nods) Yeah, kind of, I haven't figured it all out yet. I've just started dating. I've only actually gone out on two dates so far, this online dating thing is scary enough for me. After that talk with Nat . . . I started to worry and cancel dates, thinking that someone in my family would somehow show up wherever I was. I'm seriously going crazy.

Clinician: You aren't going crazy; I think that living in a world that is still homophobic and unsafe means that you are always having to be careful and cautious. If you decide to not come out to your parents, your worries make a lot of sense. I think sometimes there is this pressure or this idealized idea that to be happy means to be fully out to everyone. Living your authentic life sometimes means only being out to the ones you feel safe to be out to. You aren't required to follow someone else's path just because it works for them.

Ella: So . . . you're saying I don't have to come out to my parents?

Clinician: I think the best decision will be the one that fits your life, your desires and your needs, one that makes sense for your life; and because life is always changing that means it's also OK if you have to revisit this idea again in the future too. I hope that you can trust your expert opinion as a member of your family and an expert in your own life to make a decision that ultimately is best for you while knowing what consequences you are willing and not willing to face Coming out to your parents might give you relief from the worry of them finding out on their own, but it might also mean there are other things you'd have to consider.

Ella: I know they wouldn't kick me out. But honestly it hasn't been in my plans to come out to them; I know that I'm not ready. Maybe I might be in the future, who knows? . . . I think Nat's experience just made me wish I was either ready or that like . . . my parents weren't the way they are.

Clinician: Coming out isn't some destination; it's a continuous process. You are allowed to adjust what is right for you as you walk along this path. It must be painful to see how different it could be if you knew your parents were accepting of your sexuality. At the same time, it sounds like you have a good understanding of what your needs for yourself are. We can discuss ways to keep you feeling safe while still finding a way to have a meaningful dating life.

Ella: (starting to tear up) It's strange; I know that no one has ever said to me "Here are the rules for being gay," but hearing you say that has made me realize that I've always felt this pressure to come out to everyone and that I'm not complete if I don't. . . . It's exhausting and overwhelming to hear the opposite . . . exhausting, but in a good way! I feel less guilty, almost like I'm lighter.

3. Recognizing Fear and Rejection: Addressing the Need to "Belong" and Feel "Wanted"

While Canada is often perceived as an open, accepting, and welcoming place for sexual minorities, the reality is vastly different. Racialized sexual minorities, such as Ella and Kevin, are often positioned at the fringe of Canadian society due to their intersecting disadvantaged status as both a sexual and ethnic minority (Poon, Li, Wong, & Wong, 2017; Huang & Fang, 2019). Research by Nakamura and colleagues (2013) highlight the barriers that Asian men who have sex with men (MSM) face when trying to integrate both their ethnic-cultural and gay communities in Canada, such as rejection, discrimination, and social isolation. This inability to integrate can often result in negative mental, emotional, and physical health outcomes for Asian MSM (Nakamura et al., 2013).

Traditional values and morals are often the root of the inherent rejection of homosexuality in some Asian cultures, as homosexuality threatens and challenges traditional patriarchal gender roles and the continuation of familial lineage (Nakamura et al., 2013; Boulden, 2009). This is further exacerbated in situations where the family's religious affiliation influences homophobic behaviors while reinforcing traditional cultural ideology (Nakamura et al., 2013). These factors can force Asian LGBTQ+ individuals to remain hidden in the closet, to reject their own sexual orientation and/or gender identity, or to live a "double" life as a means to stay connected and supported by their ethnic-racial communities.

In addition, Asian LGBTQ+ folks have reported experiences of racism and sexual fetishization within the LGBTQ+ community (Huang & Fang, 2019;

Nakamura et al., 2013). While Asian MSM often report receiving messages such as "No Asians" in various dating/hook-up websites and applications, they may not necessarily attribute this as a systemic issue but rather isolated incidents of racism (Nakamura et al., 2013). On the contrary, some Asian MSM may deliberately seek out older White men knowing that they are "fetishized" by them, thereby engaging in internalized racism through rejecting other Asian sexual minorities as sexual and/or romantic partners (Wilson et al., 2009; Nakamura et al., 2013). As such, clinicians need to be aware and sensitive towards the intersecting identities of Chinese LGBTQ+ individuals and the impact on their sense of belonging and acceptance. While not all folks of Chinese LGBTQ+ background living in Canada experience the same form of racism, sexual/gender discrimination, and xenophobia, it is important to recognize and understand the legitimacy of their fears, in addition to the stigma (external and internalized) and social isolation they face. As clinicians, we must understand and factor in the risks of "non-belonging" for Chinese LGBTQ+ and the importance of boundary setting in their lives. Supporting the growth of a client's self-concept and fostering their sense of belonging within the community are aspects that clinicians must be able to do without forcing Chinese LGBTQ+ individuals to choose between their ethnic-racial and sexual communities.

Systemic and Intersectional Issues for Consideration

1. Therapy as Inherently Westernized and Eurocentric

The majority of psychotherapy training programs across the world utilize Westernized models of practice originally developed through a Eurocentric lens that is predominately intended for a White-dominant society (Wieling & Rastogi, 2004). The act of therapy itself is a very individualistic activity, and for many Chinese GL clients who are new to therapy, it may be the first time these clients have been asked to seriously think about their own needs above others. This can pose a challenge for clinicians who enter a therapeutic space with individualistic ideals towards what it means to achieve "well-being." This is exemplified when clinicians focus on "what is best" for an individual. For example, in situations where the clinician supports their client's desire to fully come out of the closet without considering and discussing potential repercussions, they may risk guiding their client towards a decision with long-term consequences that have not been considered (i.e. getting kicked out of family home, social rejection/isolation, loss of financial support, etc.). Being attuned to this multiplicity of factors is not only important as a best therapeutic practice, but it also ensures that clients are making an informed decision that factors in their mental and physical safety.

2. Structural Violence and Mental Health Stigma in Asian Communities

The mental health needs of Chinese and other Asian immigrants are rarely met due to the social stigma, shame, and victim blaming that are often associated with mental illness (Kramer, Kwong, Lee, & Chung, 2002; Hansson et al., 2010). Chinese and other Asian men have to navigate through traditional gender ideology that associates help-seeking behaviors as a sign of weakness, which deters Chinese and other Asian men from seeking mental health services (Connell & Messerschmidt, 2005; McCusker & Galupo, 2011). Clinicians need to understand how systemic issues of structural violence and mental health stigma directly impact the microaggressions that Chinese LGBTQ+ individuals face in their daily lives.

Microaggression refers to the experience of daily and brief assaults on people belonging to minorities or marginalized groups, both socially and environmentally; these acts can be intentional or unintentional, verbal or non-verbal (Sue et al., 2007). Microaggressions experienced by racialized sexual minorities include three key themes: (a) racism in sexual minority communities, (b) heterosexism in racial-ethnic minority communities, and (c) racism in dating and close relationships (Balsam, Molina, Beadnell, Simoni, & Walters, 2011; Huang & Fang, 2019). As such, clinicians need to recognize the impact of microaggressions both within and outside of therapy for their clients. More importantly, clinicians need to be self-aware of their own behaviors and actions so that they do not unconsciously or unintentionally engage in behaviors that may be perceived as acts of microaggressions when engaging with their clients.

Therapeutic and Educative Approach

1. Therapeutic Alliance and Cultural Sensitivity/Humility

An important aspect of working with Chinese GL youths involves therapeutic alliance, which is defined as a collaboration and consensus between practitioner and client (Horvath, Del Re, Flückiger, & Symonds, 2011; Sprenkle & Blow, 2004). Therapeutic alliance is achieved "when therapists use strong joining skills (i.e. warmth, empathy) and knowledge of clients' cultural background (i.e. communication styles, collectivist values) as well as their needs in order to build collaborative interactions with the clients" (Sprenkle et al., 2009, as cited in Epstein et al., 2014, p. 202). This alliance plays an integral role towards therapeutic success and reduced dropout rates for clients who belong to culturally and/or sexually marginalized groups (Horvath et al., 2011; Escudero, Friedlander, Varela, & Abascal, 2008; Ma, 2000; Epstein et al., 2014).

To improve the therapeutic outcome and alliance with Chinese GL youths, a clinicians' ability to conduct therapy that is culturally sensitive becomes an absolute necessity (Epstein et al., 2014). This is where the concept of cultural humility becomes essential to alliance building. *Cultural humility* refers to the lifelong reflexive process whereby clinicians examine and acknowledge similarities and differences between their own beliefs, values, and goals with those of their clients (Schuessler, Wilder, & Byrd, 2012; Adelstein, 2015). Clinicians who practice cultural humility "approach clients with respectful openness and work collaboratively with clients to understand the unique intersection of clients' various aspects of identities and how that affects the developing therapeutic alliance" (Hook, Davis, Owen, Worthington, & Utsey, 2013, p. 354). Clinicians don't have to become the experts in their client's culture, but having a familiarity with both Chinese and Western beliefs and values allows clinicians to have a deeper understanding of cultural formulation and its influence on client dilemmas (Jim & Pistrang, 2007; Cheung, 2000; Lee, 2011). Furthermore, clinicians with an understanding of cultural humility can foster a stronger therapeutic relationship with their clients by acknowledging their own limitations and a willingness to learn. In fact, levels of cultural humility have been associated with a better understanding of the client's change process, and ultimately with improvements in therapeutic outcomes (Hook et al., 2013; Lee, 2011).

Mental health clinicians, especially those who work with Chinese GL youths need to engage in continuous self-reflection and practice cultural humility by learning about different cultures and cultural practices both within and outside the therapy room. This responsibility should fall on the clinician in order to prevent burdening clients by taking on the teaching role or treating clients as the "token minority" in therapy. While there is no perfect formula to help determine when clinicians should utilize knowledge gained from external sources versus when it is permissible to learn through the expertise of the client, navigating that balance is a crucial skill to hone. As such, it is important to acknowledge the growing need for clinicians to practice with greater cultural humility as a means to foster therapeutic success.

2. *Including Health Education and Health Promotion as Part of the Therapeutic Approach*

Providing therapy and empathizing with LGBTQ+ clients is only one aspect of the therapeutic role. Working with Chinese GL youths and other racialized LGBTQ+ individuals requires clinicians to also address and be aware of the differences in their client's identity and healthcare needs. Showing that you are open to being educated about their needs and the right words to use (i.e. gender pronouns) is one important aspect to demonstrate continuing competency. Another aspect that clinicians need to recognize is that racialized

LGBTQ+ individuals have specific healthcare needs, which is to be treated in a non-heteronormative manner.

While it is not the role of mental health clinicians to treat their client's healthcare needs, those working with Chinese GL youths and other racialized LGBTQ+ clients should be educated on sexual health promotion, in addition to developing a list of referrals for LGBTQ+-inclusive healthcare providers. Existing research suggests that LGBTQ+ individuals, specifically gay and bisexual men, engage in more frequent high-risk sexual activities, such as condomless sex, and have increased risks for HIV and STI transmission (Al-Bargash, 2019; Chawla & Sarkar, 2019). Mental health clinicians need to be aware of specific LGBTQ+ healthcare needs that can enhance their clients' overall well-being, such as providing information and referrals for STI and HIV testing, and addictions/substance use programs offered by local hospitals, agencies, and clinics.

Case Application: Kevin

Supporting Kevin's main concerns while establishing and prioritizing physical safety and support was essential in the first session of therapy:

Clinician: OK, Kevin, from what you've shared it sounds like you don't have a lot of people to turn to for support at this time. You're struggling to meet your basic needs in having a safe place to stay and having enough money for food. You also are concerned about your drug use that is associated with hooking up with other guys so that you can stay over. Am I missing anything?

Kevin: No, that's pretty much all the crap I have to deal with. Honestly, I'm scared because I don't even know who to trust at this point. I feel so disconnected and out of it all the time. I don't know if it's because of the drugs or because I'm so emotionally and mentally drained. I really don't know what to do!

Clinician: It sounds like you're encountering stressors from all aspects in your life, and this is perpetuating a cycle of negative feelings that you feel like you can't escape. When you're meeting guys online and hooking up, I wonder is this because you want to or because you feel like you have nowhere else to go?

Kevin: Most of the time, it's because I have nowhere to stay. When you go on Grindr and ask people if you can stay over, they expect you to have sex with them. Sometimes I don't want to, but I feel forced or obligated. I usually end up taking meth or GHB to numb myself through the whole thing.

Clinician: Do you typically use condoms during these encounters?

Kevin: I ask them to, but most of the time guys want bareback sex. I know it's not safe and I'm afraid of getting HIV, but I don't have a choice.

Clinician: I appreciate you being honest with me, Kevin, and thank you for trusting me with this information. I can't imagine all the fears and thoughts that are running through your head, but I'm going to try and support you in figuring out how to move forward. As I mentioned before, there seems to be this vicious cycle where you're constantly looking for a roof over your head, worrying about money and food, and having to hook up in high-risk situations that often include substance use. It sounds like a lot to navigate, so let's try to work through this and make it feel less overwhelming. Which factor feels the most distressing for you right now?

Kevin: Definitely housing and having somewhere to stay long-term. It's hard when I have to unpack and repack my duffel bag all the time. I can't afford to lose any of what stuff I managed to keep with me when I got kicked out.

Clinician: Is there a relative other than your parents that you can stay with?

Kevin: There's my older brother and his family, but I'm scared I'll be a burden to him, and he might not accept me for being gay.

Clinician: Has your brother made any negative comments about you being gay?

Kevin: No, he's never said anything like that. I guess I'm just scared that he might because we've never been very close.

Clinician: That's something we can work towards in terms of overcoming your fears that people are judging you. In the meantime, how do you feel about reaching out to your brother and asking to stay with him in a while?

Kevin: Is that something you think I should do?

Clinician: I can't tell you what you should or shouldn't do, but you've identified finding a stable shelter as your priority need, and I believe it would be important for you to find a place that feels safe to sleep and rest in. If you feel that your brother may be someone who you can lean on for support, do you feel strong enough to reach out and speak to him? You don't have to disclose all the stuff you've been through to him, but at the very least, you can let him know that you need a safe place to stay and to be around someone who you trust.

Kevin: I guess I should call him now, then, because I don't know if I can do it later when I'm alone. But I don't know what to say, and I'm kind of nervous?

Clinician: If you would like, we can talk a little more and plan out what you would like to say to your brother. You can even call him here in session. I can sit with you while you make the call if that helps.

Kevin: That would actually be really helpful. I think I'd like that—thank you!

Clinician: Of course. I'm more than happy to do that for you.

Counseling Strategies

1. Cultural Humility: It's Okay to Not Be the Expert

The following recommendations may help clinicians to become more reflexive in their practice and to better support Chinese GL youths in addressing their intersecting needs.

- Clinicians should recognize and validate a client's unique identity. In cases where there are multiple intersecting identities, clinicians need to recognize and acknowledge how those intersecting layers of oppressions may impact the way the client views their own identity(ies).
- When appropriate, utilize self-disclosure to emphasize your understanding of the client's perspective, to normalize their experience, to build trust, and/or to reduce shame associated with self-stigmatizing behaviors and thoughts.
- Learn to seek other points of view by exploring narratives and experiences that may differ from your own personal beliefs and values. Take the opportunity to listen and hear from different perspectives that can enrich your understanding of how individuals with different identities may experience oppression and discrimination and/or stigma in their daily lives.
- Check in with clients to see if you have understood them in the way they intended to be heard. Taking the time to verify the client's feelings validates their experiences and lets them know that they are fully heard.
- Avoid the use of oversimplified assumptions, perceptions, and stereotypes of people in both your personal and professional lives by working towards using inclusive language consistently.
- Become an ally and get involved with various LGBTQ+ and community-based organizations and associations to learn about the needs of LGBTQ+ individuals. Listening and deferring to those who live with intersecting identities will strengthen your understanding of their needs.
- Acknowledge when you have gaps in cultural understanding, and seek the appropriate action to improve your competency (i.e. self-disclosing to client, doing own research into the topic outside of therapy, seeking appropriate supervision, asking clients to share, and reflect on the impacts of their own experiences).

2. Creating a Safe Environment

Chinese GL youths and other racialized LGBTQ+ clients need to feel safe before they can develop a trusting therapeutic relationship with the clinician.

Here are some suggestions to help create a safe environment for LGBTQ+ clients in your practice.

- Demonstrate and promote a safe space for LGBTQ+ clients in your clinic/office. This includes the use of inclusive language on intake forms, ensuring appropriate language is used by all staff members, and making visible LGBTQ+ affirming materials or signages in office space.
- Don't leave it up to the client to take the first step of disclosure. Be open and non-judgmental when asking clients about their sexual orientation and/or gender identity, and provide encouragement when they share this information with you.
- Be knowledgeable and up-to-date on current LGBTQ+ mental health and health issues. Remaining knowledgeable on current LGBTQ+ research, news, and events will let clients know that you are invested in supporting their needs, thereby reducing the need for clients to educate you on these relevant topics.
- Develop linkages and partnerships with LGBTQ+ and ethno-racial community organizations and agencies. Know where you can refer clients for additional support and resources.

Lessons Learned by the Author

While this chapter is intended to enhance mental health clinicians' knowledge and understanding of Chinese GL youths, we want to highlight several limitations and critiques to consider when applying these guidelines into your own clinical practice. We want to acknowledge that the experiences and suggestions described in this chapter are very much confined to the knowledge of our own clinical experiences working with Chinese GL youths in the Greater Toronto Area. The experiences highlighted in this chapter are not meant to be fully representative of all Chinese GL youths or other racialized LGBTQ+ individuals seeking out therapy within the Westernized context.

We also recognize that we were unable to address intergenerational differences in the experiences of older Chinese GL clients. Furthermore, only the L (lesbian) and G (gay) experiences of the Chinese LGBTQ+ communities were highlighted in this chapter. We cannot stress enough that other members of the Chinese LGBTQ+ have their own unique experiences, challenges, and issues that we regrettably did not have the space to highlight and address. Nonetheless, in considering these limitations, we look forward to expanding our own knowledge and research into these nuanced areas of the Chinese LGBTQ+ community in Canada.

Critical Questions for Readers to Consider

1. What are your own cultural biases when working with Chinese GL youths or other racialized sexual minorities? How do your past experiences influence your beliefs, values, and morals when working with these individuals?
2. Examine the therapeutic models you were trained in and currently utilize. Do they account for the diversity of people's cultures, values, beliefs, and norms? What gaps in consideration might they hold, and how can you improve your competency when working with Chinese GL youths and other racialized sexual minorities?
3. What does cultural humility look like in your current therapeutic practice? How do you engage in continuous reflexive practice to improve your knowledge and practice when working with Chinese GL youths or other racialized sexual minorities?

Suggested Readings and Additional Resources

1. Culturally Sensitive Supervision and Training: Diverse Perspectives and Practical Applications by Kenneth Hardy and Toby Bobes
2. Counseling the Culturally Diverse: Theory and Practice by Derald Wing Sue, David Sue, Helen A. Neville, and Laura Smith
3. My Grandmother's Hands: Racialized Trauma and the Pathway to Mending Our Hearts and Bodies by Resmaa Menakem
4. Voices of Color: First-Person Accounts of Ethnic Minority Therapists by Mudita Rastogi and Elizabeth Wieling
5. Waking Up White, and Finding Myself in the Story of Race by Debby Irving

References

Adelstein, J. (2015). Cultural humility: A lifelong process for professional nurses. *Senior Honors Projects*. Paper 426. Retrieved from http://digitalcommons.uri.edu/srhonorsprog/426

Al-Bargash, D. (2019). Recent increases in rates of gonorrhea in Toronto, Ontario, 2012-2018. *Sexually Transmitted Infections, 95*, A301.

Balsam, K. F., Molina, Y., Beadnell, B., Simoni, J., & Walters, K. (2011). Measuring multiple minority stress: The LGBT people of color microaggressions scale. *Cultural Diversity and Ethnic Minority Psychology, 17*, 163–174.

Boulden, W. (2009). Gay Hmong: A multifaceted clash of cultures. *Journal of Gay & Lesbian Social Services: Issues in Practice, Policy & Research, 21*, 134–150.

Cass, V. C. (1979). Homosexual identity formation: A theoretical model. *Journal of Homosexuality, 4*(3), 219–235. doi: 10.1300/J082v04n03_01

Chawla, N., & Sarkar, S. (2019). Defining "high-risk sexual behavior" in the context of substance use. *Journal of Psychosexual Health, 1*(1), 26–31.

Cheung, F. M. (2000). Deconstructing counseling in a cultural context. *Counseling Psychologist, 28*(1), 123–132.

Connell, R. W., & Messerschmidt, J. W. (2005). Hegemonic masculinity: Rethinking the concept. *Gender and Society, 19*(6), 829–859.

Dias, J., Chan, A., Ungvarsky, J., Oraker, J., & Cleare-Hoffman, H. P. (2011). Reflections on marriage and family therapy emergent from international dialogues in China. *The Humanistic Psychologist, 39*(3), 268–275.

Epstein, N. B., Curtis, D. S., Edwards, E., Young, J. L., & Zheng, L. (2014). Therapy with families in china: Cultural factors influencing the therapeutic alliance and therapy goals. *Contemporary Family Therapy, 36*(2), 201–212. https://doi.org/10.1007/s10591-014-9302-x

Escudero, V., Friedlander, M. L., Varela, N., & Abascal, A. (2008). Observing the therapeutic alliance in family therapy: Associations with participants' perceptions and therapeutic outcomes. *Journal of Family Therapy, 30*(2), 194–214.

Hansson, E., Tuck, A., Lurie, S., & McKenzie, K., for the Task Group of the Services Systems Advisory Committee, Mental Health Commission of Canada. (2010). *Improving mental health services for immigrant, refugee, ethno-cultural and racialized groups: Issues and options for service improvement.* Retrieved from www.mentalhealthcommission.ca/sites/default/files/Diversity_Issues_Options_Report_ENG_0_1.pdf

Hook, J. N., Davis, D. E., Owen, J., Worthington, E. L., & Utsey, S. O. (2013). Cultural humility: Measuring openness to culturally diverse clients. *Journal of Counseling Psychology, 60*(3), 353–366.

Horvath, A. O., Del Re, A. C., Flückiger, C., & Symonds, D. (2011). Alliance in individual psychotherapy. *Psychotherapy, 48*(1), 9.

Huang, Y., & Fang, L. (2019). "Fewer but not weaker": Understanding the intersectional identities among Chinese immigrant young gay men in Toronto. *The American Journal of Orthopsychiatry, 89*(1), 27–39.

Jim, J., & Pistrang, N. (2007). Culture and the therapeutic relationship: Perspectives from Chinese clients. *Psychotherapy Research, 17*(4), 461–473.

Kramer, E. J., Kwong, K., Lee, E., & Chung, H. (2002). Cultural factors influencing the mental health of Asian Americans. *The Western Journal of Medicine, 176*(4), 227–231.

Lee, E. (2011). Clinical significance of cross-cultural competencies (CCC) in social work practice. *Journal of Social Work Practice, 25*(2), 185–203.

Ma, J. L. (2000). Treatment expectations and treatment experience of Chinese families towards family therapy: Appraisal of a common belief. *Journal of Family Therapy, 22*(3), 296–307.

McCusker, M. G., & Galupo, M. P. (2011). The impact of men seeking help for depression on perceptions of masculine and feminine characteristics. *Psychology of Men & Masculinity, 12*(3), 275–284.

Nakamura, N., Chan, E., & Fischer, B. (2013). Hard to crack: Experiences of community integration among first- and second-generation Asian MSM in Canada. *Cultural Diversity and Ethnic Minority Psychology, 19*(3), 248–256.

Newman, B. S., & Muzzonigro, P. G. (1993). The effects of traditional family values on the coming out process of gay male adolescents. *Adolescence, 28*(109), 213.

Poon, M. K.-L., Li, A. T.-W., Wong, J. P.-H., & Wong, C. (2017). Queer-friendly nation? The experiences of Chinese gay immigrants in Canada. *China Journal of Social Work, 10*, 23–38.

Ritter, K. Y., & Terndrup, A. I. (2002). *Handbook of affirmative psychotherapy with lesbians and gay men.* New York: Guilford Press.

Schuessler, J. B., Wilder, B., & Byrd, L. W. (2012). Reflective journaling and development of cultural humility in students. *Nursing Education Perspectives, 33*(2), 96.

Sprenkle, D. H., & Blow, A. J. (2004). Common factors and our sacred models. *Journal of Marital & Family Therapy, 30*(2), 113–129.

Sprenkle, D. H., Davis, S. D., & Lebow, J. L. (2009). *Common factors in couple and family therapy: The overlooked foundation for effective practice.* New York: Guilford.

Sue, D. W., Capodilupo, C. M., Torino, G. C., Bucceri, J. M., Holder, A., Nadal, K. L., & Esquilin, M. (2007). Racial microaggressions in everyday life: Implications for clinical practice. *American Psychologist, 62*(4), 271.

Tiwari, S. K., & Wang, J. (2008). Ethnic differences in mental health service use among white, Chinese, South Asian and South East Asian populations living in Canada. *Social Psychiatry and Psychiatric Epidemiology, 43*(11), 866.

Wieling, E., & Rastogi, M. (2004). Voices of marriage and family therapists of color: An exploratory survey. *Journal of Feminist Family Therapy, 15*(1), 1–20.

Wilson, P. A., Valera, P., Ventuneac, A., Balan, I., Rowe, M., & Carballo Diéguez, A. (2009). Race-based sexual stereotyping and sexual partnering among men who use the internet to identify other men for bareback sex. *Journal of Sex Research, 46*, 399–413.

7

REDEFINING SEXUALITIES OF MIGRANT LATINX AND MIDDLE EASTERN WOMEN IN THE UNITED STATES

Estefanía Simich Muñoz

Key Terms

Latinx: a person of Latin American descent
Middle Eastern: the region of the world that includes Western Asia and all of Egypt
aldea: a small community/township
cariño: affection
Borrón y cuenta nueva: a commonly used Spanish expression that means "Erase and start over"
Cierra las piernas: "Close your legs and don't have sex"
calientes: hot blooded
haram: sin
masjid: a mosque, place of worship for people of Islamic faith

Introduction

In this chapter, I intend to explore the complex construction of sexual scripts of migrant Latinx and Middle Eastern women through their shaped identites as members of a specific community. It is important to note that in Latin American and Middle Eastern cultures, the role an individual plays within their community is embedded in the individual's identity and linked to their role in that society. These embedded roles act as core codes of the individual's sexuality. Gender inequality across Latin America and the Middle East creates an environment where women face social barriers and high exposure to gender violence. Educational and economic work barriers caused by the

DOI: 10.4324/9781003034063-8

introduction of neoliberal markets make women and adolescent girls susceptible to financial dependency and various forms of abuse (physical, psychological, emotional, and sexual) that could eventually lead to a need to migrate. Although this is not the case for all migrants, it can be said that these are some of the most common circumstances that cause the migration of thousands of Latinx women.

The complexities of sexuality are always linked to various factors that influence the behaviors and preferences of individuals. For Latinx and Middle Eastern women, the constructed sexual identities are based on dynamics of patriarchal socities that uphold rape culture and impose socially accepted gender roles. Various cultures around the globe have unique views on sexuality, depending on the place where an individual comes from. This allows us to understand that a change in geographical location—such as migration—can significantly impact perceptions and views on sexuality. When migration occurs, the culturally acquired identity that was created to function within a specific cultural system is challenged. The identity that was developed within the old community no longer exists, as physical distance creates a disconnect from friends, family, and all they knew. This distance allows the individual to create a unique identity that can assist them in negotiating between their two worlds. This constant negotiation is at the center of the integration of the sexuality of a migrant Latinx and Middle Eastern woman.

The intent of this chapter is not to generalize migration processes or sexualities based on cultural factors, but rather to share a couple of cases that illustrate how the migration process might have influenced and impacted the sexuality of a Latinx and a Middle Eastern migrant client, as well as predisposed the outcome of sex therapy. Sexuality is as simple or complex as our social and cultural environments indoctrinate us to view it. Once migration occurs, the interactions with other cultural and social environments allows us to mold and shift from our constructed sexual scripts. Both Carrillo (2017) and Espín (2006) mention that the adaptation process to a new culture comes with the loss of old identities and gaining new ones through finding the desired freedom or emotional stability. It is through the process of migration that new and old sexual scripts are constantly negotiated between two places to create a migrant's sexual identity.

Some overlapping themes between these two cultures are patriarchy, conservative religious beliefs, and rigid gender roles. The use of an intersectional approach to all these cases was important to address the needs and desires of the clients from a cultural lens. In my private practice, I have had the pleasure of working with women from both cultures. My experience with all of them has been a familiar sense of understanding and connecting through similarities of my own culture.

As a sex therapist and educator working with migrant clients, you should get familiar with the different phases of migration and how each one could have impacted your client. A comprehensive understanding of your client's journey through migration will help you better address their needs and concerns. The migration process of Latinx and Middle Eastern women should not be analyzed as a linear concept, but as a complex system that comprises several dynamics including the reasons for migration, when this migration ocurred, where the client is from, and where they migrated to. Engaging in discussion around all of these queries should be part of a complete assessment of your client's background.

Why Did the Client Migrate?

There are mutiple reasons why Latinx and Middle Eastern women migrate. From seeking new job opportunities, schooling, fleeing gender violence, getting married, moving with family, or simply wanting to experience living in a different place. Regardless of the reason, the migration process a Latinx and Middle Eastern woman goes through as she mobilizes herself, adapts, and eventually settles into her new life in her new country is complex. This process impacts every aspect of her being including her sexuality. Understanding of the motivations for the migration of your client will provide insight into their experiences of gender violence, oppression, discrimination, torture, or other forms of violence that your client has lived through.

What Was the Client's Migration Experience?

Depending on the type of route of the migration process, several dynamics could have taken place. Identifying voluntary versus involuntary migration is key to the presenting circumstances of migration. Voluntary migration could involve someone who wants to move somewhere else for a purpose. Involuntary or forced migration is mostly experienced by refugees and asylum seekers. Both types involve different considerations such as access (or lack of) to services, experiences of oppression, and violence—these can impact the client's well-being and drastically influence their sexuality.

When Did Migration Occur?

The experiences of a child, an adolescent, and an adult in the migration process will vary significantly due to age of migration and the age of arrival to the place of destination. The age of migration and how an individual adjusts to lived experiences and surroundings of their new environment are essential factors to consider in sex therapy. For example, a migrant adolescent from Guatemala could have a broader perspective on sexuality as their peers begin to talk about sex in a more unrestrictive manner than in their home country. This leads into questioning learned concepts of sexuality and comparing them against the culture they live in. This process may create a conflict with conservative parents who might not be able to have a conversation about sex. This same scenario can be applied to adolescents across the globe, but the main significance is that the circumstances in their country of origin differ by geographical location. As described by Espín (1997), the adaptation of immigrant Latin American women to the United States creates a shift in the views of their sexualities. She states that "during the acculturation process sexuality may become the focus of the parents' fears and the girl's desires" (p. 175). Thus, family culture surrounding the internalized messages of intimacy, connection, language, discourses on sexuality, migration, and other culturally learned factors impact the way individuals experience pleasure and how this might contribute to or hinder their sexuality.

From Where Did Your Client Migrate and to Where Did They Migrate?

Identifying where your client comes from is as significant as any other data that you would need to identify your client's needs. For example, the client may have moved from a war zone or a gang-infested society or they may be fleeing from political oppression. These are all important factors. As a therapist, it is your homework to research and recognize factors that might have influenced your client's migration and their sexual health. Furthermore, the geographical location where a Latinx or Middle Eastern woman arrives in the United States also creates a specific impact on the social environment they identify with and involve themselves in. For example, a client from a small town moves to a large US city. The pace, influences, and exposure to different experiences might prove more challenging than a slower-paced environment. A small town could present its own challenges, for example, lack of transportation and limited access to services in their native language.

Why Is All This Information Important?

Throughout the migration process, Latin and Middle Eastern women construct unique identities that allow them to integrate into their newly found context and negotiate between cultures. Identifying this process with your clients will help you acknowledge their experiences and the influences on sexual behaviors as they adapt. As a mental health and sex therapist, I have worked with several migrant women who seek services—not only in their native languages—but from culturally knowledgeable providers. This allows us to build trust as they start their journey towards healing and growth. Sex therapy is not only a foreign concept to most of my female clients, it is also challenging, considering that the connection with the therapist is an important tool to reach the client's desired outcome. Again, Espín (1997) explains that Latin American bilingual women speak Spanish as their emotional language. If sexuality is linked to emotion, then the cultural background of that individual will significantly impact their sexual experience.

Another consideration with the complexities of migration is intergenerational cultural inheritance. The expectations after migration are more significant since these women carry not only their family's messages, but also the push and pull factors of adapting into their new adopted culture. Carrillo (2017) speaks of how participants crafted new lives and identities while still maining things that they enjoyed from their lives before migration. In a sex therapy setting, understanding intergenerational cultural inheritance from a biopsychosocial model may be a helpful framework to approach a client's needs. It is also important to consider the impact of culture and migration that influences the individual's sexuality and what supports would be needed for the client's needs. All of this can influence the outcome of therapy.

Case 1: Melinda

As previously mentioned, the migration process has a significant impact on the mental health and the well-being of any individual. The change in geographical location experienced by migrants causes new challenges as they adapt to their new surroundings and heal from their wounds. Migration impacts our lives by challenging our sexual scripts, as demonstrated in the case of my client, Melinda.

Melinda is a 25-year-old from El Salvador and has a child from a previous relationship. Three years ago, she migrated to the United States, fleeing domestic violence and brought her 8-year-old son with her. She was forced into marriage by her family when she got pregnant at 16. Raúl (the father of her child) was ten years older than her and well known in their community. Everyone respected him as the son of the local *aldea* (township) pastor. Melinda noted that he was charming, and she fell in love with him quickly. After a few months of living together, everything changed, and the violence began. She tells how the violence escalated over time. While pregnant, Raúl punched her in her stomach, telling her he did not believe the child was his. He would come home drunk, threaten her with violence, and lock the main entrance door, which left her trapped in her own home. She shared that during her pregnancy, she was not allowed to seek prenatal or medical care, and every time Raúl physically assaulted her, she would clean up her own wounds. Due to the physical violence, her son Diego was born prematurely. Melinda's family and people in the aldea (township) noticed the violence, but no one spoke about it—leaving Melinda with no way to leave the relationship. At one point, Melinda's cousin, who lived in the United States, was visiting family. Melinda was moved to share with her about the abuse she suffered, and her cousin agreed to help Melinda leave that situation and flee to the United

States. She put her in contact with Julio, a childhood friend of theirs who also lived in the United States. He arranged the journey for Melinda and Diego, and she escaped this abusive relationship. During her migration journey, Melinda witnessed and experienced violence. While her son slept, the leader of the migrant group approached her and threatened her that if she did not have sex with him, he would not allow her or her son to continue the journey. She had to endure being raped by this person on many nights while her son slept. She was violated by this man who was taking her to a place where she would feel free of violence. Once arriving in the United States, Melinda was separated from her son and detained by ICE (United States Immigration and Customs Enforcement) while her son was sent to one of the ORR (Office of Refugee Resettlement) shelters across the country. After two months of being detained, she was released under a bail bond and obtained custody of her son again. Throughout this process, Julio (the friend who arranged their passage to the US) was emotionally and financially supportive of them, and Melinda was deeply thankful. After a few months of living in the same home, Julio proposed to Melinda. She was caught off guard by his proposition but thought this would provide stability for both her and her son. After marrying, they had a daughter. She shared that initially she avoided having sex with Julio for many months, until she felt she had to do it as part of her duties and to pay Julio back for everything he had done. The first time Melinda had sex with Julio, she experienced pain and an out-of-body experience. She didn't know what was happening, as this was new for her. She was concerned that Julio might be upset at her for what she was feeling. Even now, each time they have sex, she does not enjoy it, is triggered by his touch, and wishes she never had sex again. She shared that she has never felt pleasure, and her main concern is that Julio feels frustrated, as he wants her to feel pleasure. She says that she feels dirty and broken—and can't imagine enjoying sex since that's not been the case. Melinda wants to be present and get satisfaction out of her sexual encounters with Julio. She wishes she hadn't experienced sexual abuse from her former partner and the man who helped them cross the border.

Goals for Sex Therapy

- Melinda identified that she wanted to work towards healing her past sexual abuse and to be present with Julio. She feels *cariño* (affection) towards Julio, and for the first time in her life, she feels safe.
- Melinda identified that she wanted to work on her self-image, as she has low self-esteem and body image concerns associated to the abuse she experienced.
- Melinda wanted to explore what it means to feel pleasure.
- Melinda wanted to learn how to tell Julio about being triggered by certain touch.

- Melinda wanted to work on her frustration about her sexuality. She used the phrase *borrón y cuenta nueva* ("erase and start from scratch") as what she wanted to achieve.
- Melinda wanted to learn how to be assertive to invite Julio to future sessions.

Insights and Guiding Principles

Clients like Melinda who have a heightened arousal state often experience barriers to connecting sexually to their partners. In this case, my first insight was to revisit the healing she had achieved due to her trauma. Melinda had engaged in some trauma work prior to seeing me—this took place while in ICE detention—and more recently due to the sexual assault. Allowing Melinda to tell her story as she experienced it and in her native language created trust in our relationship, where she felt comfortable addressing sexual concerns.

At the start of our sessions, Melinda came to get a psychological evaluation for her immigration case; at the end of our sessions is when she shared that she did not expect to work on other issues after the evaluation was done. When we began meeting, she was reluctant to talk about her history of sexual violence and mainly focused on the physical, emotional, and psychological abuse. As a sexual trauma and sex therapist, Melinda's not mentioning her sexual history was a red flag for me. I know that in Latin American countries, gender violence in domestic relationships encompasses multiple forms of abuse (physical, emotional, sexual, psychological, and financial). For Melinda, having a therapist who understood her story without questioning her was key to building a therapeutic relationship that gave her the opportunity to heal. I understand gender roles in Salvadorian society; this helped me recognize that she didn't have options to get out of the relationship. Gender violence in Salvadorian society is prevalent—the rate of femicides and gang violence are amongst the highest in the world. The strong social influence from her environment also played into why she stayed.

Melinda had extreme trust issues due to the abuse and violence she experienced, so opening up sexually to Julio would not be easy. She didn't want Julio to see her naked, because this would hinder her from engaging in any sexual contact. My first thought about this was that she wanted to feel good in her own skin before she would open herself up to Julio.

Approach to Melinda's Case

A therapeutic and educative approach was used for this case. Melinda's construction of sexuality was created through her experiences of violence. She did not have anyone talk to her about sexuality while growing up, so she had no clue what to expect for her first sexual encounter (her first time with her former partner). Her father never spoke to her about sex, and her mother always told her, *"Cierra las piernas"* ("Close your legs"). None of her friends spoke about sex, as this was considered taboo in her culture. These messages, along with the sexual abuse, were the only ways that Melinda had experienced sex. These negative sexual messages were explored during our sessions. Over time, Melinda worked hard to construct a new approach to sexuality that was positive and affirmed that sex could be a pleasurable experience. We discussed consent and boundaries and how all these should be considered within her relationship.

In our sessions, it became apparent that Melinda's gender-role norms were challenged by taking ownership of her own sexual pleasure. In Latin America, the concept of owning your own pleasure is a more recent discussion, and it clashes against conventional intergenerational patriarchy that allots the pleasure to men. As we talked about this, she was able to identify that she was worthy of pleasure, and that sex was not only about the other person. It was about her and her relationship with her body. She explored her history of traumatic situations before and during migration that impacted her well-being, self-esteem, and sexuality. Through a therapeutic approach, Melinda was able to break away from familiar patterns of questioning her self-worth and started opening up to explore her sexuality with Julio.

Finally, the component of work that Melinda used to help her healing process was using a psycho-educative approach about dissociation and grounding techniques. This was key—during our sessions and for her at home—to ensure she was able to feel safe and reconnect with her body and eventually connect with her husband.

Systemic and Intersectional Issues

Fear of deportation: Melinda is an undocumented migrant in the United States; as such, she lives with the constant fear of being deported at any time. She struggles with finding stability in her current life, as much is unknown. She wonders if she will be separated from her children or have to face her ex-partner. She wants to study and do more for herself but feels her life depends on an immigration case. Feelings of instability in her current life were always present during sessions.

Lack of support system: Melinda's disconnect from her support system in her home country impacted her ability to establish new relationships that would provide support. Even though she developed a few friendships, she felt lonely at times. The friendship dynamics in her home country were completely different from these in Baltimore, and this proved to be a challenge—especially when she wanted to have a date with Julio but had no one to care for their children.

Access to health care: As an undocumented migrant in the United States, Melinda has no access to health care/insurance and had a hard time finding an OBGYN who did a sliding scale. Since the birth of her daughter, she shared that she has incontinence and feels embarrassed and ashamed. She has not told Julio about this, so when they are intimate, she fears leaking urine and that Julio will be disgusted. Not having access to health insurance is a common struggle amongst undocumented migrants.

Language: Like other migrants in the United States, Melinda experiences language barriers, with English being her second language. A bigger factor, however, is the loss of not speaking her native language to express herself and her identity. Melinda feels lucky to be able to do therapy in her own language. She expressed concern that her son needs homework help and that she can't help him. Towards the end of treatment, Melinda decided to take a free placement English as a Second Language (ESL) class at the local community college.

Sample Dialogue with Melinda

Therapist: Would you be open to exploring touch without clothes on?

Melinda: No way; I would never dare to show Julio my body.

Therapist: Why is that?

Melinda: Because is disgusting; I don't like it! I even pee at times.

Therapist: How do you have sex with Julio now?

Melinda: I get under the sheets with my pajamas and just let him do what he wants. I don't participate. I just lay there and wait until he is done.

Therapist: What does Julio do?

Melinda: He says, "Chiquita te quiero" and then he kisses me. But I never let his hands touch me; that reminds me of the times that others have touched me.

Therapist: And what would you want for him to do instead?

Melinda: I would want him to hug me and just hold me, not to touch me everywhere. I need him to understand that's what I need so I can feel safe.

Therapist: Have you told him?

Melinda: He will say that I am crazy, that it is not what he wants to hear. You know how men are . . . "calientes."

Therapist: What would it take for you to ask for what you need in bed?

Melinda: I don't know; I don't think I can ask. I feel afraid that he might not like that; no man likes that.

Therapist: But based on what you shared with me, Julio is a supportive partner, correct?

Melinda: Yes, he will do anything I ask of him. He adores me, but I'm afraid.

Therapist: But if you don't ask him, then you would never know.

Melinda: That is true; maybe I can bring him here, and you can tell him. (smiles)

Therapist: (smiles back) I won't be able to tell him, but I can facilitate the space where you can share your sexual needs with him and go from there. How does that sound?

Melinda: I think that would be easier than doing it by myself, and that way we can ask other things if we need.

Therapist: You are doing hard work, and bringing Julio into session will assist in finding a way to do this together.

Melinda: Maybe you are right. I will ask him, but I'm not sure what he will say.

Therapist: We never know until we ask.

Melinda: Maybe he will like the idea. (smiles) But I'm still afraid.

Melinda exemplifies the story of thousands of migrant women from Latin America—women who risk their lives and those of their loved ones to be free from gender violence. If a therapist is unaware of the oppressive systems and culture these women come from, a positive outcome of therapy may be difficult. Latinx women want to connect to others by being able to see themselves in them. Being supported by someone who understands their struggles and life in their home country will help them open up and process what needs to heal. After working with Melinda for a long time, she brought Julio three times to our sessions. He's been supportive of Melinda's need for intimate connection. She has been able to open up more, has shared her incontinence concerns, and has started asking for what she needs. She also learned how to let Julio know when she wants to be held/cuddled instead of having sex. Both Melinda and Julio have started having open conversations in which they share their needs.

Case 2: Fatimah

After migration, the adapting phase (into a new culture, ideas, and experiences) happens. In the case of women migrating to the United States, that means learning how to create lives by incorporating your own culture and understanding the new culture you live in. This can create serious distress that impacts the mental and physical health of the individual. This is the case for my next client, Fatimah.

Fatimah is a 28-year-old woman from Egypt who moved to the United States at the age of four. She was raised in a conservative Muslim household, and family is a strong and important part of her life. She shared that during high school she was confronted with significant peer pressure from her friends who were experimenting with boys, and she got into trouble with her parents due to hanging out with her friends. In high school, she'd change clothes when she arrived at school and was always concerned that her parents would find out. Fatimah liked a boy, and a couple of times after school they made out. From then on, Fatimah began exploring her body through masturbating, and she knows what she likes. As a college student, she lived at home (the accepted norm in her household). She recalls her mother talking to her on a couple of occasions about sexuality in Islam and how she needed to find a good husband to share that with. She always avoided masturbating when anyone else was in the home and would stay home purposely sometimes to have time for herself. When she completed college, Fatimah became more conservative—by changing her outward appearance (conservative clothes and wearing hijab), as well as attending her local Masjid (Mosque). As a result of this deeper approach to her religious practices and beliefs, she has questioned herself about masturbation and whether she is committing *haram* (sin). She feels she's been dishonest with herself and is extremely concerned about her upcoming marriage to Ibrahim, the son of a family friend. Ibrahim was raised in Syria and migrated to the US after high school. Fatimah likes Ibrahim, and they communicate frequently (texting/talking). Ibrahim often visits her home with his family, which is part of a traditional courtship of a Muslim family. She came to therapy seeking help to work on her fear and anxiety, and to determine whether she needs to tell Ibrahim about her past experiences before marriage. She's overly concerned he might not accept her if she shares these experiences. This level of self-doubt and questioning has created high anxiety. Ibrahim's family is very well-known in the Muslim community, and people look up to them. Fatimah feels that if she reveals this information to him, it will not only impact the outcome of her marriage—as she might never be suitable for marriage—but her family might be outcasted from their social circle.

Goals for Sex Therapy

- Fatimah seeks to reconcile between her past experiences of sexual encounters and masturbation and her religious faith/beliefs.
- Fatimah wants to enjoy what she has discovered about her sexuality with her future husband.
- Fatimah would like to decrease her anxiety about her past experiences.
- Fatimah wants to explore whether it is necessary to tell her future husband of her experiences.

Insights and Guiding Principles

My first impression of Fatimah was that she was fearful and wanted a quick solution. She was concerned that she was doing something wrong and questioned why it felt so good. Fatimah also shared her worry about possible rejection from her future husband. My initial thoughts were to work with Fatimah to identify masturbation from an Islamic perspective as well as a Western perspective. By providing psychoeducation on masturbation, the intent was to normalize the concept of masturbation, by grounding the fact of her masturbation not involving anyone else. This would decrease Fatimah's fear of not being pure. For me, discussing and addressing Quranic teachings on body, purity, and sexuality was going to part of my own homework. As a therapist, I needed and wanted to reassure her that I respected her beliefs, which was essential as she felt she had sinned.

Another factor to explore was the shame and guilt attached to her high school experiences. Normalizing what she experienced as part of sexual development was key to reconciling Fatimah's feelings with the pleasure she felt. Consolidating her cultural and religious beliefs along with her own acquired beliefs from being raised as a migrant in the United States was essential for this journey. Fatimah realized that her migration at such a young age exposed her to different values than hers, which she was comfortable with. Finally, an important piece was to support Fatimah's ownership of knowing what she likes as a strength and not a weakness. Her awareness of her own body and what is pleasurable to her was a tool she could bring into her marriage.

Approach to Fatimah's Case

As in my previous case, I used both a therapeutic and educative approach. Fatimah had many questions regarding sexuality and felt at ease working with a Muslim convert sex therapist; I understood both the Western perspective and her culture and religious upbringing well. She had many questions regarding interpretations and meanings of Quranic passages; throughout our sessions, she'd make a list of what she wanted to research.

In our sessions, Fatimah was open in sharing her experiences with me, which indicated that she could work with some of her anxiety-producing thoughts. Through therapy and psychoeducation, she discovered new ways to conceptualize her sexuality and decrease her anxiety of sharing her experiences with Ibrahim. She took it upon herself to understand and deconstruct the concept of virginity. This process helped her see how social norms influenced her. She was able to create a new sexual script that fit her way of thinking about sexuality and purity without challenging her faith.

Systemic and Intersectional Issues for Consideration

Role of community: Fatimah is a practicing Muslima, and her faith and community hold a significant role in her life. Her family and their name in the community have a deep impact on her identity. If a therapist was narrow and utilized mostly Western-focused perspectives, Fatimah might have walked away from therapy if she were told to forget what she experienced and move on regardless of what others thought. This approach removes the importance of Fatimah's connection to her community, which could be detrimental to her well-being. In her case, her family and future husband were the main people she needed to stay connected to as a main part of her social identity.

Islamic teachings on pleasure: Islam teaches the importance of equal pleasure for both men and women. This was another layer Fatimah had not considered prior to being in therapy. The realization that understanding her own sexuality influences her pleasure and her husband allowed her to feel less restricted and more affirmed in her own sexuality.

Identities: Fatimah came to the United States as young child, which was a unique situation where her family and social roles at times conflicted with her identity. This created distress and, in therapy, she was able to reconcile both identities to obtain the emotional stability needed to make decisions.

Sample Dialogue with Fatimah

Therapist: What do you envision Ibrahim would say about your experiences?

Fatimah: That is something dirty that no Muslim should do, and he will not marry someone like me because who knows what I might have done in the past.

Therapist: Have you ever talked to him about sex?

Fatimah: No way; we haven't even held hands. I think it would be really hard to talk to him about this stuff. I don't know what he thinks about it.

Therapist: How do you envision your marriage to him would change things?

Fatimah: I hope our friendship grows, that we support and love each other, and that we trust each other enough to share things like this.

Therapist: Do you feel that part of growing is to share everything?

Fatimah: Yes, especially when it comes to sexuality. He will notice from the first time we kiss and have sex. He will notice that I know too much and that I am not pure. Then you know what will happen . . . he will return me to my family.

Therapist: How he will notice what you are describing?

Fatimah: By the way I would kiss him and touch him, he will just know. I don't think he is stupid. I don't know how much experience he has with women either.

Therapist: What if I tell you there is no way to know?

Fatimah: There is no way? Don't you bleed the first time when your hymen breaks? What If I broke my hymen while masturbating? Now that would be really bad.

Therapist: What if I tell you that no hymen "breaks" and that not all women bleed during their first sexual experience?

Fatimah: You don't? But that is the normal thing that happens, If it doesn't then that means you are not a virgin, right?

Therapist: It doesn't mean anything because some women bleed, and others don't.

Fatimah: I think I'm going to read about this. You know in my culture they might want to check the sheets we slept on during our first night, and if there is no blood that could be a problem.

Therapist: I understand your concern. Having accurate information about sexuality is really important and needed especially when myths are being reinforced. I encourage you to read about it. Let me look up some information that could be helpful for you.

Fatimah: Thank you for understanding. I'm sure you think I'm being silly, but these are real concerns.

Therapist: I know, Fatimah, and I'm here to support you through this process.

Fatimah was in therapy for a few months while exploring her questions. She was proactive and had notes from research she had done prior to our time together. She shared that, as her marriage date approached, she felt more secure of her friendship and love towards Ibrahim, and was less anxious and less focused on her previous experiences. Near the end of therapy, Fatimah felt more at ease with her sexuality. While she wasn't sure whether she would tell Ibrahim about her past experiences, her fear of him finding out had significantly diminished. She ended therapy right before getting married, no longer questioned herself, and appeared to be in a good, emotionally stable place.

Counseling Strategies

- **You cannot and will not know it all.** Seek consultation from other colleagues who have experience working with certain migrant populations.
- **Reach out and ask questions.** Connect with people in your community who may be familiar with the culture or are from the same culture as your client.
- **Educate yourself.** Be aware of your client's needs—if there's something you do not understand about your client's culture, just ask. Most will be happy to tell you.
- **Think Decolonial Sexuality.** When working with migrant clients with different backgrounds, be clear about not letting Westernized power dynamics surface in your sessions.

- **Listen.** Your client's migration journey is crucial to hear and to listen to—this provides a bigger picture of your client's needs and will assist you in connecting with them.
- **Put on magnifying glasses.** Allow an integral approach to sex therapy or education that encompasses the intersectional identities of your client.
- **Speak "their language."** Being able to communicate with your client in their native language could yield a higher positive impact on their processing of emotions. Use words that describe and express their sexuality based on their upbringing—this will be more impactful. Also note that some clients might not have the words to describe certain things because they do not exist in their own language or dialect.
- **Know the culture.** Take time to understand the culture that your client comes from—this is one of the most important tasks. The term *culturally sensitivity*—as well-intentioned as it is—can create condescending dynamics. Just ask your clients if you have questions.
- **Do not make any assumptions.** Although cultural dynamics can be similar, clients are always different.
- **Most of the time, it is not about sex.** The main concern that a Latinx or Middle Eastern client would come to therapy for is most likely not about sex. Consider other relational or systemic concerns as the main stressor.

Lessons Learned by the Author

As someone who has experienced migration, working with migrant clients has always been my passion. The time and dedication your migrant clients will need may exceed that of other clients. The work and time you put into understanding and connecting with your clients will make a difference in their lives. All cases are different and unique, so make sure to have resources to support you in this work, too. Dive in deeply with your clients—they need your sex therapy and education expertise as well as your assistance to navigate complex systems as they create a sense of community.

Critical Questions for Readers to Consider

- Have you asked your client to share their migration journey with you?
- Have you considered how your client's migration journey might have impacted their sexuality?
- Has the client ever avoided talking about their migration experiences?
- Do you understand the concepts of the way of life that the client is sharing with you?
- Do you have further questions regarding your client's life before their migration?

Reading Suggestions

Akande, H. (2015). *A taste of honey. Sexuality and erotology in Islam*. London: Rabaah Publishers.

Carrillo, H. (2017). *Pathways of desire: The sexual migration of Mexican gay men*. Chicago: The University of Chicago Press.

Espín, O. (2018). *Latina realities: Essays on healing, migration, and sexuality*. New York: Routledge Press. (Original work published in 1997).

Mohanty, C. T. (2003). *Feminism without borders: Decolonizing theory, practicing solidarity*. Durham: Duke University Press.

Mignolo, W. D. (2005). *The idea of Latin America*. Oxford: Blackwell Publishing.

Said, E. (1979). *Orientalism*. New York: Routledge Press.

References

Carrillo, H. (2017). *Pathways of desire. The sexual migration of Mexican gay men*. Chicago: The University of Chicago Press.

Espín, O. M. (1997). *Latina realities. Essays on healing, migration, and sexuality*. New York: Routledge Press.

Espín, O. M. (2006). Gender, sexuality, language, and migration. In *Conference on immigration and psychology* (pp. 241–257). Anne Arbor, MI, April 2003. University of Michigan.

8

TRANSGENDER BLISS

From Gender Dysphoria to Gender Euphoria Through Decolonizing Gender

Jaxx Alutalica

Key Terms

gender identity: how one identifies with and or constructs their gender through social roles, individual expression, and felt sense of identity, within or beyond the gender binary, and regardless of the sex they were assigned at birth

gender expression: the ways in which an individual performs gender to the outside world through social roles, behaviors, dress, and other secondary sex indicators; may or may not be aligned with one's gender identity

transgender: an adjective describing someone whose gender identity is variant from the gender they were assigned at birth; may or may not choose to pursue social or medical transition

trans: an umbrella term used to define people who identify along the spectrum of not being cisgender; may or may not also identify as transgender

gender non-conforming: an individual who experiences gendered traits that are in contrast to the expected traits of their gender assigned at birth

Two-Spirit: a label that surfaced in the 1990s as a term to bridge the understanding between Indigenous and Western understandings of gender, with varying definitions depending on Native American Nation; used to refer to gender variation outside of the Western gender binary

gender dysphoria: an individual's experience of discomfort, incongruity, or dissociation from how one's body, social roles, or perceived gender align with their gender identity

DOI: 10.4324/9781003034063-9

A note on gender dysphoria: The aim of this chapter is not to discount the experience of gender dysphoria in trans and gender non-conforming bodies; this is an important part of many transgender people's experience and is not to be minimized. Rather, I aim to integrate the concept of gender euphoria as an alternative, pleasure-centric approach to coping with symptoms of gender dysphoria and redeveloping a relationship with one's self, one's body, one's history, and one's cultural environment.

gender euphoria: the experience of being aligned with and comfortable with the relationship with one's gender identity and gender expression; a feeling of congruence, validation, and authentic self-expression

internalized transphobia: negative beliefs about transgender or gender-variant people that are passed down through collective cultural conscience and internalized by transgender and gender non-conforming individuals, thus resulting in self-hatred and self-judgment

decolonizing gender: the act of deconstructing how the validity of "gender transition" is determined (i.e., box jumping from male to female) and instead exploring the variations of gender expression outside of Eurocentric binary gender standards; removing standards of gender expression that are bound up in Westernized ideals of what constitutes a man and what constitutes a woman

Background

Understanding Colonization and Gender

In order to understand the etiology of gender dysphoria and how mapping a path towards gender euphoria is paved, we must first understand what is meant when we reference "decolonizing gender." The gender binary operates through White supremacy. According to Lugones (2007), through the Eurocentric lens everyone is racialized and gendered. However, in many other parts of the non-Western world, this didactic separation does not occur. The idea of gender dimorphism is largely tied to the idea of being civilized, which is a construct of colonization (Dietz, 2014). Therefore, the construction of the gender binary is a tool utilized to civilize and colonize non-Western cultures who would not otherwise operate within this imposed division. This is not to say that all non-Western cultures do not abide by their own divisions of gender, but rather that they are often inclusive of multiple genders and a greater variance of gender roles. In many Indigenous cultures, people of gender variance are celebrated and given special roles in society (see: Two-Spirit, Hijram, Muxes, etc.).

The predominant amount of literature regarding decolonizing gender focuses largely on feminism and the roles of men and women in society. While this is certainly relevant to transgender studies, none of the literature I encountered directly addressed the role of gender decolonization as it relates to transgender and Two-Spirit populations and their well-being. I arrive at the conclusion that gender colonization is an issue of importance to transgender populations because many of the manifestations of gender dysphoria are also likely to be stereotypically gendered expressions, or lack thereof, of self and identity. The large amount of gender dysphoria is often rooted in not performing a particular gender in congruence with its assumed gender presentation and roles.

The following are some examples of colonization of gender as it relates to transgender and Two-Spirit people:

- The notion of "passing" as one's identified gender in order to be taken seriously and as valid in their transgender experience
- Box jumping, or the idea of transitioning "from one gender to another"
- Physical/sexual dysphoria and the disconnection between one's identity and one's body parts
- Secondary sex characteristics and what identifiers are associated to be male or female (i.e., facial hair, breasts)
- Character traits and aesthetic expressions benign inherently coded as male or female

    Through decolonizing gender we ask, what could gender look like if it didn't have to follow norms and scripts? How then, could we shift the language behind gender and sex therapy to better cultivate a wide range of gender expressions and affirmations?

Trans vs. Two-Spirit

It is impossible to talk about decolonizing gender without also addressing the delineation between trans and Two-Spirit. *Two-Spirit* is a label that surfaced in the 1990s as a term to bridge the understanding between Indigenous and Western understandings of gender. Its definitions are depending on Native American Nation, but in general it is used to refer to gender variation outside of the Western gender binary. It is a word exclusive to Indigenous populations, and it encompasses a vastness of gender expression, identity, and performance. *Trans* is an umbrella term used to describe someone who does not identify with their assigned gender at birth, including binary male-to-female and female-to-male transgender people and also people who are non-binary, gender queer, agender, etc. While there are similarities between the two, there are also important differences. *Two-Spirit* is a word reserved for those of Indigenous background to identify with their gender in a way that shirks the cloak of colonization. While it might be correct to say that Two-Spirit people fall under the trans umbrella, not all trans people are or should identify with being Two-Spirit.

It is relevant here to note that while many fields of study have used the term *transsexual* or *transvestite* to refer to this population, it is now considered more correct, and is preferred by the trans population itself, to use the term *transgender* or *trans* in lieu of previous terms. For this reason, I will use the term *trans* throughout this chapter unless directly quoting an author who has used another term.

Gender Dysphoria—The Making of a Pathology

Transgender bodies have been an often-polarizing point of conversation for the medical and mental health fields alike. In the long history of transgender people's existence, reports on transgender bodies and experiences have been characteristically pathologized, criminalized, and dehumanized (Cauldwell, 1949). This is a direct product of how a White-supremacist lens influences the perception of these populations. That is to say, trans bodies are seen as an abnormal topic of study rather than a lived human experience of variance and complexity. Through this colonizer psychology, trans bodies are often seen as incongruent expressions of self, indicators of hysteria, or dissociations of identity (American Psychiatric Association, 2013).

Psychoanalysis was one pioneering field in the interpretation of unconscious sexual desire, the development of sexuality throughout the lifecycle, the repression of sexual pleasure, and the pathological development of gender identities (Freud, 1927). In his "Three Essays on Sexuality," Sigmund Freud believed the infant to have a "psychic bisexuality" and that gender identity development relied on socializing influences, implying that the healthy child would cleanse themselves of the other gender throughout their well-supported development (Freud, 1927). Trans bodies, then, were the unhealthy product of this psychic bisexuality, never appropriately individuating in childhood. In Freud's statement "Anatomy is destiny," he summarizes his belief that natural gender identity development results in heterosexuality and a joining of opposites, and that trans identity was a result of a person's inability to attach to the same-gender parent appropriately, thus lacking the ability to differentiate their gender beyond a psychic bisexuality into a binary gender-congruent expression of self (Freud, 1927).

Psychoanalysis has a fraught history with trans bodies, especially considering the reliance on mental health practitioner approval that comes with any medical transition, which is bound up in the idea that the mental health professional can determine more about the validity of one's gender than the transgender patient (Walker et al., 1990; World Professional Association for Transgender Health, 2012). Some psychoanalysts turn to Jaques Lacan and his theory of sexuation to relate to transsexuality, emphasizing the instability and uncertainty of sexual identity (Carlson, 2010;

Dean, 2000; Elliot, 2001, 2010; Gozlan, 2011; Salamon, 2010; Shepherdson, 1994). Still, much of psychoanalysis perceives the trans identity as a fantasy, and surgery or medical intervention as a harmful confirmation of that fantasy (Elliot & Roen, 1998).

Cited as one of the first pieces of literature about transgender bodies, the 1949 publication of "Psychopathia Transexualis" utilizes the vernacular of eugenics to suggest that transgender people possess poor hereditary background with a highly unfavorable childhood environment (Cauldwell, 1949).

Cauldwell is one of many to describe transgender people as narcissistic and self-obsessed, building on Freud's pathologizing of the transgender body as a perverse sexual expression (Freud, 1927). Similarly, physician Harry Benjamin reported that his transgender patients displayed traits of psychological conditioning, infantile trauma, childhood fixations, and arrested emotional development (Chang, Singh, & Dickey, 2018). While Benjamin took credit for the significant contribution of differentiating sex and gender, previously delineated by John Money's advocacy for the concept of gender in 1957, he was overly fixed in creating a single psychological narrative about transgender people. He coined the terms *transsexual, transsexualism,* and *transexualist* to describe those whom he considered to have a "rare psychological condition" (Chang et al., 2018). In his publication, he suggests the most effective treatment for this condition to be the development and reinforcement of realistic ideas and circumstances, subsequently invalidating the reality of a transgender person and infantilizing their perception of self. As a part of his work, Benjamin developed a rating scale for gender variance, sexual orientation, and desire to alter one's body (Walker et al., 1990). In this singular-narrative measurement scale, patients were required to report feelings of being "born in the wrong body" and were only considered a true transsexual (and subsequently awarded care) if they desired genital surgery (Walker et al., 1990).

This interpretation of gender incongruity will go on to evolve into the clinical understanding of gender dysphoria that we have today. Interestingly, Benjamin is cited as a monumental contributor in transgender health care and an ally to the equal treatment of transgender patients, perhaps given the progressive nature of his research and his desire to give transgender people a voice at a time of high stigma. Benjamin will go on to be credited for the development of the WPATH Standards of care, which outline the appropriate treatment for transgender individuals in medical and psychological fields, and his work will be cited as the pinnacle of transgender advocacy. Ironically, having to affirm that one is in the wrong body and desires genital surgery completely undermines a great number of transgender folks' desires and too narrowly defines the experience of transgender.

The Wrong-Body Narrative

This is a relevant place to dissect one of the most colonized transgender myths, a product of the aforementioned pathology, and a critically anti-pleasure discourse: *The Wrong Body Narrative*. The "wrong-body narrative" is a dichotomous explanation of a complex and vivid experience of gender, diluting the transgender identity experience and bifurcating it into a binary expression of right and wrong, male and female, certain or uncertain. The wrong-body narrative is criticized at length by feminist, queer, and transgender theorists (Engdahl, 2014). The critique concerns the gatekeeping, which this narrative uses to determine whether one is truly "transexual," as seen in Harry Benjamin's determination of transexuality and the pervasive existence of gender dysphoria and its similarly diagnosable counterparts throughout the DSM (Walker et al., 1990; American Psychiatric Association, 2013). This narrative is also seen in the *International Statistical Classification of Diseases and Health Problems*, 10th ed. (ICD-10) as: "A desire to live and be accepted as a member of the opposite sex, usually accompanied by a sense of discomfort with, or inappropriateness of, one's anatomic sex, and a wish to have surgery and hormonal treatment to make one's body congruent as possible with one's preferred sex" (World Professional Association for Transgender Health, 2012).

The problem with this diagnostic standard and its "Diagnostic and Statistics Manual" counterpart, Gender Identity Disorder, is that it makes many impactful assumptions about transgender bodies. The wrongness presumed here implies that the transgender person feels wholly and completely disconnected from their body and the ways in which their gender has been assigned to them, and that this wrongness can only be corrected through medical and surgical intervention across the binary to the other gendered body. This is an essentialist perspective that reinforces the norms of the gender binary and results in the misrecognition of gender variant bodies, thus disputing the realness of the transgender spectrum of experiences (Engdahl, 2014). This is not to say that gender dysphoria is not experienced by some transgender people, nor that medical intervention is not a lifesaving and important milestone for many, because that certainly is the truth for many transgender people. It is, however, to say that the wrong-body narrative creates a standard of mistruth and clinical evaluation that is dehumanizing and limits access for transgender people, regardless of their relationship with gendered body parts. This narrative also implies that the transgender person only becomes "real" once they have received the necessary interventions to "correct" the body/experience misalignment, that the "transgender" body is non-existent but rather an incomplete process on the way to the opposite side of the binary, made whole only once it is unidentifiably transgender. It leaves little to no space for cultural experiences of gender, social roles, personal meaning, or the diversity and humanness of the transgender experience entirely unique from the interpretation of transgender experiences by medical subjectivity.

Most relevant to the argument at hand, the wrong-body narrative leaves little place for pleasure-centric experiences without relying on the default narrative of binary gender transition. Throughout this journey, it is evident that much of the academic literature relies on post-medical intervention to determine sexual satisfaction and pleasure in transgender sexuality, presuming that the relationship with one's body prior to such intervention left little to no space for pleasurable sexual experiences (Reay, 2016; Prosser, 1998). This is a common discourse within the medical and academic literature, even when it is pleasure-focused (Reay, 2016). Hence, the importance of recognizing the existence and validity of pleasure in pre-operative or non-operative transgender bodies is often left up to personal narratives of pleasure and transgender storytelling to rewrite the wrong-body narrative (Bellwether, 2013; Roche, 2018).

Decolonization Through Pleasure

The erotic is a tool for self-healing (Driskill, 2011). The transgender body does not belong to academic researchers, gender confirmation surgeons, psychoanalysts and psychiatrists, or TV talk shows. There is a creativity to being transgender that is unique to the experience of being in a gender-expansive body and is often overlooked by non-transgender sexuality researchers and academics alike. Halberstam describes the transgender person's ability to "morph, shift, change, and become fluid" as a paradox of visibility and temporality (Halberstam, 2005). When the transgender person is seen as transgendered, they are both failing to pass and exposing a rupture between the temporal registers of past, present, and future (Halberstam, 2005). I believe that it is in the liminal space described by Halberstam where the evasiveness of transgender pleasure exists, in broadening this liminal space by expanding conceptions of transgender sexuality and decolonizing the means through which we understand gender in its entirety.

The erotic is a source of power and information, of self-reclamation and identification (Driskill, 2011). In her iconic essay "Uses of The Erotic: The Erotic as Power" Audrey Lorde (2000) speaks of the erotic as a resource rooted in power that offers the ability to feel deeply and fully into one's life and vitality (2000). For transgender people, who have been culturally neutered, a reclamation of the erotic is an opportunity to attune to an intimacy of the self, which has the power to liberate structural oppression and accept less powerlessness (Lorde, 2000). The concept of the "sovereign erotic" suggests that the erotic bridges the gap between "individual desire, wounding, and longing and collective histories of dispossession, imposition, and removal" (Driskill, 2011). Again, for transgender individuals, sexuality healing cannot be separated from the ongoing process of decolonizing gender (Money, Hampson, & Hampson, 1955), but rather the experience of the erotic is a personal and systemic process of liberation.

Claiming our eroticism is a reclamation of our own power, something that structural oppression fears. Therefore, shifting the dialogue about transgender bodies away from the wrong-body narrative and gender dysphoria is a threat to the systems that rely on transgender powerlessness. This is why shifting conversations about transgender sexuality towards pleasure is not only an intriguing script flip, but it is a critical act of erotic liberation and structural deconstruction. Sovereign erotics relates our bodies to the nations, traditions, and histories from which our ancestors originate (Driskill, 2011). It is a decolonized perspective that offers our gender relationship to be one of complex, creative expression rather than the colonized, binary, stereotyped expressions of male and female (Driskill, 2011) Lorde posits, "As we begin to recognize our deepest feelings we begin to give up, of necessity, being satisfied with suffering and self-negation, and with the numbness which so often seems like their only alternative in our society." When we begin to create space for transgender narratives of pleasure in contrast to narratives of numbness and pain, erotic knowledge empowers a more complete, embodied expression of self. The greatest indicator of sexual satisfaction is one's feeling of empowerment and satisfaction with their relationship with self. Therefore, erotic liberation and pleasure-centric narratives have the potential to create a cyclical positive feedback loop where erotic empowerment feeds sexual satisfaction, and so on. This positive feedback loop is in direct opposition to the ways gender colonization keep transgender bodies repressed and oppressed.

Gender Euphoria: A Pleasure-Centric Counter-Narrative

This is an intriguing place to introduce a counter-narrative to gender dysphoria: gender euphoria. In my research, I found an absence of conversation about gender euphoria in academic or peer-reviewed literature. Instead, it is a concept that exists largely on community-run platforms like Reddit and Tumblr. This is significant to note because gender euphoria is a pleasure-centric alternative to gender dysphoria, which is rising in popularity amongst how transgender people talk about their bodies and in particular, their sexuality. Its absence from the academic literature is indicative of the oversight academic has for in-group dialogue and transgender-driven theory. Gender euphoria is the feeling of being seen in one's gender in a way that is congruent with how one identifies, commonly reflected in social or intimate situations where one is addressed by the appropriate language and treated in a manner congruent with their gender identity

(Lester, 2013). The presence of gender euphoria does not imply that said person does not experience gender dysphoria or that they never feel at odds with their body. Certainly, the two can exist concurrently or independently. It does, however, introduce a pleasure-focused lens through which to view the transgender experience, as moving towards satisfaction instead of avoiding discomfort (dysphoria). Gender euphoria is an essential component because it highlights the creativity required to feel sexual embodiment when one is navigating sexuality in a gender non-congruent body and exploring means by which their sexual expression feels affirmative (Bellwether, 2013). It is also a critical discourse to introduce into the conversation of decolonization because the experience of pleasure is innately in direct contract to colonization. In the cases following, I will explore how a migration from a pleasure-negative narrative to an embodied pleasure-centric narrative (gender dysphoria to gender euphoria) is both the product and the propellent for decolonizing gender on transgender and Two-Spirit bodies.

CASE 1: Juanita and Kim

In this case study, we explore how the sexual manifestation of gender dysphoria can be addressed using narrative techniques as well as reframing the experience through a decolonizing lens.

Kim and Juanita are a couple in their mid-thirties. Juanita (she/her) is a cisgender Mexican-American woman, and Kim (he/him or they/them) identifies as Two-Spirit, and he is currently struggling with societal expectations of masculinity. The couple have been together approximately 7 years. Two years ago, Kim came out as trans and began to take testosterone. Since, they have had complex feelings about the balance of masculine and feminine energy they experience and how to appropriately express his identity. The couple presents now in therapy because they are having troubles with their sex life. Juanita reports that the two of them have been struggling to connect sexually because whenever they begin to have sex, Kim becomes distant. Even when it appears that they are both enjoying themselves, Kim will stop abruptly and change the activity. Juanita expresses a frustration behind her expectations of Kim to be the more virile partner because of his testosterone levels and her perception of a more masculine demeanor. Kim reports that his experience of his body feels incongruent, and when they have sex he feels a sense of disconnect from the sexual acts that are occurring. Kim states that he enjoys the feeling of what he would call "women's sexual acts," including penetration, but feels judgment and shame around his masculine identity and being perceived as transgender enough. Kim reports that Juanita has expectations that he will always initiate sex, and this feels frustrating to him. Both partners report still having a sexual desire for one another.

Hopes for this couple are for them to both release gendered expectations about sex, bodies, and the right kind of sex for those bodies. Goals for the couple are as follows:

- Decentralize the focus on masculine roles and body parts and create space for the construction of a new narrative
- Help Kim build a positive somatic relationship with his body so that he is better able to remain present during sex
- Reconstruct ideals around types of sexual intimacy being gender-affirming from a pleasure-centric approach (i.e., this is gender-affirming because it feels good).

The guiding principle of this case is the belief that the gendered expectations and disconnection Kim is feeling in his body is a direct reflection of the ways colonized gender ideals have taught him gender is validated. In order to begin to deconstruct these beliefs around gender, we must first examine their origin and the role they've played in the client's development. With Kim, he is struggling to enjoy sex because he is finding himself pigeonholed by the gendered expectations he has, including masculine partners initiating sex, certain sex acts being gendered, and an overall disconnect from his body due to a complex relationship with gender. It is likely that Kim will experience a more satisfying relationship with his gender if he is able to reconstruct narratives around sexuality and develop a more positive relationship with his body as a whole. In Kim and Juanita's case, I believe the predominant work is around shifting their stories and creating space for new narratives to exist.

I have chosen narrative therapy as the therapeutic approach that I will use with Kim and Juanita. I have chosen this because both partners are struggling with stories of what sex must look like and each partner's role in that sexuality. Because of these stories, Kim has become distant, and Juanita has become in pursuit. To shift this for the couple, we must break down the stories that are contributing to their understanding of gender and begin to reconstruct them with a decolonized lens in mind. This means targeting beliefs around sex for both partners and the history behind these beliefs, examining how they may be causing a disservice and choosing to replace the useless part of these beliefs with new ones. As a clinician, my role is to support the clients as they deconstruct the belief systems that have been imposed on them by colonized gender expectations. In this instance, these colonized gender beliefs include Kim being the only initiator of sex, Juanita taking on a passive role in sexual encounters, and Kim feeling distant from his body because the sexual activities he enjoys are incongruent with how he perceives his gender identity. By shifting these stories, we give the client permission to live outside of the norms of gendered expectations. Decolonizing their belief systems involves restructuring their understanding of themselves as individuals and a couple within the larger purview of gender and giving them permission to act beyond it.

There are a few important systemic intersectional issues for us to consider here. First, Kim and Juanita come from different cultural backgrounds and therefore have different understandings of gendered expectations. Furthermore, Kim is a transgender non-binary individual, and Juanita is a cisgender female. The two of them have markedly different experiences of the world, however they were both raised as female in the United States and have internalized values and beliefs from this background. They are both in their early thirties and have a long history of sexual partners; however Juanita is Kim's first sexual partner since transitioning, which is presenting novel challenges for them both. Collectively, they are attempting to navigate the intersection of culture, gender, and identity within sex.

In this case, we see how shifting the narrative around sexuality towards one that creates space for diverse gender expression instead of pigeonholing Kim into one type of gender expression helps to liberate ideals around sex, leading to more cathartic pleasure and an accessibility to sexuality that was not previously present. Decolonizing ideals around gender expectations also allows Juanita to witness the complexity of Kim's gender and engage with it accordingly. Both partners are able to shift their relationship with gendered expectations and be more conscious of Kim's lived experience rather than expectations around Kim's gender identity.

CASE 2: Tammy

In this case study, we explore the impact of colonized gender and dysphoria on an individual's sexual relationship with herself and how she might restructure that relationship through somatic practices.

Tammy (she/her) is a 46-year-old black trans female. She was assigned male at birth and began transitioning in her late thirties. She has recently undergone gender reassignment surgery and is struggling to develop a healthy relationship with her body and sex since surgery. While her body feels congruent now, she has spent so much time disconnected from a body that she was taught was not worthy of receiving touch or affection that she feels entirely dissociated from sexual touch or pleasure. Tammy recalls learning early on in transition that transgender people should feel disconnected from their bodies and that their bodies were only a source of distress, not pleasure. Tammy presents in therapy because she wants to learn how to be able to masturbate so that she can develop her sexual relationship with herself. She reports that prior to surgery she would never touch herself for pleasure because she believed her penis was a shameful reminder of her gender incongruence. Now that she has had surgery, she is struggling to bypass the disconnection she has developed with her body in order to better be able to enjoy sex and feel embodied in her gender.

My hope for this client is to redevelop a relationship with touch that refutes her belief that transgender people do not deserve pleasure and allows her to reconstruct her relationship with her body. My goals for this client include:

- Develop a healthy self-touch practice to feel more embodied and connected with herself
- Establish a practice of embodiment that focuses on her relationship with her full body
- Deconstruct colonized ideals that her body must look or be touched a certain way in order to enjoy masturbation and self-pleasure

Tammy is a black trans woman living in the United States of America, a place where it is very dangerous to be herself in the current sociopolitical climate. Because of this, Tammy is likely spending the majority of her life in a hypervigilant survival mode; this presents a challenge to somatic embodiment, which asks the client to drop into their lived experience and channel vulnerability in order to more fully experience sensation and connection. This is a critical consideration when working therapeutically with her. In addition to somatic work, it is imperative to connect Tammy to community resources and safer places for black trans women for any somatic work to be effective.

Through working with Tammy we are able to witness how somatic awareness helps her develop more presence in her body and an ability to shift her relationship with sexuality and masturbation. By doing so, Tammy is able to transition into experiences of gender euphoria and embodiment that were not previously accessible to her.

Counseling Strategies Highlights and Recommendations

The clinical pathway I suggest here is broken into three parts, assessing for the presence of gender distress, exploring the role of colonization, and transitioning to the lens of gender euphoria. Within those three parts are substeps that help guide the clinician along the path towards helping the client decolonize their relationship with gender. I predominantly utilize narrative therapy strategies, Queer Theory, and somatic therapy practices to structure my clinical work (see Table 8.1).

Table 8.1 A potential outline for clinical pathway to decolonizing gender

Stage 1: Assess for the presence of gender-related distress (gender dysphoria).	Substeps: - Explore the client's relationship with their own body as it relates to gender. - Identify how the distress manifests in their daily life. - Acknowledge the significance this distress has on client's daily functioning.	Clinical tools: - Perform comprehensive assessment of how symptoms of gender dysphoria may arise for the client. - Create space for the complexity of feelings and pain experienced by the policing of gender expression and identity through colonization. - Understand the ways in which experiences gender dysphoria have impacted the client's ability to express and experience their gender.
Stage 2: Explore the role of colonization in the client's relationship with their gender.	- Identify cultural expectations and gendered stereotypes that the client feels bound by. - Deconstruct the values behind gendered expectations. - Address internalized colonization by investigating how messages about gender affect the relationship with self.	- Take a comprehensive history of gender socialization and messages client has received about their gender through a colonized context. - Utilize narrative tools to tell the story of how colonization has impacted their understanding of acceptable gender expressions.
Stage 3: Transition to the lens of gender euphoria.	- Give permission to client to engage in gender expression that feels authentic to their lived experience instead of scripts they've been taught to internalize. - Develop a connected relationship with the body that allows the client to feel embodied pleasure symptoms of gender dysphoria may arise for the client. - Reconstruct narratives around gender to be inclusive of gender variance and non-White interpretations of identity.	- Grant permission to break perceived boundaries of gender expression. - Utilize somatic techniques like sensate focus to increase awareness of the body and enhance positive associations with touch. - Catalyze the ability to critique how colonized gender arises in one's body, and challenge it with positive narratives of self and somatic experiences of embodiment.

Lessons Learned by the Author

In exploring this topic I learned two major lessons. The first is that decolonization is as much of an internal practice as it is a social liberation. In order to practice decolonizing the state, we must also decolonize the mind. The second is that while it is not irreverent to consider decolonization of gender as primarily Indigenous work, all who are affected by colonization (read: everyone) benefit by decolonizing their minds and subsequently the systems they operate within.

Critical Questions for Readers to Consider

How has this client been impacted by colonized (White Western culture) ideas of what gender should be and how gender should look? How can unpacking this internalized transphobia help with the retelling of a client's story?

In what ways can this client use somatic strategies to reconnect with the physiological experience of their body? What parts of their body produce pleasurable experiences aside from those that create dysphoric experiences?

How can the therapist empower the client to use alternative strategies to centralize pleasure in their experiences of gender to highlight experiences of gender euphoria?

References

American Psychiatric Association (2013). *Diagnostic and statistical manual of mental disorders: Diagnostic and statistical manual of mental disorders* (5th ed.). Arlington, VA: American Psychiatric Association.

Bellwether, M. (2013). *Fucking trans women.* Scotts Valley: CreateSpace Independent Publishing Platform.

Carlson, S. T. (2010). Transgender subjectivity and the logic of sexual difference. *differences, 21*(2), 46–72.

Cauldwell, D. O. (1949). *What's wrong with transvestism?* Girard, Kansas: Haldeman-Julius Publications.

Chang, S. C, Singh, A. A., & Dickey, L. M. (2018). *A clinician's guide to gender-affirming care. Working with transgender and gender nonconforming clients.* Oakland: New Harbinger Publications.

Coleman, E., Bockting, W., Botzer, M., Cohen-Kettenis, P., DeCuypere, G., Feldman, J., Fraser, L., Green, J., Knudson, G., Meyer, W. J., Monstrey, S., Adler, R. K., Brown, G. R., Devor, A. H., Ehrbar, R., Ettner, R., Eyler, E., Garofalo, R., Karasic, D. H., . . . Zucker, K. (2012). Standards of care for the health of transsexual, transgender, and gender-nonconforming people, version 7. *International Journal of Transgenderism, 13*(4), 165–232. https://doi.org/10.1080/15532739.2011.700873.

Dean, T. (2000). *Beyond sexuality.* Chicago: University of Chicago Press.

Dietze, G. (2014). Decolonizing Gender—Gendering Decolonial Theory: Crosscurrents and Archaeologies. *Decoloniality, Postcoloniality, Black Critique: Joints and Fissures,* 245–269. Frankfurt-on-Main; New York: Campus-Verl.

Driskill, Q.-L. (Ed.). (2011). *Queer indigenous studies: Critical interventions in theory, politics, and literature.* Tucson: University of Arizona Press.

Elliot, P. (2001). A psychoanalytic reading of transsexual embodiment. *Studies in Gender and Sexuality, 2*(4), 295–325.

Elliot, P. (2010). *Debates in transgender, queer, and feminist theory: Contested sites*. Surrey, UK: Ashgate.

Elliot, P., & Roen, K. (1998). Transgenderism and the question of embodiment: Promising queer politics? *GLQ, 4*(2), 231–261.

Engdahl, U. (2014). Wrong body. *Transgender Studies Quarterly, 1*(1–2), 267–269.

Freud, S. (1927). Some psychological consequences of the anatomical distinction between the sexes. *International Journal of Psycho-Analysis, 8*, 133–142.

Gozlan, O. (2011). Transsexual surgery: A novel reminder and a navel remainder. *International Forum of Psychoanalysis, 20*(1), 45–52.

Halberstam, J. J. (2005). *In a queer time and place. Transgender bodies, subcultural lives.* New York: New York University.

Lester, S. W. (2013). *Gender euphoria: An embodied practice of painting & drag performance* (Doctoral dissertation), University of British Columbia.

Lorde, A. (2000). *Uses of the erotic: The erotic as power*. Tucson, AZ: Kore Press.

Lugones, M. (2007). Heterosexualism and the colonial modern gender system. *Hypatia, 22*(1), 186–209.

Millot, C. (1990). *Horsexe: Essay on transsexuality* (K. Hylton, Trans.). New York: Autonomedia.

Money, J., Hampson, J. G., & Hampson, J. (1955, October). An examination of some basic sexual concepts: The evidence of human hermaphroditism. *Bulletin of the Johns Hopkins Hospital,* Johns Hopkins University, *97*(4), 301–319.

Prosser, J. (1998). *Second skins: The body narratives of transsexuality*. New York: Columbia University Press.

Reay, B. (2016). Transgender orgasms. *Feminist Formations, 28*(2), 152–161. doi: 10.1353/ff.2016.0034.

Roche, J. (2018). *Queer sex a trans and non-binary guide to intimacy, pleasure and relationships*. London: Jessica Kingsley Publishers.

Salamon, G. (2010). *Assuming a body: Transgender and rhetorics of materiality*. New York: Columbia University Press.

Shepherdson, C. (1994). The role of gender and the imperative of sex. In J. Copjec (Ed.), *Supposing the subject* (pp. 158–184). London: Verso.

Walker, P. A., Berger, J. C., Green, R., Laub, D. A., Reynolds, C. L., & Wolman, L. (1990). *Standards of care*. Sonoma, CA: Harry Benjamin International Gender Dysphoria Association.

9

DE-PATHOLOGIZING THE BLACK SUPERWOMAN'S KINKY SEXUAL FANTASY

Lexx Brown-James

Key Terms

Black Feminist Thought: Black Feminist Thought is a theory based on the commonality of Black women's experiences developed by Collins (2009) that articulates black women's voices, struggles, and histories by valuing Black women's abilities to know and measure the world through their unique concrete experience.

Black woman: To reduce the definition of a Black woman down to a few simple sentences is necessary for the brevity of this chapter, although a true, holistic, and all-encompassing definition of a Black woman does not readily exist. Therefore, for the remainder of the chapter, the term *Black woman* refers to a woman who self- identifies as Black within her own communities and believes she has some genealogical connection to members of the African race who were a part of the Transatlantic Slave Trade.

chattel slavery: A system where people were the personal property (chattel) of an owner and were bought and sold as if they were commodities (Gasper & Clark Hine, 1996).

explicit power-sex belief: "The conscious belief that consensual sex inherently involves power (i.e., either domination or submission)" (Chapleau & Oswald, 2010, p. 68).

manumission: When a slave owner grants freedom to a slave (Gasper & Clark Hine, 1996).

New World: A name used to reference the Western hemispheres specifically in regard to the Americas; popularized in the 16th century (Davidson, 1997).

DOI: 10.4324/9781003034063-10

rape: An act of aggression and power combined with some form of sex, where a person forces another person into sexual contact through verbal coercion, threats, physical restraint, and/or physical violence where not given consent (American Law Book Company, and West Publishing Company, 2002).

rape fantasy: The term *rape fantasy* refers to fantasies that include the use of physical force, incapacitation, or threat of force to coerce a person into sexual activity against his/her will (Hawley & Hensley, 2009; Sanday, 1981). Haskell (1976) describes that the integral difference between rape in reality and rape in fantasy is control. He maintains that in fantasy the woman constructs the terms of existence and therefore is able to edit the fantasy to meet her needs; whereas, in reality violations take place against the woman's will (Haskell, 1976).

sexual fantasy: A mental image or pattern of thought that stirs a person's sexuality and can create or enhance sexual arousal (Leitenberg & Henning, 1995). This includes all thoughts and images that alter our emotions, sensations, or physiological states erotically (Maltz & Boss, 2008).

sociohistorical context: The term *sociohistorical* means "of, relating to, or involving social history or a combination of social and historical factors" (Merriam-Webster, 2013).

sexual scripts: Socially constructed ideas of how males and females are supposed to interact with each other, including how each gender should behave in sexual or romantic situations (Wiederman, 2005).

power: The capacity or ability to empower or transform oneself and others (Allen, 2011, para 17).

Background

When you put *Black + woman + rape fantasy* together, for most clinicians, this equals pathology. To most people, including the Black women who experience rape fantasy, this fantasy about power exchange can be uncomfortable, scary, and yet pleasurable. Research primarily studies Black women's sexuality from a pathological standpoint: prevention of disease, prevention of pregnancy, prevention of hypersexuality, and treatment of traumatization, specifically (Bean, Perry, & Bedell, 2002). Clinical treatment of Black women's sexuality also has been pathologized. As a result, the full experience of Black women's sexuality still needs thorough exploration and support in therapy instead of being treated from a deficit. According to Patricia Hill Collins, Black women exist at the intersections of racism, classism, and sexism from birth. I contend, however, that Black women (and girls) from birth are subject to racism, classism, sexism, sizeism, texturism, and colorism.

Judgments about Black women and their sexuality rely on how the culture of power has construed their value in each of these realms. Because these systems and their inherent function to strip Black women of power, it makes sense that Black women have been socialized to amass as much power as possible. The accruing of this power, however, creates a tenuous situation where Black women have minimal places of safety to be completely themselves and sans power—including with their own sexuality. In my office, I see Black women come in afraid of the power they relinquish in their fantasy—afraid of the fantasies that give them pleasure and looking for a cure, a remedy or, what I typically offer, validation. The socialization of Black women around sexuality has taken a new path.

The baby-making Mammy, wonton Jezebel, and ball-busting Sapphire archetypes for Black women's sexuality have paved the way for the asexual Black Superwoman. Black women are now socialized to be Superwoman out of all the archetypes of Black women's sexualized tropes. The Black Superwoman is the only archetype that does not have an inherently attached sexual script. She is asexual—by force or choice—and unassured that she is entitled to her own pleasure. The Black Superwoman is viewed as powerful as a daughter of Krypton. Unlike the actual Superman, she cannot dodge speeding bullets, leap tall buildings, or use X-ray vision, but instead she is expected to feed an entire community on her salary alone, work full-time while taking care of her own children and others, and make any house a home—all while navigating White society to conquer systemic capitalism, all while remaining in a pleasant mood. The mothers and grandmothers of Black women have often been the sole provider for, or contributed to the survival of, the family; therefore, independence and self-sufficiency become traditionally reinforced lessons (Woods-Giscombé, 2010). Without the abilities of self-sufficiency and independence, there is fear that the Black family fails (Woods-Giscombé, 2010). This archetype, unlike the others, developed within Black culture. Being a Superwoman can be honorable in comparison to the other denigrating stereotypes generated by the culture of power (Beauboeuf-Lafontant, 2009). The value and regard for the Black Superwoman creates an expectation and desire for Black women to raise their own daughters with the same expectations of becoming a Black Superwoman; thus, perpetuating the archetype. The perpetuation takes place because the Superwoman is juxtaposed to the normative, damsel, fragile, White woman (Beauboeuf-Lafontant, 2009). Beauboeuf-Lafontant (2009) posits that the Black Superwoman is rooted in difficult assumptions such as the idea that strength is a natural quality of Black women and that having strength accurately summarizes Black women's motivations, behaviors, and sexuality. For Black women who have adopted the archetype of the Black Superwoman, understanding the collection, maintenance, release, and retention of power is integral to understanding Black women's unique experience and their fantasies about rape.

Bond and Mosher (1986) report that when a woman fantasizes about rape, she "imagines a sexually desirable man, motivated by passion that is aroused by her sexual attractiveness, who uses just enough force to overcome her resistance and to promote her pleasure" (p. 163). Kanin (1982) concluded that erotic rape fantasies exist in a dichotomy, erotic versus aversive fantasy types. In Kanin's *erotic* category, a dominant and attractive male desires a woman so intensely that he must act on his passion to overcome her (Kanin, 1982). In this fantasy, women can feel or express non-consent but present minimal resistance. Ultimately, all the women studied succumb, which takes 15–30 minutes according to Kanin (1982). In the *aversive* category (a fantasy that is suggested to last only a few minutes), the male perpetrator is an unattractive stranger who is coercive and forceful (Kanin, 1982). Kanin (1982) also concluded that in this aversive fantasy, the victim fights the aggressor attempting to prevent painful violence; this fantasy elicits no sexual arousal for the fantasizer. To be clear, the Black Superwomen typically present with *erotic* rape fantasy, shame, and minimal sexual satisfaction.

For Black women, the internalization of the Superwoman can be a leading cause of depression (Beauboeuf-Lafontant, 2009). This depression may partially be due to the Superwoman's requirement of less from lovers, especially when they are the "endangered Black males," suggesting Black men have enough issues to deal with without their Black women expecting true sexual gratification (Randolph, 1999). Randolph (1999) further suggests that a cultural crisis exists for Black women, stemming from the inability to determine whether their power is a desired benefit or a cumbersome burden. The next case studies will examine the phenomena of Black women who experience rape fantasy and its relationship with their sex-power belief and how to work with it in therapy to reduce harm and increase pleasure. Learning about consensual power exchange, fantasy, and Black women's sexual relationship with power increases a clinician's offering regarding sexual pleasure for Black women.

Case 1: Delores

In my practice, every second session with a client is a sexuality interviewing session. Centering on permission gaining and giving, I ask questions about the past, current, and desired future experience with sexuality. This always includes asking about sources of sexual pleasure for a client. Sometimes this is hard for clients to pinpoint and, often rooted in shame and perplexity, they share in hushed tones and with downcast eyes. Despite doing these interviews, I was able to learn that Delores (68) and Santana (22) both experienced pleasurable force fantasy, and throughout our work with their depression and exploration while working to dismantle the Superwoman archetype, we were able to explore their roles with power.

Delores is a Black woman from the northern United States who has been married for over 30 years. Delores is a cisgender Black, Christian, post-menopausal woman who has never had a truly high sex drive according to her report, but who has always had a vivid sexual fantasy life. She presented in therapy with depressed mood and was struggling with reconnecting to her husband in his recent retirement. She was a stay-at-home mom (which I always call a "domestic engineer," if you will) and raised their family and helped with grandchildren. She led an active life outside of the home once the family was successful. She has earned many rewards and a reputation in her community. For her husband, she still wakes up after 30+ years together with him for coffee in the a.m. and ensures dinner is ready in the evening. She felt fulfilled through a variety of philanthropy and by providing care for her husband as needed. She had not connected with him sexually of her own regard; for her, he was always the pursuer. During our sessions, she noted that sex had always been just okay and that it just wasn't a priority for her anymore. She also noted that she did masturbate a few times monthly and her fantasies were what she used during that time. She presents physically as youthful and full-figured with straight black, shoulder-length hair and mocha-brown skin.

During our fifth session Delores talked about her feelings of longing regarding her husband as she just experienced a feeling of sexual rejection. She was feeling unsure about how to connect with him during this retirement and whether approaching him sexually was "appropriate" after so many years of not initiating sexual play. During this session her fantasy about rape came up as an admission.

Therapist: So, those feelings of rejection can be very hard and distancing. How do you self soothe after feeling hurt?

Delores: Usually I get busy doing something else. The hot feelings pass, and we come back together in our own way. I don't even know if he realizes I'm a little put out.

Therapist: Hmm? I'm a little shocked that with such a leading presence and long relationship your lover doesn't know when you're hurt or when you want pleasure.

Delores: Maybe I'm better at keeping this things from him. I have never wanted to burden him; he's a good man. A good husband, my other girl-friends some of tried a few and still ain't found the right one, and others have just . . . well . . . settled. I don't feel like I did any of that. I love him and he loves me, so what's a miss or a dropped ball every now and again?

Therapist: That's fair. I want to explore your sexual pleasure with your lover a little more, is that OK?

Delores: Go ahead, Doc.

Therapist: Thanks. What do you want for your future sexual pleasure with your lover?

Delores: That's a good question. I don't know.

Therapist: If it could be anything, anything you wanted. What would your pleasure look like sexually?

Delores: (nervously) Well, and I haven't told no one this. I have this fantasy that comes up every so often. I'm in our room just toiling around putting up laundry, and he walks in just hot for me. I shoo him away, and he won't take no for an answer, ya know. Like he has to have me. He pushes up on me, close and hot. I push him away, and he kisses me dizzy and although I'm trying to get back to this laundry, he has to have me. We end up all in passion.

Therapist: That is some fantasy. And, actually, a quite popular one. A lot of women who are leaders like you have this fantasy, it was even a number one fantasy amongst some women surveyed. The idea of not having to make decisions and that you have pleasure even though you didn't seek it out, some folks say is a release.

Delores: Yes, this "fantasy" as you call it, is something that plays in my head when I'm at my hottest, I can usually just enjoy it and move on, but it's getting more stuck in my head now.

Therapist: Have you enacted that with him?

Delores: Oh no, Doc. My husband is gentle, no muss, no fuss, and I can count the minutes by this stage in our relationship. Two times a month and that's about it. Like clockwork.

Therapist: So there is some regularity and he desires you. These are great signs in a marriage of longevity. I also heard you state that he is a good husband and that you want more. What makes you think he won't rise to meet this need of yours too?

Delores: Well, now that's a question isn't it? How do I talk to him about it though?

And we ended that session talking about ways to bring up the conversation with her husband to help alleviate some angst around talking about sexuality and normalize her desire for pleasure. We continued to work together, and eventually Delores' partner came in for a few couple's sessions to work on understanding and meeting her needs differently, while expressing his wants. We ended work when a grandchild took ill and the couple had to support their child and grandchild for a period of time.

Case 2: Santana

Santana is a 22-year-old Afro-Latina who is darker in complexion with kinky hair. She is thin and has no noted disabilities. She is seeking therapy for wanting to explore her sexuality. She identifies as pansexual, cisgender, ex-Catholic. She is interested in BDSM. She reports no history of sexualized trauma. She has had this sexual fantasy of being abducted and forced to engage in erotic rape since she was about 18 years old. She is currently wanting to become a therapist and is seeking out therapy to help her explore what this means for her sexually. She is hoping to understand where some of her sexual desires come from and to build a sexual community where she can navigate her exploration of kink.

Santana: OK, Doc, lemme tell you about this, and I wanna know what you think.

Therapist: OK, shoot.

Santana: So, I dunno where it comes from. Wait, that's not true. OK, when I'm like super nervous or feeling real overwhelmed with all the things, I swear the best fantasy pops in my head. I use it to cum, and it's really just so amazing that I think I want to have it happen, but it's weird. Don't put me in the hospital OK?

Therapist: I'm never *trying* to put you in the hospital. What's the scene though?

Santana: OK, like, so I'm in my house and none of my roommates are at home. I'm in like some shorts and whatnot walking around the house, and I never get to do that for real. So I'm comfy and come in and there is this hot, I mean, hot guy just in my living room. He sees me and, *Ping!* Instant erection. I can feel my cooch get tight and I'm just like whoa, but also like, who is you?! And he comes over in the kitchen and pushes me against the cold fridge, and we making out and I'm pushing him away and none of it is working. I fight him a bit and he takes the kitchen thread—you know to tie up chicken when you cook it—and ties my hands behind me. And then I'm helpless, but it's how. So I just like let it happen and it is the best f*** of my life. I wake up, and I feel that throb and have to take care of it. The release is just the best. What is wrong with me?

Therapist: Santana, thank you for sharing such a moving fantasy with me. Force fantasy also known as rape fantasy is really popular. You have to remember that you have been socialized to always fight. Fight racism, classism, sexism, colorism, texturism, all of that. In your fantasy, it is safe to be powerless—you don't have to be a Superwoman in that moment, and although it seems like his pleasure is centered in your fantasy, he does all these things that you want. Bondage, aggressive kissing, harder penetration—equal things on your list of enjoyment.

Santana: Damn. That's true, but (and here's the part that worries me a bit) I kinda wanna have it happen in real life. Like I don't want to be raped at all, that's not what I'm saying. I want this experience though.

Therapist: I get you. And there is a whole community where you can explore this fantasy of consensual non-consent.

Santana: What do you mean?

Therapist: I mean that there are folks, just like you, who have these same fantasies and desires. There is even an event here where people can sign up to get taken during the event, tied up, and pleasured. They have a discussion beforehand about what would be interesting for them. I do not think they have physical intercourse in the play space, but I do know they engage in this kidnapping, force-type behavior.

Santana: Where do I sign up?

Santana found a few events that she was able to go to with a trusted friend and had a great time. We processed each experience afterward, and she found that some of her anxiety stemmed from lack of community within the kink world. By meeting the need and normalizing her desire for play, we were able to find safe ways for her to explore her rape fantasy and build lasting bonds with others who also validate her desires.

Counseling Strategies

A clinician should assess—not judge or diagnose—the level of the Superwoman experience for their Black women clientele. Being vulnerable is antithetical to the internalized Black Superwoman. So, to perform a successful assessment, a clinician must create the proper holding environment to allow for the necessary vulnerability it will take for a Black woman with Superwoman characteristics to feel safe. Doing so may help a Black woman be more willing to be open and honest with information in general because she finds the clinician empathetic and relatable. Furthermore, if the clinician finds that power-sex beliefs and Superwoman beliefs are elevated, the client might struggle with sexual surrender. Struggling with sexual surrender could also indicate a lack of sexual satisfaction and feeling safe in sexual vulnerability. Additionally, if internalized power-sex beliefs and Superwoman characteristics are high, the client may also struggle with satisfaction and feelings of safety within other relationships outside of sexuality. The clinician should work with the client on creating a relationship where she can intentionally choose to relinquish power. By creating this relationship with the clinician in a safe and caring environment, ideally, women with high power-sex and Superwoman beliefs can start to choose surrender in relationships, both sexually and globally.

Further, this research necessitates that clinicians review their own lenses in which they view Black female sexuality when doing therapy. For clinicians who approach Black sexuality from a pathological standpoint, it is important to externalize those views and instead use a sex positive lens for understanding Black female sexuality, as it has been pathologized enough.

When working with women in therapy who present with possible distress around rape fantasy and who demonstrate characteristics of the Black Superwoman applying the Sociohistorical Cultural Perspective can be useful. Grounded by Black Feminist Thought, the Sociohistorical Cultural Perspective provides clinicians with a global, sex positive, non-deficit-based framework to comprehend the position of their Black female client by understanding how power dynamics are pertinent to their Black female client's existence and sexuality. Using the Sociohistorical Cultural Perspective, a clinician will be able to provide psychoeducation and intervention to alleviate distress or increase awareness related to the power dynamics involved in rape fantasy for Black female clients. By using the sex positive framework of the Sociohistorical Cultural Perspective, clinicians will be more aware of their own biases and able to help Black women who exist in an environment rife with classicism, sexism, racism, sizeism, colorism and texturism—to say the least about the oppressions Black women face.

When working with Black female clients, both individually and in partnerships, the clinician will have to gain permission from the Black woman to explore her understanding of power. For Black women who exist within the continuous sextuple oppressive context, permission to explore her own perception of power is integral in assisting, supporting, and bonding with her. Without her permission, a Black woman can feel unsafe, which reinforces the notion that it is necessary to accrue and never relinquish power in order to maintain safety and survive (whether that is physical, emotional, spiritual, or psychological). Furthermore, in couples' spaces, a clinician not only needs permission for the exploration of the Black woman's power dynamic but also has to be careful to not devalue the lived experience of the partner or imbue their own ideas regarding power if they stem from a framework involving intersectional identity oppression. Doing so again reiterates the oppressive conditions the Black woman exists within and reinforces the need for the internalized Superwoman to exist.

Lastly, when working with Black women, clinicians must seek to understand the sociohistorical context in which Black women have existed. By understanding the historical, cultural, and current social context Black women exist within, clinicians will be able to use non-deficit-based theory in treatment to empower Black women's sexual prowess and pleasure. Clinicians can use the Sociohistorical Cultural Perspective by educating themselves on the history of Black women, working to become an ally to Black women in spaces (especially when the space is devoid of Black women's voices), and beginning to understand the role power has in the lives of Black women, not just in sexual fantasy, but also in everyday occurrences and interactions—beginning with the therapy room Black women might present in for help. This examination creates the foundation necessary for clinicians to help Black women navigate through relationships, expand their own internal view of self, and explore places where the lack of safety in surrender results in rigid power dynamics and loss of pleasure.

Lessons Learned by the Author

These cases taught me that rape fantasy and desire have no age and do not have to stay in just the fantasy realm. Further I realized that, although I do a sexual history interview for every client, I do not want to ask about this fantasy until further rapport is gained, as many of the women who disclose this fantasy hold some shame and doubt about it. I further realize that I, as a clinician, needed to be more aware of the various types of BDSM community that I could refer my clientele to who wanted to enact the fantasy in real time. Lastly, the more I work with Black women, I am finding that the desire to relinquish power is great, but the only safe place to do so is often in sexual fantasy versus any type of reality outside of my office.

Critical Questions for Readers to Consider

- What do you believe about Black women's sexuality?
- How do you feel about consensual non-consent actions?
- When it comes to something that may seem traumatic and yet is pleasurable, how do you work to not condemn or shame the desired behavior?
- What more socio-cultural historical information do you need to consume in understanding the sexuality of marginalized folx?
- How do we support exploration of Black women's sexual power and fantasy in reality if it is desired?

Suggested Readings and Additional Resources for Consideration

Sexuality Educators:

- Mollena Williams-Haas
- Orpheus Black
- Robin Wilson-Beattie
- Shakti Bliss Bunny

Critelli, J. W., & Bivona, J. M. (2008). Women's erotic rape fantasies: An evaluation of theory and research. *Journal of Sex Research, 45*(1), 57–70. doi: 10.1080/00224490701808191

Cruz, A. (2016). *The color of kink: Black women, BDSM and pornography.* New York: New York University Press.

Friday, N. (2009). *Beyond my control: Forbidden fantasies in an uncensored age.* Naperville, IL: Sourcebooks, Inc.

References

Allen, A. (2011). Feminist perspectives on power. In Edward N. Zalta (Ed.), *The stanford encyclopedia of disorders of sexual desire*. New York: Brunner/Mazel, 1979. Philosophy (Spring 2013 Edition), Retrieved from http://plato.stanford.edu/archives/spr2013/entries/feminist-power/

American Law Book Company, and West Publishing Company. (1936). *Corpus Juris Secundum: A complete restatement of the entire American law as developed by all reported cases*. St. Paul, MN: West Pub. Print.

Bean, R. A., Perry, B. J., & Bedell, T. M. (2002). Developing culturally competent marriage and family therapists: Treatment guidelines for non-African American therapists working with African-American families. *Journal of Marital and Family Therapy, 28*, 153–164. doi: 10.1111/j.1752-0606.2002.tb00353.x.

Beauboeuf-Lafontant, T. (2009). *Behind the mask of the strong Black woman: Voice and the embodiment of a costly performance*. Philadelphia: Temple University Press.

Bond, S. B., & Mosher, D. L. (1986). Guided Imagery of rape: Fantasy, reality, and the willing victim myth. *Journal of Sex Research, 22*, 162–183.

Chapleau, K., & Oswald, D. (2010). Power, sex, and rape myth acceptance: Testing two models of rape proclivity. *Journal of Sex Research, 47*(1), 66–78. doi: 10.1080/00224490902954323

Collins, P. (2009). *Black feminist thought: Knowledge, consciousness and the politics of empowerment* (1st ed.). New York: Routledge.

Davidson, M. H. (1997). *Columbus then and now, a life re-examined*. Norman: University of Oklahoma Press, p. 417.

Gasper, D., & Clark Hine, D. (1996). *More than chattel: Black women and slavery in America*. Bloomington, IN: Indiana University Press.

Haskell, M. (1976, November). The 2,000-year-old misunderstanding: Rape fantasy. *Ms.*, 84–96.

Hawley, P. H., & Hensley, W. A. IV. (2009). Social dominance and forceful submission fantasies: Feminine pathology or power? *Journal of Sex Research, 46*(6), 568–585. doi: 10.1080/00224490902878985.

Kanin, E. J. (1982). Female rape fantasies: A victimization study. *Victimology: An International Journal, 7*, 114–121.

Leitenberg, H., & Henning, K. (1995). Sexual fantasy. *Psychological Bulletin, 117*, 469–496.

Maltz, W., & Boss, S. (2008). *Private thoughts: Exploring the power of women's sexual.* Charleston: BookSurge Publishing; Reissued edition (May 2, 2008).

Randolph, L. B. (1999, July). Strong black woman blues. *Ebony, 54*, 24.

Sanday, P. R. (1981). The socio-cultural context of rape: A cross-cultural study. *Journal of Social Issues, 37*(4), 1540–4560, Blackwell Publishing Ltd. doi: 10.1111/j.1540-4560.1981.tb01068.x

Wiederman, M. W. (2005). The gendered nature of sexual scripts. *The Family Journal, 13*(4), 496–502. doi: 10.1177/1066480705278729.

Woods-Giscombé, C. L. (2010). Superwoman schema: African American women's views on stress, strength, and health. *Quality Health Research, 20*(5), 668–683.

10

MORE THAN EBONY AND IVORY

Complexities of Sex Therapy with Interracial Relationships

Anne Mauro

Key Terms

mixed race/interracial couple: a union between individuals of different ethnicities and/or races

intercultural: relationships between individuals of different cultural backgrounds

interfaith relationships: relationships between individuals of different religious backgrounds

homogamy: partnerships between individuals of similar culture, race, and/or religion

White body supremacy: the phenomena of White bodies being the dominant population, thus seen as "normal" while non-White bodies are seen as "other;" with White body supremacy comes systemic racism, discrimination, and the oppression of "other" groups

BIPOC: Black, Indigenous, People of Color

homogeny: a union between individuals who have similar positions of power

ethnosexuality: a term by Joane Nagel referring to the intersection and interaction between ethnicity and sexuality

BBC: an acronym for Big Black Cock, which is a sexualized racial stereotype commonly used in contemporary porn and other forms of erotica to depict men of African descent with large penises

DOI: 10.4324/9781003034063-11

selective amnesia: For the purpose of this chapter, it means boxing away or selectively losing memory of racialized incidents and distress. There may be a desire to appear like a "normal" couple who does not struggle with the complications around race.

This chapter was born out of personal discovery. Discovery of the self, the systems I am a part of, my nation's gruesome history, and the field of sex therapy and education's tardiness to understand it all. Please understand that I have completed this chapter as a novice, sharing with you a personal reflection of myself and work. In a gesture to amplify BIPOC, I have deliberately chosen to use a lower case "w" for white persons.

When I opened my private practice in 2016, I was the only clinical sexologist specializing in couples counseling and sex therapy in Tacoma, Washington. Clients who were unable to travel to Seattle, where there were many sex therapists to choose from, would seek out my services. My clients exhibit an array of presenting problems that include out of control sexual behavior, infidelity, mismatched desire, sexual trauma, consensual non-monogamy, fetishes, sexual dysfunction, and performance anxiety to name a few.

Mixed race relationships or *interracial relationships* consist of partners of different ethnicities and/or races. Here, in the Pacific Northwest (PNW), it is common to see a combination of White, Asian, Black, Hispanic, Middle Eastern, African, European, Indian, Indigenous, biracial, or multiracial couplings. The number of mixed-race unions is on the rise, and we have never seen this many multiracial people in American history (Parker et al., 2015). According to Ridley and Gambescia (2020), "Western society is becoming a multi-cultural, multi-ethnic, multi-religious blend where attention to and an understanding of each other's family and culture of origin is essential" (p. 29). With the continuous blending of racial borders, we need to remain inquisitive about each relationship's experience without imposing stereotypical interracial narratives upon them. Interracial couples typically struggle with the same relational issues as their homogenous cohort. However, in addition they must navigate through the multifaced terrain of their differences all while carrying the burden of how they have been treated within the systems to which they belong: their society, culture, peers, and family of origin will likely all play a part, among others. Each mixed-race couple lives a reality that is unique to them. To understand some of the complexities of treating mixed-race partnerships in a clinical setting, we need to look at the socio-political history of interracial unions in the United States.

When white European settlers arrived in North America, they brought a more rigid, ritualistic sexuality intended mainly for procreation. They were accustomed to laws criminalizing alternative aspects of sexuality, and they publicly shamed those who broke their sexual rules. Upon arrival, the settlers were both repulsed and intrigued by the sexualities of the Indigenous, and later, Black peoples (Smith, 2003; Solomon, 2017). As Africans were brought to North America via the slave trade, Indigenous and African people quickly became sexualized by racial stereotypes that perpetuated sexual assault and coercion. Black and Indigenous men were seen as sexual savages that White women needed to be protected against (D'Emilio & Freedman, 1997; Nagel, 2000; Ross, 2004). Black and Indigenous women were seen as hypersexualized exotic temptresses' just asking for their bodies to be taken. Sexualized stereotypes from colonial times have assisted in the perpetuation of objectification of BIPOC and have been used as justification of sexual assault on Black and Brown bodies.

Present day, there are noticeable echoes of this racist past hidden in our ourselves, our client's sexualities, and at times, overtly displayed in our society. Sexual violence against BIPOC is an obvious indicator of one of the countless bequests colonization has given us. The transgenerational legacy of sexualized trauma has impacted the oppressed, oppressor, and bystanders of many generations of Americans and Canadians. We can see remnants of our traumatic past locally in the PNW with the missing and murdered Indigenous woman and girls (MMWIG) epidemic. Sadly, Seattle leads the US as the city with the highest number of MMIWG cases. Of the highest number of MMIWG cases statewide, my state, Washington, ranks second, after New Mexico. A study done by the Urban Indian Health Institute (2006) found that 94% of Seattle's Indigenous women have been coerced into sexual activity in their lifetime. The majority of the perpetrators were non-Native individuals, and most of these criminal instances happened on reservations. We know that even while Black women are underreporting sexual assault, they are still 35% more likely to be the victims of a sex crime than their White counterparts (Woman of Color Network Facts & Stats: Domestic Violence in Communities of Color, 2006). This disparity in cases between BIPOC and whites has a direct correlation to colonization.

Menakem's (2017) term *White body supremacy* may be misinterpreted as referring to White extremist groups. However, given that white bodies make up the majority of the US population (US Census Bureau, 2011), they have been in the position to create the dominant discourse and dictated what "normal" bodies, relationships, and sexuality look like. With the promotion of *homogamy*, any relationships where one person was White and the other was not has called attention and undergone scrutiny. Some people felt so strongly about the mixing of races that they criminalized interracial marriage. The trafficking of African bodies for the slave trade in the 1600s led to enslaved Africans becoming the largest minority racial group in the United States, eclipsing the Indigenous people (Solomon, 2017). Anti-miscegenation laws arose from fear of racial mixing and were established to prohibit sexual relations and marital unions with persons outside one's own race.

Marital segregation laws were not isolated to America; South Africa, the Middle East, Asia, and Europe shared similar deprivation of marriage equality. Relationships viewed as outside dominant discourse have had a long history of being pathologized even by therapists and educators (Killian, 2013). Although legally sanctioned, there are still people today who do not think races should mix (Livingston & Brown, 2017).

People who found concern with mixed race partnerships have often had positions of power that were able to influence others and their views on these couples. The media has a long history of censoring mixed-race couples. In early Hollywood, the Hays Code—a pre-set list of film industry standard moral guidelines—forbade depictions of miscegenation. This law prohibited whites from showing affection—such as kissing—to BIPOC on screen. In the documentary *They Got to Have Us* (2018), Harry Belafonte explains the bravery and creativity it took to play the love interest opposite a white woman, Joan Fontaine, in the film *The Island in the Sun* (1957) with strict rules in place around demonstrations of affection towards Black bodies. He brilliantly describes a scene where the two of them share a fresh coconut and, when it was his turn to take a drink, he carefully placed his lips in the exact same spot her lips so recently departed. "I handed her the coconut; it was my rebellion to the idea that we couldn't kiss. To find a way to do it as sexually and seductively as I possibly could to make it fill the space in the absence of a kiss and making sure that the audience would get it and it would be hard to edit that moment out . . . by drinking from that, it kinda set the message through a lens that we were having an orgasm. It was a delightful moment to beat the system" (Connolly & Frederick, 2019). This was an ingenious effort to mimic a kiss and express to the audience the sexual passion and desire they shared but were not allowed to display on screen. These subtle messages viewers consume are bursting with erotic hints of secret lust and desire.

Through cinematic history, dominant discourse has reinforced "othering" by censoring, sexualizing, and eroticizing BIPOC. This began with the erasure of interracial intimacy in print and film, which later set the precedence to allow a sense of taboo when mixed-race couples finally appeared in sexually connected ways on screens. On screen, stigmatizing and making fun of interracial relationships is commonplace as seen in *The Jeffersons*, *Guess Who*, and *Mixedish*, where racial microaggressions and name-calling are almost expected. The media strongly impacts *ethnosexuality* by perpetuating sexualized stereotypes in their portrayal of interracial relationships. Regressive, racialized sexual stereotypes continue to be projected onto interracial couples as seen in movies like *Jungle Fever* or television shows similar to *Modern Family*. Portraying interracial intimacy as out of the ordinary allows people to believe that it is something to make fun of, to hide, romanticize, or sexualize.

Similar to the media's representation of interracial couples, research has mainly been characterized by a combination of Black and White persons (B/W) (Childs, 2008; Killian, 2001; Killian, 2013). However, there is a wide variety of ethnic/racial combinations of partners of present day. In the United States, it is among Blacks, Asians, and Hispanics where the highest increase in interracial marriages is seen (Livingston & Brown, 2017). Literature examining relationships outside the "standard" B/W interracial configuration is sparse, and data comparing interracial relationships with other interracial relationships of different racial configurations is almost non-existent (Bratter & Rosalind, 2008).

Having understudied populations as clients can be a challenge, leaving clinicians without a set of best practices in sex therapy for interracial couples. In this case, using ecosystemic therapy (Killian, 2001; Killian, 2013) or intersectionality theory as a lens can assist in examining different identifiers, such as education level, gender, race, socioeconomic status, religion, birth country, etc. Using these models, we can place individuals' identifiers on a hierarchy of power. The collection of these points allows us to view their ecosystemic axis of power and how it interacts with their partner's (Zimmerman, 2012), thus offering a view of the power relations between them. In a relationship, many points of power within an individual interact with their partner's ecosystemic axis points. Due to the complexities and nuances within each interracial couple, these theories act as an informational guide that is helpful for assessment.

Additionally, both models are trauma-informed and allow for sociopolitical and historical considerations which are critical when working with mixed race couples. However, both theories offer too little on the topic of sex. In relationship and sex therapy, it is important to look at how the axis points of each partner interacts with sexuality on an individual and relational level.

Case 1: Walter

Potential clients often choose me due to my specialization in human sexuality or because they are seeking services from a BIPOC therapist. The clients in the case that follows chose me for both reasons. Walter, a 40-year-old cisgender African American and Samoan man is married to 39-year-old cisgender Caucasian woman named Hannah. They have been my clients for nearly two years. In the beginning of our work together, they reported that race/culture/ethnicity was not a factor in their presenting problems. However, through our time together, they have highlighted incidences where they indeed experienced racialized distress.

It took six months for them to share anything about their racial differences or their experience as an interracial couple—there was a prerequisite trust-building needed to secure our therapeutic alliance before this couple disclosed any racialized incidents. The couple sought out therapy due to Hannah having panic attacks during sex. We had begun in hopes of decreasing anxiety and panic while increasing communication around sexual wants and needs. Here is a passage from a session a few days after their eighth wedding anniversary:

Therapist: It sounds like you two had a great time on your anniversary. You've been together for a while now; you overcame many hardships together and really evolved both as people and as a couple. Would you say your sexuality has changed or evolved over the years?

Walter: I'd say so. At the beginning, the problems were definitely with me.

Hannah: I wouldn't say that.

Therapist: What do you mean, Walter?

Walter: (looks down) I really struggled with my body and penis size.

Therapist: If you're comfortable, would you mind telling us more about that?

Walter: It wasn't big enough. (Hannah shakes head in a disapproving nod)

Therapist: Your penis?

Walter: My penis and my body. Everybody looks at me and labels me as a "Black guy," and you know what they say about Black guys?

Therapist: The BBC? (both nod) Damn those sexualized stereotypes!

Walter: Exactly. I look one hundred percent Black, but I am also Samoan. The smallest on the Samoan side of my family. Out of the men and women! And, when we first got together, I was so skinny. (turns to Hannah) I filled out now though. (both laugh)

Hannah: He used to wear three shirts and a tank top. (looks at him) How many pairs of pants would you wear, babe?

Walter: Ha! I always had on at least three.

Therapist: Wow. What would happen when y'all would be intimate and clothes started coming off?

Hannah: That was part of the problem, the clothes wouldn't come off. Maybe a layer or two. I don't think I actually saw his penis until a year after we were started sleeping together. It seemed like he didn't really want to even use it back then.

Therapist: You guys were sleeping together for a year before you saw his penis?

Hannah: Yes, everything was done under the sheets.

Therapist: What about oral or manual stimulation of the penis?

Hannah: Nope. Nothing.

Walter: It's true. I was slick about keeping it under the covers. I even tried to put three condoms on once. It didn't work out too well.

Therapist: Wow, it sounds like you really internalized stereotypes of what Black and Samoan men's bodies were "supposed" to be and had a lot of shame associated with your body.

Walter: I did. I really did.

Therapist: It must have been difficult to not have a body that resembled these ideals.

Walter: It sure was.

Therapist: I imagine many stereotypes around minorities did not start from within the minority culture.

Hannah: Thanks, again White people. (She smiles and the therapist and Walter smile back.)

Therapist: (to Hannah) How do you think Walter's discomfort affected you?

Hannah: Hmmm, well, back then I think it made me insecure.

Therapist: Oh yea?

Hannah: Yea, I thought that his struggles around his penis were because he wasn't really attracted to me. I knew his previous partners were either Black or Samoan, and I was the first white girl. I could never *be* them.

Therapist: Oh geez, sounds like his insecurities brought out some insecurities in you? (Hannah's chin quivers, which usually precedes tears.)

Walter: I'm sorry, babe. (He places his hand on her knee. Through our work together he had learned that she appreciates him moving towards her with physical touch when she is distressed. Hannah becomes flushed.)

Hannah: I kinda forgot about that time.

Therapist: Do you think this has anything to do with your panic attacks now?

Hannah: I never thought of that.

Walter: Could it?

Therapist: There was a negative cycle happening, where you were both were influenced by your partner's feelings. I think we need to stay curious about that.

Counseling Strategies

- Join with clients to build a therapeutic alliance.
- Don't rush into talks on race or sex—meet clients where they are.
- Request consent to discuss difficult topics.
- Highlight clients' strengths.
- Allow clients to self-identify.
- Use ecosystemic/Intersectionality framework to map positions of power.
- Affirm clients' identities both as individuals and within the partnership.

  - Acknowledge their struggles.
  - Affirm sexualized and/or racialized discomfort.

- Assess for protective responses.
- Call out systems of oppression.

  - Sexualized racial stereotypes
  - Eroticization/Exotification

- Give permission to explore the topics of ethnosexuality, and leave room for further discussion.

Therapeutic Approach

On my intake questionnaire, and in the beginning of our therapeutic relationship, I opened the door to discussing ethnosexuality. Although, I did not force them to walk through the door, I allowed them space to stroll through and share what they were comfortable with when they were willing. Walking through that metaphorical door together created an intimate opportunity for the couple. They recognized the racialized pain and the effects it had on their partnership. Now, topics of race and sex come more often and without my prompting. They have also begun having their own discussions on sex and race together outside of therapy. I provided space, permission, and acceptance that promoted the idea of sharing what they were comfortable with in their own time. This fostered our therapeutic alliance and increased their trust and safety in our work together.

I start this session by drawing on the clients' strengths and acknowledging their struggles as well as the resiliency it took to overcome them. I again opened the door to talk about sexuality and let them guide the session. I stayed active and engaged while asking questions, providing supportive reflections, empathy, and validating their experiences. I held the door open so they could feel safe to explore.

I mentioned oppressive systems of power and not only called out the internalized racism Walter experienced, but gave it a name. My hope with delivering psychoeducation was to facilitate insight development around our cultural conditioning. By highlighting their negative cycle of interaction, they had a better understanding of their old patterns and problematic beliefs.

Walter and Hannah are still my clients today, and they continue to work through many facets of their relationship. They have been able to process painful relationship ruptures from the past and build a more trusting and safe relationship. Hannah has not had a panic attack in over a year, and Walter is comfortable being naked, having his penis seen, and incorporating it into their sexual play. They both have become increasingly open to addressing their ethnic and sexual differences.

Lessons Learned by the Author

On my intake paperwork, which is done online in my client portal prior to our first meeting, I ask my clients how they identify their race/ethnicity/ culture and allow them to type their response. My next question is, "How is this impacting your reasons for coming to therapy?" The majority will state that their race/ethnicity/culture plays little or no part in their presenting problems. However, through time, like with this couple, they will disclose stories of discrimination, microaggressions, and/or internalized racism that have had effects on their sexuality. This failure to disclose could be because they truly do not see a connection between their race and sexuality. With the couple described earlier, it's possible that we still needed to strengthen our therapeutic alliance, or it could have been selective amnesia. Maybe it was the socially constructed rules they abide by that have taught them to be silent on topics of race and/or sexuality. As professionals, we need to keep an eye out for these protective responses. We need to stay curious when we see minimization, hypervigilance, or hypersensitivity towards race (Killian, 2013).

This case demonstrated that messaging around stereotypical racialized sexualities still linger and sting us today. However, they can be hidden from assessment. With the body Walter had, he was unable to socially conform to the ideals that were imprinted on him, which caused both partners distress. Hannah also struggled with insecurities around her race—being white left her feeling like an inadequate lover for her partner of color.

This case demonstrates the importance of self-identification. Sometimes there is more variance than meets the eye, and we cannot gather proper data for the ecosystemic axis with assumptions. Since each interracial couple is different in their ethnicity, how they identify, and possibly, how they were raised, it is important to allow clients to tell their own stories. It is our job to remain curious and avoid assumptions. The work is partly in allowing discomfort to enter the space and holding it without trying to shoo it away. Only when we sit with the discomfort can we truly see what it is.

It is important for us to take inventory of our own biases around interracial relationships. The truth is, we all have biases. I remember being in a large-group discussion during my first quarter of grad school. A white woman in my cohort disclosed that her children were mixed. As she spoke, I imagined her cute little brown babies with curly hair. When I later found out that their father was Japanese, I initially thought to myself, "Those kids aren't mixed! I'm mixed. Black and white." I grew up knowing other mixed Black and white kids, and up until that point, when people used the word *mixed*, I made the assumption that they were referring to an individual mixed with Black and white. This was an assumption I carried with me through grad school! Yes, that woman's babies are mixed! I did not see past my own experience and bias of what "mixed" meant. I had to take the time to examine my automatic response, assumptions, and the feelings that followed. When we can deconstruct initial assumptions within ourselves, we can stop perpetuating sexual and racial oppression in our offices and classrooms.

It's also important to continually build your cultural competency. You can do this by taking inventory of your own biases, attending continuing education courses, educating yourself like you're doing now, and hiring a supervisor who has a strong multicultural competency for case consultation.

Critical Questions for Readers to Consider

- Can you identify where each client falls on the ecosystemic axis of power or power hierarchy? Does one partner have more power than the other?
- Do the partners share any of the same ecosystemic axis points? (i.e., same religion, political views, gender)
- How do their power relations interact with their sexual lives?
- Do you share any of the same exosystemic axis points or identifiable points of power with the clients (gender, race, sexual orientation, etc.)?
- How comfortable are you with talking about race? Can you acknowledge microaggression or other forms of discrimination in a clinical setting?
- Are you comfortable calling out systems of oppression within our society? Within their relationship? In the therapy room?

When discussing ethnosexuality, we are surfacing two very taboo topics in our culture: race and sex. It can be extremely difficult for some folx to talk about sex. It can be equally difficult for some to speak about race. Looking at sex through a lens of race can be uncomfortable for many. Our families, culture, religion and other systems have constructed rules for how we communicate about both.

Case 2: Jason

In this next case we will see how difficult it can be for our clients to talk about this intersection of race and sex, ethnosexuality, within the relationship. Jason, a 29-year-old, white, third-generation Mexican, and third-generation Native American identified himself as a white, cisgender, gay man. He had several previous relationships and experience with consensual non-monogamy (CNM) prior to partnering with Jay. Jay, a 35-year-old Indian, cisgender, gay man was in his first romantic relationship of one year with Jason. Jason was from Seattle, WA, Jay from Punjab, India. They were in a committed relationship that Jay classified as monogamous but that Jason had hopes of opening up. The couple came to me due to their constant arguing and lack of sex, intimacy, and connection. My hopes for them were to decrease the conflict and improve communication around sex.

In this case, you see that we immediately got into processing ethnosexuality, as they reported it contributing to their presenting problems.

Therapist: I read both of your intake documents, but I would like to take a few minutes hearing from the both of you about what brought you to therapy? Is that going to be okay with the both of you? (They turn to each other, look in each other's eyes, smile shyly, and nod yes.)

Jason: First off, I need to preface this by saying that we are two *very* different people. (Jay nods in enthusiastic agreement.) We are from different cultures, different countries, different ways of communicating, and . . . (turns to Jay) do I dare say it? (Jay puts his chin down slowly and shyly.) Different feelings about sex.

Therapist: So, you both chose to work with me because I'm a sex therapist? If I'm moving too fast, feel free to pump the breaks. . . . But, I'm wondering how comfortable you are with talking about two very difficult topics to discuss: race and sex.

Jason: I have always been able to discuss sex, but we definitely struggle, and I'm not really used to that.

Therapist: You normally feel secure talking about sex but not with Jay?

Jason: Yes, we have really struggled in this area.

Therapist: I want to hear more about how you two are struggling when discussing sex in just a moment. Do you feel comfortable talking about race? In here, with us?

Jason: As for the race bit, this relationship has really challenged me, and I've had some growth. I think I have farther to go in this department. It's not something that I have had to do at this capacity before. Well, I'm the only White guy in the room. I'm a little bit nervous that I am going to say something wrong, but I think I'm ready to take that risk.

Therapist: Thank you of sharing and for being brave, Jason. I know it can be difficult navigating conversations on race and culture. Jay, how comfortable are you talking about race and sex?

Jay: Race is something that I feel most comfortable with. Sex (loses eye contact with the therapist) is difficult. Extremely difficult.

Therapist: How are you feeling about talking about both race and sex in this space? Here with us?

Jay: Uncomfortable, but this is why we are here.

Therapist: On a scale of 1–10 with 1 being no discomfort and 10 being extreme discomfort, where are you at now?

Jay: 8. I don't think I have ever talked to anyone, aside from Jason, about sex.

Therapist: What's your number, Jason?

Jason: 5

Therapist: OK, let's all just take a few deep breaths and slow down in this moment. I like to take a few deep breaths in through my nose, exhale out my mouth, and relax my shoulders. Can we try that together?

Jay: Yes.

Jason: Sure. (We continue to take a few breaths.)

Therapist: (Sees both client's bodies relax slightly) Know that whenever that number rises, we can slow down and calm ourselves before moving forward. I'm curious if the two of you think having these different identities have impacted your sex lives?

Jay: I think it was mostly around communication. In general, Jason and his family are much more direct than myself and my family. If they have something to say, they are going to say it. We are much quieter. More reserved. And, we *never* talk about sex! Ever!

Jason: We are loud, we are blunt, but we aren't homophobes. Jay's family doesn't know he is gay.

Jay: It's true. My family doesn't know I'm gay. This is an example of our general communication differences. It's hard for me. So, when you're used to a more passive way of communicating, and you're uncomfortable talking about sex and your body in a sexual way, it's really hard to hear your partner say sexually explicit things like, "Let me see that arse." (He immediately becomes flush. Jason laughs uncomfortably.)

Therapist: I'm sure that is difficult. Have you been able to explain how you felt about it?

Jay: I think I would just shut down in the moment. It took a lot of courage for me communicate anything was wrong after the fact. I didn't want to hurt him or look too prude.

Therapist: That seems like a difficult position to be in, Jay. Jason, did you realize your word choice was making him feel uncomfortable?

Jason: Sometimes. I mainly notice it when I initiate, and I mainly do that non-verbally now. I just know that most things sexual will make him uncomfortable and can cause him to completely shut down.

Therapist: How could you tell he is shutting down?

Jason: He gets this real "deer in the headlights" look. Sometimes his body tenses, and he will stop talking.

Therapist: So, you can really see when this happens. You can pick up on some non-verbal ques.

Jason: Yeah.

Counseling Strategies

- Assess client's level of comfort talking about race and sex.
- Assess of rules around communicating around sex, bodies, and race.
- Slow down.

  - Give clients time and space for reflection and self-soothing.

- Scale questions to allow for assessment of client distress in the moment.
- Practice mindfulness.

  - Calm the room when distress increases.
  - Bring body awareness into the room.

- Assess for protective responses.

Therapeutic Approach

Using an ecosystemic framework to graph the clients' positions of power provided access to view how their intercultural, interracial, interfaith, and other axes of power are intersecting with their relational and sexual well-being. This, in turn, lends a view of where the power lies within the relationship as a whole. Seeing that Jason was positioned higher on the hierarchy of power and privilege—coupled with personality and communication differences—I felt that I needed to work on having Jay's voice heard and honored. I used solution-focused scaling questions to assess the level of distress in each person and followed this with mindfulness techniques, including a breathing exercise to calm the energy in the room. Doing this allows time for self-soothing and reflection. With my open-ended questions, I gained insight into how aware they are of their differences and their cultural sensitivity within the relationship and what narratives they have around their differing identities (Killian, 2001).

Unlike the previous case, we were able to get into ethnosexuality straight away due to it having a large influence on their presenting problems. Through our interactions, I was able to model a communication style that requests consent, permission, and slowing down with the intent to regulate and to self-soothe. The couple quickly included these skills into their own patterns of communication. They began having discussions both in and out of the therapy room that would ordinarily cause conflict. Sadly, six months into our therapeutic relationship, the couple was in a near fatal car accident causing serious injuries to both—the media coverage outed the couple as gay. When Jay's family saw this, they told Jay that the accident was punishment for him being homosexual. Jay began having nightmares, panic attacks, amaxophobia (fear of riding in cars), and an even stronger aversion to sexual touch and intimacy. After being discharged from the hospital, Jay chose to sleep in their spare bedroom. In our first session after the accident, the couple disclosed that although they truly loved each other, they no longer felt compatible for a romantic partnership and had taken action steps towards an amicable separation. I referred both to individual therapists and recommended Jay try Eye Movement Desensitization and Reprocessing (EMDR) for his PTSD symptomology.

Lessons Learned

I found examining each person's rules around communicating about sex and race valuable for increasing partner empathy and understanding around presenting problems.

Again, this theme of allowing clients to self-identify is an important factor in assessment. Jason identifying as white did not match my automatic assumption when looking at him. How he identified offered helpful insight into where he saw himself systemically positioned. I learned that Jay's quiet temperament coupled with him feeling uncomfortable discussing sex left an imbalance, where Jason's voice was the one primarily heard. Knowing this, I allowed more time and space for Jay's responses.

Highlighted Recommendations

- Model respectful communication.
- Like you, your clients may fear that they will mess up and say something wrong. Be brave, authentic, and try your best.

Critical Questions for Readers to Consider

1. When it okay for us to start talking about race?
2. How comfortable are your clients talking about sex and race?
3. Where is the power in the relationship?
4. Does the client in the underprivileged location of power have enough space to show up as their authentic self?
5. What is the couple's narrative about their differences?

Suggested Readings

DiAngelo, R. J. (2012). *What does it mean to be white? Developing white racial literacy*. New York: Peter Lang.

DiAngelo, R. J. (2018). *White fragility*. Boston: Beacon Press.

D'Emilio, J., & Freedman, E. (1997). *Intimate matters: A history of sexuality in America*. Chicago: The University of Chicago Press.

Gambescia, N., & Ridley, J. (2019). What every sex therapist needs to know. In N. Gambescia, K. M. Hertlein, & G. R. Weeks (Eds.), *Systemic sex therapy* (pp. 29–40). Oxfordshire: Routledge.

Harlow, H. F. (1983). Fundamentals for preparing psychology journal articles. *Journal of Comparative and Physiological Psychology, 55*, 893–896.

Holmes, A. (2018). Checking the boxes: The loving generation [Youtube video]. Retrieved from www.youtube.com/watch?v=PZQSc2CTdJE.

Killian, K. D. (1997). Crossing borders: The negotiation of difference and formation of couple identity in interracial. *Marriage and Family Therapy—Dissertations, 38*. Retrieved from https://surface.syr.edu/mft_etd/38.9820016.

Killian, K. D. (2013). *Interracial couples, intimacy, and therapy: Crossing racial borders*. New York: Columbia University Press.

Kort, J. (2018). *LGBTQ clients in therapy: Clinical issues and treatment strategies*. New York: W.W. Norton.

Oluo, I. (2019). *So you want to talk about race*. New York: Seal Press.

Parker, K., Horowitz, J. M., & Morin, R., Lopez, M. H. (2015, June 11). *Multiracial in America: Proud, Diverse and Growing in Numbers*. Pew Research Center. https://www.pewresearch.org/social-trends/2015/06/11/multiracial-in-america/

Rothman, D. J. (1995). *"Notorious in the neighborhood": Interracial sex and interracial families in early national and antebellum Virginia* (Doctoral dissertation). doi: 10.18130/V3MM1G.

Schatz, B. R. (2000, November 17). Learning by text or context? [Review of the book *The social life of information*, by J. S. Brown & P. Duguid]. *Science, 290*, 1304. doi: 10.1126/science.290.5495.13.

Stenbugler, A. (2012). *Beyond loving: Intimate racework in lesbian, gay, and straight interracial relationships*. Oxfordshire: Oxford University Press.

Vice News. (2017, June 13). We talk to interracial couples 50 years after Loving vs. Virginia [YouTube video]. Retrieved from www.youtube.com/watch?v=RseBL4eC0ok

Witherow, J. (2005). Conquest: Sexual violence and American genocide [Review of the book *Conquest: Sexual violence and American genocide*, by Andrea Smith]. *South End Press*, 46–49. doi: 10.1080/15377938.2016.1232209.

References

Bratter, J. L., & Rosalind, B. (2008). "But will it last?": Marital insatiability among interracial and same-race couples. *Family Relations, 57*(2), 160–171. Retrieved from www.jstor.org/stable/20456781?seq=1

Childs, E. C. (2008). Listening to the interracial canary: Contemporary views on interracial relationships among Black and Whites. *Fordham Law Review, 76*(6), 2771–2786. https://ir.lawnet.fordham.edu/flr/vol76/iss6/5

Connolly, M. (Producer), & Frederick, S. (Directory). (2019). They've Gotta Have Us [Video file]. Retrieved from www.netflix.com

Killian, K. D. (2001). Reconstituting racial histories and identities: The narratives of interracial couples. *Journal of Marital and Family Therapy, 27*, 27–42.

Killian, K. D. (2013). *Interracial couples, intimacy, & therapy: Crossing racial borders*. New York: Columbia University Press

Livingston, G., & Brown, A. (2017). *Intermarriage in the U.S. 50 Years After Loving v. Virginia: One-in-six newlyweds are married to someone of a different race or ethnicity.*

Menakem, R. (2017). *My grandmother's hands: Racialized trauma and the pathway to mending our hearts and bodies*. Las Vegas, NV: Central Recovery Press

Nagel, J. (2000). Ethnicity and sexuality. *Annual Review of Sociology, 26*, 107–133. Retrieved February 1, 2020, from www.jstor.org/stable/223439

Pew Research Center. Retrieved from www.pewsocialtrends.org/2017/05/18/intermarriage-in-the-u-s-50-years-after-loving-v-virginia/

Ridley, J. & Gambescia, N. (2020). What every sex therapist needs to know. In Hertlein, K. M., Gambescia, N., & Weeks, G. R. (Eds.), *Systemic Sex Therapy* (pp. 29–59). Routledge.

Ross, J. (2004). The Sexualization of Difference: A comparison of mixed-race and same-gender marriage. *Harvard Civil Rights-Civil Liberties Law Review, 37*, 255.

Smith, A. (2003). *Not an Indian tradition: The sexual colonization of native peoples.* Retrieved from www.racialequitytools.org/resourcefiles/NotIndianTradition.pdf

Solomon, R. (2017). Sexual practice and fantasy in colonial America and the early republic. *Indiana University Journal of Undergraduate Research, 3*(1), 24–35. doi: 10.14434/iujur.v3i1.23364

U.S. Census Bureau. (2011). *2010 census shows America's diversity.* Retrieved from www.census.gov/newsroom/releases/archives/2010_census/cb11-cn125.html

Women of Color Network Fact & Stats: Domestic Violence in Comminutes of Color. (2006, June). Retrieved from www.doj.state.or.us/wpcontent/uploads/2017/08/women_of_color_network_factsdomestic_violence_2006.pdf

Zimmerman, T. S. (2012). *Integrating gender and culture in family therapy training*. New York: Routledge Taylor & Francis Group.

11

COOKING THERAPEUTIC RECIPES WITH TWO EAST INDIAN COUPLES

Some Convention, a Dash of Rebellion, and Stir

Arva Bensaheb

Background

There once was an Indian woman who was so full of lust, she swore to wander naked until she found a lover to meet her voracious sexual appetite. Her sexual voracity was of great distress to the men around her, especially the King at the time, who was at a loss when it came to finding a solution to tame her sexual prowess. After a string of inadequate lovers, she came across a man named Koka Pandit, who with his breadth of skills and experience satisfied and domesticated her through sex. On the ordinance of the King, Koka Pandit wrote a book about how to control the "dangerous sexual appetites of all unrestrained women" (Burton, 1964). This book is called the Kama Sutra.

As the myth suggests, sexual desires of East Indian women have long been considered dangerous by the highly traditional and patriarchal societies that these women have lived in. A girl's virginity is typically viewed as a commodity that ruins or elevates a family's status. In order to protect such a precious thing, she's required to refrain from anything that might possibly allow her access to or exploration of her sexuality; and she's indoctrinated into pious roles of "good" mother, daughter, sister and the obedient and devoted wife (Jani, Gupta, Barot, & Gadhavi, 2008). She is expected to be demure, wear modest clothes that cover her body, and be an excellent cook and home maker. Masturbation, dating, and engaging with any sexual content, encounter, or even thoughts are considered taboo (Bhugra, Mehra, Silva, & Bhintage, 2007).

DOI: 10.4324/9781003034063-12

Her parents guard her "innocence" until she's married, while aunts warn the young women of the dangers of sex and out-of-wedlock pregnancy with scary metaphors and fairy tales. They keep her busy by controlling her with household chores, engage her in beauty regimens around long hair, set tight curfews, and follow her with watchful eyes. Once married, she belongs to her husband. In the same way keys to a car or home can be handed over, the custody of her entire being, including her sexuality, is handed over to her husband (who could be a total stranger given that arranged marriages are typical in India). Many a groom can be just as inexperienced as the bride, but like most East Indian men, he is raised to consider himself superior, a leader, figure head, bread winner, strong, and at times entitled (Ahmed & Lemkau, 2000). More sexual freedoms are allowed, but there's little to no education around sexuality, and the access to women is limited as they are too busy being pure. While women are raised to be chaste, virginal, and have no sense or knowledge of their sexuality, their partners don't seem to either. East Indian culture doesn't do the men or women any favors when it comes to romantic, sexual, and companionate relationships.

Introduction

Judging by the calls coming through my practice, some East Indian women have found a way through thick layers of sexual obscurity to connect with their sexual desires. They're complaining about disappointing sexual encounters with their husbands who are just as inexperienced, but for some reason also seemingly less interested in sex. Their culture doesn't condone divorce, so East Indian women cannot look for a more suitable sexual partner like the woman in Kama Sutra. Instead, present-day East Indian women are asking for their husbands to turn into Koka Pundits. Some speculate that this presenting complaint is particular with East Indian clients knocking at my door. If you are a sex therapist who works with diverse clients, be prepared. Indian women are asking for help because they want to have more satisfying sex.

Through two cases, I'd like to highlight the rocky road to sex therapy for couples who straddle between Eastern and Western cultures. Although my traditional Western training has many necessary ingredients for good sex therapy, I've found it insufficient if I miss the nuanced cultural pieces that the clients come in with. This point got lost when I was hired to resolve a complicated case of two people who disliked each other yet want to have satisfying sex with each other.

Case 1: Akash and Amani

Akash called to schedule an appointment for he and Amani, his wife of 20 years. He had reached out—at Amani's insistence—to say that they needed to work on their sex life, and that they needed to do something about getting them help. At intake, Amani was vocal and stated in no uncertain terms that Akash's penis was the identified patient. It was weak, unreliable, crumbled under pressured, and selfish; it came too quickly only to tuck back into its shell after ejaculating without any regard for her needs. It had failed her repeatedly, left her dissatisfied, full of unmet sexual desires and resentment. For this crime, the penis deserved to be disparaged until it learned to rise to the occasion and take better care of her. As I listened to Amani, it was clear that her description of his penis also served as a metaphor for how she saw him as a person, father, partner, and professional.

Amani and Akash met at college. He was few years her senior, and it wasn't love at first sight for him. Their decision to get married was based on practical considerations; for him, it was time to find a wife. When he met Amani, he thought she fit certain categories: the right religion at a school in Bangladesh where Hindus were a minority, she was "a good age for marriage," and he found her attractive. As he got to know her, he felt she was better than him, which became his least favorite thing about her. He disliked her ambition, the fact that she was smarter than him, more attractive, and belonged to a higher caste. This was difficult, because as a traditional East Indian man, he needed to be better than her. He fantasized that after they married, she'd be too busy with house work and child rearing, that her physical appearance would fade, and her ambition wouldn't have an outlet. He, on the other hand, would be the "bread winner" and, by proxy, outshine her. For him, the factors in favor of asking her to marry him edged over his dislike for her superior competence and ambition. However, time proved him wrong. Amani held her beauty, she was an excellent mother, held a better job—one that allowed her flexible hours for child rearing while working less—and her income closely matched his.

Amani agreed to marry Akash as a calculated decision; for her, it was important to prevent getting stuck with a suitor of her older sister's choosing. Amani had lost both her parents when she was young, and her care was left to her older sister, who was harsh but a conscientious caretaker. She made sure Amani went to the best schools, spent money on her education as directed by her late father's will, and even moved out of the comfort of her village to a big city to chaperone Amani while she went to school. However, Amani's sister reminded her how she was a burden and how she couldn't wait to marry her off to a "village idiot." As she came of age, the pressure to get married was building. So, when Akash pursued her and asked her to marry him after a few weeks of flirtatious conversations, she hastily accepted his proposal. She was relieved at the prospect of getting out from under her sister's claws. She found Akash attractive enough; and given he was at the university made her hope he was modern in his thinking and would support her ambitions. Akash was of a lower caste than Amani. This issue of caste difference bothered Amani's family, but her older sister agreed to the proposal because it was one sure-fire way to remind Amani of her shortcoming for marrying a man beneath her caste.

As they told me about their life together, their reasons for making any major decision together seemed based in "have-tos." They married each other based on these respective "have-tos;" they had children because it was expected; they moved to the United States because they *had to* fulfill Akash's father's aspirations about his son moving to America. And, despite their acrimonious dynamic, they stayed together because they *had to*. Divorce was not an option culturally, religiously or traditionally. And, now they were sitting with me because Amani wanted better, satisfying, and pleasurable sex—but it *had to* be with Akash. I also learned that for them, sex *had to* involve penetration. Akash—rather his penis—*had to* be the one to give her an orgasm.

Essentially, I was trying to help two people—who seemed to deeply dislike each other—have sex, preferably where both were orgasmic, and where Akash was the initiator. This was their goal for treatment. As an East Indian woman, there was the expectation that I not only understood but shared their belief in the importance of this goal. As their sex therapist, I had to help them get to this goal. I wanted to help them but didn't think I had to help them achieve their goal of satisfying sex the way they envisioned. Sadly, I thought I would help more, but things didn't go well. Much like their sex life, their sessions with me left them frustrated, resentful, no better than how they started, with Amani's needs unfulfilled. We ended prematurely.

I couldn't accommodate their clear goal of wanting to have sex regardless of whether they liked each other. This might be due to my application of a North American, sex therapy centric mindset, as I tried to help them become a more intimate, sexual team (McCarthy & McCarthy, 2020). With so much discord between them, it seemed sensible to start working on emotional intimacy. I hoped this would make space for vulnerability, playfulness, and a forgiving environment so they could enjoy sex with each other. I started by addressing emotions rather than sex, hoping to reduce his anxiety and her anger. We worked on interpersonal skills and did role plays with exercises for approaching each other respectfully, asking for preferences without demanding, and tolerating ruptures with the radical acceptance that relationships have ruptures and reliance on others can be inherently disappointing (Ellis, 1988). They were obedient clients. They role played as directed in session and did their homework outside of session.

As their self-reported interpersonal dynamic seemed to ease up slightly, they were eager to get to sex. Their partnered sexual history was littered with mine fields of disappointments. Sex took place at night, in the dark, before bed and neither of them knew of or participated in foreplay because there was no consideration for anyone's desire or arousal. Akash didn't wear deodorant and Amani hated the way he smelled—it was a turn-off for her, and he refused to shower before bed despite her asking. Despite her distaste for his hygiene, she was eager to have an orgasm. When he approached her, she complied but was disappointed when it ended quickly. Akash couldn't sustain an erection when it was time for penetration. To him, ejaculating was successful sex, so when he could hold an erection long enough to achieve penetration, he was eager to cum quickly because he worried about losing it. Once he was "done," he didn't know what to do about Amani and had no idea why he had these difficulties with partnered sex. He felt more successful at having sex than Amani gave him credit for because he was able to ejaculate and had fathered three children. He had been cleared of any medical concerns, thought he was healthy, and was only in treatment because he was forced by an unhappy spouse.

Amani was expectedly angry and predictably dissatisfied with him. The meaning Amani ascribed to Akash's erectile difficulties was that he was less than a man and didn't care about her. She was frustrated that he didn't work on his issues around ED (erectile dysfunction) and general sexual incompetence, and she felt that if he cared about her, he would seek help. His response of turning around and falling asleep after his orgasm left her alone to deal with her emotions and dissatisfaction. In their early years of marriage, sex happened once every few weeks. As the years went by, the frequency declined. For the last few years, they've slept in separate rooms. At one point, Akash had taken an initiative to acquire Viagra. A quick assessment suggested he'd taken the pill expecting it to work on its own; when it didn't, Amani berated him even more. That was the first and last time he tried medication, and it was the last time they had attempted to have sex, which was about a year ago.

Given this history, I recommended a continued partnered sex hiatus and reinforced exercising good sensibility to not return to a disastrous experience. I started with psycho education around sex, attempting to address the myths and misconceptions they had. I introduced ideas around sex for pleasure—to be playful and not orgasm-focused. I highlighted the importance of foreplay, the need for good hygiene, and being pleasing to one's partner and helped them recognize desire and arousal as well as the disastrous effects of anxiety and anger on arousal. As their eyes glazed over, I decided to give them something that was more hands on. I shifted our work to helping them each become experts on their own bodies. We discussed masturbation as a way of knowing one's own self and important for partnered sex. Akash was finally interested and on board; he had been masturbating successfully since adolescence and felt good about having an edge on Amani since she'd never masturbated and was squeamish and resistant for a bit before agreeing to try it. Akash was wonderfully patient, which softened her towards him as she battled with old myths about masturbation being dirty. She also wondered why she had to masturbate when she had a husband around. Once she started masturbating, she enjoyed her experience and felt more relaxed about waiting to have partnered sex. Eventually, Amani became an expert on her own body—she'd share videos she found online with me and was giggly and playful when telling me how she followed the videos' directions to her orgasmic satisfaction. I'd look to Akash to see his response to her being more pleasant and self-sufficient in this arena, which meant she was less disparaging and demanding of him to give her what she needed. Akash was hard to read and responded with a cool smile when asked how he felt about Amani's newly learned skill, delight, and better humor. I didn't push Akash when he was tacit, and Amani's gushing took up space. I reinforced their work and suggested they were working up to becoming a well-matched team, where both players were equally skillful and took up space together. However, this was my mistake because I missed something crucial—Akash was once again bested by Amani.

In what was their final session, they arrived with severe expressions. They had attempted to have sex—we'd not discussed ending their sexual hiatus in therapy. Akash had insisted on having sex one evening and Amani went along. It felt like they went back to an old pattern, and a familiar story unfolded where "all went wrong for her and right for him." Amani was angry at Akash again. However, this time, Akash wasn't anxious—he was angry and more vocal in session. In no uncertain terms, he expressed his disappointment about therapy and at me. He shared his displeasure with Amani's recently discovered sexual freedom—it was *unladylike* and a *turn off*. He talked about how he, as the man, was supposed to be more knowledgeable, skillful, and better at sex than her. Once again, this was not the case. He didn't think therapy had helped him get better, and I failed at helping him with their goal.

I was struck by his words—he was right in that they *had* asked me to get *him* better. Instead, I'd been focused on teaching them how to get better at the same time. Instead, the competition tilted in Amani's favor, and they both seemed displeased with this outcome. As I looked back, I realized their goal was for Akash to rise (no pun intended) to the occasion. He was supposed to get and be better than her. That was their pact, following the tradition of a man leading sexually. This was something deeply steeped into their relationship. My goal for them was to have better sex and intimacy as defined by a Western sex therapy rhetoric, and this caused a culture clash that contributed to things going sour.

Akash was angry as he talked about this experience, and then he switched topics to talk at length about a wall in their home that had plumbing issues. Before I could interject, Amani gave him a look; and at that point, he took a breath and said this was our last session because their wall repair was unexpectedly expensive. I expressed my surprise and attempted to validate his frustration. Amani interrupted me by standing up, and Akash and I followed. She came over and hugged me, with an apology (for what I couldn't imagine). Akash said goodbye, shook my hand, and left, with Amani following her husband.

This ending was deeply unsettling, and as I've had many thoughts about this case, I'd like to offer a few realizations:

First, it's possible that their goal was unrealistic given their level of discord. Treatment may have failed for them no matter what. Second, it's also possible that I was unable to stick with the goal for Amani to "have satisfying sex with my husband regardless of likability" because I used a Westernized idea where I attempted to work on their intimacy to increase tenderness and likability first. I also tried to increase their skills individually, hoping that if they each were more knowledgeable about their own bodies (through masturbation and self-exploration) and if they liked each other and enjoyed spending time together that they would work to have the type of sex they wanted with each other. In doing this, I probably interjected treatment goals around intimacy that complicated things for them. It surely recreated conditions that perpetuated the very pattern they came to work on in therapy. Unfortunately, this therapeutic solution highlighted their problem, and going back to what they knew may have felt better to them. I needed to listen better to hear what they asked for—which was to teach Akash how to have mutually enjoyable penetrative sex with Amani. I didn't do that.

As luck had it, a second chance came knocking at my door. I had a chance to treat another East Indian couple, Kapil and Payal. Determined to learn from my past, I chose to focus on a treatment approach that centered the couple's unique and nuanced complaints about their sex lives. I couched my Western sex therapy training within this couple's cultural background and planned my treatment by keenly tracking their sense of what needed to be treated.

Case 2: Kapil and Payal

Kapil and Payal were a couple in their late twenties who came in wanting to work on their sex life. Payal called to schedule, and at the outset it appeared their primary complaint was discrepant desire. Payal wanted sex more often than her husband and was dissatisfied about the frequency and quality of their sex life. She was also upset about having to initiate sex; as the man, this was her husband's job. Kapil agreed with Payal's perspective but didn't know how to address it. He acknowledged that he didn't know how to have sex in a "good way"—his erections were "unreliable." He couldn't help but "finish first," and this left Payal frustrated. They had never been to therapy but collectively decided to come to work on their sex life. I was chosen because I shared their cultural background.

Kapil and Payal had a combination of traditional and egalitarian expectations of themselves and each other. They grew up in India but attended college in the US. While they were used to walking between traditions and expectations from two different worlds in other things, when it came to romantic relationships, they stayed true to tradition. They met on campus during college and fell in love only after confirming economic, religious, and cultural compatibilities between their families. They dated for a brief time with minimal physical contact and decided to get married with their parents' permission. They had sex for the first time after marriage and got to know each other better after becoming husband and wife. Theirs was a "love marriage," not arranged; nonetheless divorce was not a consideration, and this relationship was "it." Kapil and Payal had watched how the "this is it!" sentiment between their parents turns into complacency and silent resentment between two people bound by tradition. They decided to use that example to work on their marriage. Their relationship, much like their sex life, was not in the best shape. But Kapil said, "If we have to be with each other for the rest of our lives, I want us to be happy." Although neither had witnessed a long-term, committed relationship where spouses communicated openly with each other, shared chores, effectively resolved conflict, enjoyed things together, supported each other, and had sex for pleasure, they wanted to learn how to achieve this in their relationship. Before anything, Kapil needed to learn to be at the helm of their sexual journey. They hoped that a sex therapist from their culture could teach them how.

In many ways, working with Kapil and Payal was easier than Akash and Amani. Kapil and Payal were motivated and overall more open to receiving psychotherapy. It was easier to give them feedback that encouraged self-reflection and insight into their contingencies, get them to challenge old ways of thinking, and help them consider adapting to new ways that were functional for them. While they didn't exactly like each other, they didn't hate each other either. I recalled my experience with Akash and Amani to firmly remind myself that this couple's primary treatment goal was to improve their sex life by improving Kapil's sexual skill. I hope I learned something about my past failure and would focus on helping the man to be better in bed.

I started by debunking common sex myths. Most of their misconceptions were typical—what you'd expect in an inexperienced couple. For example, sex was supposed to be natural and spontaneous, orgasm was the goal and the marker of successful sex (penetration) was necessary, orgasm via penetration was ideal, and the man had to initiate. They were shocked to learn that these were myths and misconceptions. I presented ideas that were new to them about sex being playful, exploratory, primarily for pleasure, and not orgasm-focused. This was eye opening and relieving to them. Using a psycho-education about sex and sexuality, we dialed down the focus on penetrative sex, and instead expanded sexual scripts that allowed both parties to initiate when the mood struck. While this was helpful to hear, Kapil insisted on wanting to initiate. To that end, we taught him how to recognize his desire, arousal, and interest, and I invited Payal to do the same. We worked on mindfulness exercises to learn and zone in on internal sensations. Kapil used this to focus on finding out when he was aroused or horny. We discussed how he could approach Payal verbally and also non-verbally, e.g., by a type of look or a deeper kiss to suggest something more was desired and being offered. We also talked about the importance of learning to make time for sex and preparing oneself mentally and physically as well as adjusting one's environment like they did when they were dating.

The idea of planning for sex helped Payal a lot; she'd started to worry about Kapil's spontaneous approach of her between body waxing appointments. She said as an Indian woman, she was hairy and this helped her to prioritize self-care as they moved towards becoming a sexually active couple. Kapil grew up in India, where wearing deodorant or "man-scaping," wasn't typical. The conversation around preparing the body for sex was helpful in educating him about his personal work on his own hygiene and grooming to be pleasing to his partner. Kapil wasn't always receptive immediately to corrective suggestions, but he appreciated having the knowledge. I learned when to push and when to let him be. Kapil and I spent a lot of time alone talking about the female anatomy. I provided him with readings and suggested videos to watch so he could start to recognize what was interesting to him and what he would be comfortable doing. These systematic psycho educational/didactic sessions were a key element for treatment progress. There were times when Payal came to these sessions and listened patiently, and there were times we all decided Kapil would attend alone.

As they both learned new ways of thinking about sex, Kapil also learned new skills on his own to excel in the bedroom. In joint sessions, conversations shed light on new knowledge and old learnings. Payal said, "We never thought of sex this way." When asked to go deeper, Kapil said, "Actually it's funny; we never thought of sex in any way because we were taught not to think about sex. It was dirty and taboo, and now we are just confused about it." I validated their confusion and used cognitive behavioral interventions to help them evaluate the utility of "old" and "new" learning while allowing them to decide what they wanted to keep and what they wanted to let go. They accepted the idea of sex being playful and pleasurable. They both wanted Kapil to keep initiating sex and felt that he should be responsible for Payal's orgasm. Even though Kapil appreciated Payal initiating many things in their life, they both wanted him to take the lead during sex. Payal felt less feminine for being the sexual aggressor, and Kapil felt less masculine. And remembering my experience with the previous couple, I respected their right to this choice.

As Kapil educated himself with books and videos (including porn) about sex, he felt better around what to do. His mood and confidence improved as did their relationship. They hadn't had sex since therapy started, but Payal remained patient and supportive. She understood her husband was a perfectionist and needed to feel accomplished at a certain level before having partnered sex. To help her cope with waiting, we discussed the notion of waiting with anticipation and growing desire. We joked about how this was similar to how they connected prior to getting married. Humor and what felt like "girl talk" was helpful with her, as Payal didn't have conversations with girlfriends about sex. For Kapil, we worked on his perfectionism, along with didactics on the "how tos" of sex. His therapy focused on changing his mindset to align with positive perfectionism, where success was the goal and how mistakes on the way to success were important for learning. This reframed negative perfectionism, where failure was never allowed because success was the only option. Relevant examples related to different situation—not just sexual—were used to make this point. We worked on mindfulness, breathing exercises, and other practices that helped him focus and learn how to control his body. In therapy, Kapil learned to recognize his common thinking errors and didn't fall back into old behaviors of trying to mind-read or forecast Payal's responses if things didn't go well. He battled with labeling himself "less of a man" if he lost his erection, so we worked on reframing the issue of lost erections more realistically and used them as opportunities for growth and progress. Together, we crafted helpful self-statements he believed in. For example, we used cricket and tennis superstars who Kapil admired, noting that occasionally they'd had less-than-ideal performances. We discussed how they were able to garner sympathy and love from their fans during an "off day." These analogies helped Kapil understand that when things didn't go perfectly, vulnerabilities could be endearing rather than shameful. In validating Kapil, I was careful to consider his emotional temperature about validation; he said that the validation around his emotional experiences felt reassuring; he liked it but at the same time he didn't trust its value in helping him with his treatment goal, as it felt "very American." He was still resistant to validation or self-compassion as culturally he was used to the stance of "Chin up" or "Don't worry; you'll be fine." I slowed things down when he got to this place and validated his experience by way of self-disclosure. I told him about my own discomfort with validation when I first moved to the United States. I told him how strange it felt when people mirrored my emotions, took care of them, told me things like "It makes sense you feel this way," and allowed me to either feel what I felt or even process emotions further. We agreed how this was not typical where we grew up. We shared stories and humor around how our parents would sound if they tried validating us. We both agreed it would be a comical disaster. We imitated an accent and used native words while imagining their clumsy attempts at trying to validate our emotions. This brought some much-needed lightness to his solo sessions, and he appeared receptive to therapy after these chats.

About halfway through a session, Kapil and Payal shared that we needed to shelve sex talk because Payal's parents would be visiting for a couple of weeks, which was stressful on their relationship. Payal's parents were critical of Kapil by saying that "he wasn't good enough for our Payal." Kapil felt that Payal sided with them when they criticized him, which she admitted to doing. She explained that while she didn't agree with her parents, she couldn't oppose them out of respect. She also felt an immense need for their acceptance and validation. This required a temporary fix for them to survive the parental visit. Over the next two sessions, we created a plan for them to remain united, discussed how they'd reassure each other, and talked about how to repair feelings that might be harmed while maintaining outwardly appearances of parental respect.

This plan was more important than any of us expected. Payal held up their part of the plan, which made Kapil feel so supported that he spontaneously initiated sex. They reported that it was a "surprisingly wonderful time." I hadn't placed them on a sex hiatus—they made that decision and then broke it on their own. I was happy to hear about their satisfying experience. Kapil noted he felt more skillful in navigating his anxiety, his erection lasted longer than before, and after his orgasm, he focused on Payal's pleasure. While his penis didn't give her an orgasm, he used his hand(s); it wasn't perfect and a little clumsy. Payal was open to the experience and didn't shame him for having an orgasm first; nor did she insist on a penetrative orgasm. She said the session content came to life for her in bed and saw hope for a better sex life.

This positive experience cemented my relationship with them at a deeper level. We continued to meet and work towards their goals for sex, and added other targets about overall relationship dynamics and emotional intimacy. They saw how factors around sex and emotional intimacy interconnected and reinforced each other. Starting their therapy by focusing on the couple's goal of improving Kapil's sexual competency and being the sex initiator set the right tone. This helped them relax their anxieties around other issues. I earned cultural and academic credibility as they saw their work bear fruit in their sexual lives and home. And, to their credit, Kapil and Payal remained open to working on goals for emotional and sexual intimacy. Using Kapil's skill around sexual intimacy was key—the tweak that helped traditional sex therapy work in a culturally sensitive manner for this East Indian couple. While the ingredients for sex therapy remained the same, the prioritization and titration made a difference.

Discussion

These two couples presented a unique challenge for a sex therapist trained in North America. Helping two people who don't particularly like each other have orgasmic sex with each other seems tricky. There is not much, if anything written about how one does this, and I'm learning with trial by fire. While I understand the concept of the presenting complaint, I grew up between India and Dubai, two extremely sexually repressed countries where marriage is paramount and having children is a given. There is no discussion or education around sex, and young people are chided and shamed for talking or thinking about sex. Most couples I know interact like co-workers on an assembly line, making a parallel life work while exchanging few words. Many couples didn't seem to like each other very much; growing up I never wondered, *How does this work? Do you ever have sex? What happens behind those closed doors?* Now, I am thinking, *How can two people, married for life, have good sex if they don't really like each other?* This presents a challenging but exciting opportunity for research where the outcome could help couples who struggle with this predicament regardless of their culture of origin.

Until then, this enigma around helping people who insist on having sex with a particular partner regardless of desire or attraction is here to stay. Options are necessarily limited by their culture—it's sex with their spouse or no sex at all, and couples need help right now. If I encountered Akash and Amani now, I'd focus on their stated goals. Akash may have needed individual therapy for his issues, but since he was opposed, I should have observed that my Western sex therapy training was limiting. I could have spent more time with him in preparation for partnered sex, in an approach similar to the one I used with Kapil. There were myriad skills to help Akash be ready for the occasions successfully (e.g., as start-stop methods, reading or watching videos on ways to pleasure a woman, using fantasies). Perhaps these skills might have worked even if he wasn't attracted to Amani. That, in combination with opening up Amani's sexual script to include manual and oral stimulation, would have helped this couple. Also, it would have helped if Akash became an expert of Amani's body before she did. While I may not have fully agreed with that, I have to remember the customer is sometimes right. My presuppositions based on my training led me to ignore or invalidate their request, and while my intent was well meaning, the impact of my therapeutic treatment of Akash and Amani was misguided.

Considerations for Readers

Like the couples described in this chapter, the current generation of newly wed East Indians, especially those who immigrate to the West, is likely caught in the flux between Eastern and Western values. They may not know the impacts of two currents on how they feel. As sex therapists, being aware of the push and pull of traditional and Western values could help us guide our clients through this fusion of values more effectively. Understanding and respecting our clients' cultures will inevitably help establish our credibility with clients from diverse backgrounds.

India is largely a traditional and patriarchal society, and at least with the generation of clients at this time, we may notice that even though the woman is in charge of problem identification, there is a reliance on the man to solve the problem. This may not be because of dependency or a lack of autonomy; rather, it seems to be wrapped in cultural meanings around being wanted, loved, or cared for by a partner. Protocols around assertiveness and autonomy within romantic or erotic realms are misplaced and don't work well with East Asian clients.

Perhaps the Kama Sutra texts were about subjugating women's desires as Barton suggested. Another interpretation is that the Kama texts inform men that women are sexual beings and are encourage men to work on their sexual skills so that like Koka, they could satisfy their female partner. Perhaps the Kama Sutra teaches us that a woman's desires aren't dangerous or untoward; they are hot, sexy, and the stuff of legends.

Lessons Learned

I offer that we view the presenting complaints of our patients with a cultural lens that allows us to see where Western sex therapy may fail. We need to put the sex back in sex therapy in a culturally appropriate way—for East Indian women and those who want to make better lovers of their men. Would it be enough? What else may come? We may let the couples tell us what happens next and what they need. For the present, sex therapy needs to address the challenge of transforming a husband into Koka so that both he and she are blissfully satisfied.

Suggested Reading

Althof, E. S. (2014). Treatment of premature ejaculation. In Y. M. Binik & K. S. K. Hall (Eds.), *Principals and practice of sex therapy* (5th ed., pp. 112–137). New York: Guilford Press.

Avasthi, A., Kaur, R., & Kulhara, P. (2008). Sexual behavior of married young women: A preliminary study from North India. *Journal of Community Medicine, 33*(3), 163–167.

Avery-Clark, C. (2017). *Sensate focus in sex therapy: The illustrated manual.* New York: Routledge.

Bader, M. J. (2002). *Arousal the secret logic of sexual fantasies.* New York: St. Martin's Press.

Baptiste, D. (2005). Family therapy with east Indian immigrant parents rearing children in the United States: Parental concerns, therapeutic issues, and recommendations. *Contemporary Family Therapy, 27*(3), 345–366.

Buongpui, L. R. (2013). Gender relations and the web of traditions in Northeast India. *The NEHU Journal, 11*(2), 73–81.

Burton, R. (1964). *Translated: The perfumed garden of the sheikh of Nafzawi.* New York: Castle Books.

Burton, R., & Arbuthnot, F. F. (1984). *Translated: The kamasutra of Vatsyayana.* New York: Putnam.

Jaiya, & Hanauer, J. (2008). *Red hot touch. A head-to-toe handbook for mind-blowing orgasms.* New York: Broadway Books.

Mintz, L. (2017). *Becoming cliterate. Why orgasm equality matters and how to get it.* New York: HarperCollins Publishers.

Morin, J. (1995). *The erotic mind.* New York: HarperCollins Publishers.

References

Ahmed, S. M., & Lemkau, J. P. (2000). Cultural issues in the primary care of South Asians. *Journal of Immigrant Health, 2*(2), 89–96. doi: 10.1023/A:1009585918590.

Bhugra, D., Mehra, R., Silva, P., & Bhintage, R. V. (2007). Sexual attitudes and practices in North India. A qualitative study. *Journal of Sexual and Relationship Therapy, 22,* 83–90.

Burton, R. (1964). *Translated: The perfumed garden of the sheikh of Nafzawi.* New York: Castle Books.

Ellis, A. (1988). *How to stubbornly refuse to make yourself miserable about anything—yes, anything!* New York: Kensington.

Jani, C. B., Gupta, S., Barot, H., & Gadhavi, J. (2008). Retrospective study of cases of drunkenness with emphasis on procedure and interpretation of results. *Journal of Indian Academy of Forensic Medicine, 30*(3), 128–135.

McCarthy, B., & McCarthy, E. (2020). *Rekindling desire, third edition.* New York: Routledge.

12

SEXUAL SOVEREIGNTY AND EROTIC SURVIVANCE

Two-Spirit Sexual Health and Vitality

Roger J. Kuhn

This chapter was written on occupied Esselen, Ohlone, and Pomo territory in what is now known as California and specifically Monterey County, San Francisco County, and Sonoma County. I acknowledge the land as an integral entry point in any decolonial framework.

Introduction, Background, and Key Terms

The study of human sexuality (including sex therapy and sex education) is transdisciplinary and examines the socio-cultural, religio-political, and physio-psychological aspects of the human experience. Recently I finished reading a book titled Sex *Therapy with Erotically Marginalized Clients* (Constantinides, Sennott, & Chandler, 2019). I appreciated the nine principles to engage critical thinking among mental health professionals around sexuality and learned a great deal to bring to my work as a sexuality educator and psychotherapist. I was also struck with the thought, *What about working with the erotically colonized?* I define erotic colonization as the form of eroticization wherein power, control, and force are used to perpetuate patriarchal and heterocentric settler colonial ideologies on Black, Indigenous, and People of Color (BIPOC) especially as it relates to women/womyn, trans, and Two-Spirit and/or LGBTQI Indigenous peoples.

When we fail to process the erotic, it become eroticized. What I mean by this statement is that we conflate the idea of the erotic with the sexual, and while the erotic might contain the sexual, and the sexual might be erotic, they may also exist on their own. I call this conflation *projective eroticism*, and I believe it is at the root of settler ideologies on Native sexuality. Projective eroticism is a form of ethnocentrism and has clinical implications

DOI: 10.4324/9781003034063-13

including misdiagnosis and failure to understand cultural context. This chapter reflects the socio-cultural aspect of human sexuality and examines the intersecting issues of race, culture, pleasure, sex therapy, sex education, and mental health. Two-Spirit Indigenous[1] sexuality will be used as the grounding focus with the goal to decolonize sexuality and reclaim sexual sovereignty through erotic survivance. *Two-Spirit* is an umbrella term used by some Native American/First Nations people to signify gender and sexual orientation variance and/or an LGBTQ+ identity. Two-Spirit is an addition, not a replacement for Indigenous terminology that describes gender and sexual orientation variance. *Two-Spirit* was derived from the Northern Algonquin phrase *niizh manitoag*, which has been translated to mean "two spirits" (Balsam, Huang, Fieland, Simoni, & Walters, 2004).

Throughout this chapter, I use the following terms: *decolonizing sexuality*, *sexual sovereignty*, and *erotic survivance*. These concepts are not of my creation. Rather, they are continuations of the resiliency, determination, and knowledge that BIPOC communities have experienced through attempted genocide and colonization, and I honor and recognize the activists, community organizers, community members, and academics who have created entry points for decolonization discourse to thrive.

To decolonize sexuality is to challenge the dominant discourse surrounding human sexuality and to forge a new narrative. I define decolonizing sexuality as a multi-tiered process of challenging dominant narratives of sexuality in order to advocate for sexual sovereignty and erotic survivance. Decolonizing sexuality is an engaged process that includes the emotional, somatic, spiritual, and sexual experiences that all colonized, oppressed, and marginalized people have a right to explore and claim as part of their sovereignty and lived experiences. Sexual sovereignty is a direct challenge to settler colonialism and heterocentric idealism, which fail at understanding how Indigenous communities experience gender and sexuality. Sexual sovereignty is also a claim that Two-Spirit bodies have a right to identify with gender and sexual orientation fluidity and the physical acts of intimacy, pleasure, and sex as an extension of decolonization and a return to Indigenous roles, identities, and practices that existed prior to first contact. Erotic survivance is an extension of Vizenor's (2008) work and creates space for Two-Spirit people to share and express how their sexuality (gender, orientation, practice) has been an important aspect to their story of survival. Further, erotic survivance is the stories, poetry, prose, songs, dances, medicine, and the gatherings Two-Spirit people and communities engage in to celebrate their resiliency, survival, sexual expression, and sexual sovereignty. According to Tuhiwai Smith (1999), "Decolonization . . . does not mean and has not meant a total rejection of all theory or research or Western knowledge. Rather, it is about centering our concerns and world views and then coming to know and understand theory and research from our own perspectives and for our own purposes" (p. 39). Wilson and Yellow Bird (2005) state, "The first step toward decolonization is to question the legitimacy of colonization" (Wilson & Yellow Bird, 2005, p. 3). This question around legitimacy is applicable to sexuality because it welcomes a critique of the discourse surrounding sexological understandings of how colonizing perspectives of gender and sexual orientation are rampant in the field of psychology and psychotherapy. Wilson and Yellow Bird (2005) further their position by stating, "Current institutions and systems are designed to maintain the privilege of the colonizer and the subjugation of the colonized, and to produce generations of people who will never question their position within this relationship" (p. 1). The privilege of the colonizer can be seen in academic discourse when the history of sexuality is started from and explained through a Eurocentric perspective, without the acknowledgment of multiple ways of acquiring and disseminating knowledge. From this framework, decolonizing sexuality means dismantling the exploitative practices, policies, and discourse that subjugate and colonize the sexuality of Indigenous people, including those who identify as LBGTQ and/or Two-Spirit.

The following cases illustrate a decolonial approach to working clinically with issues relating to sexuality and gender expression. All identifying characteristics of the clients have been altered to ensure confidentiality.

Clinical Cases

Case 1: Tommy (Indigenous Knowledge and Language Reclamation)

How has erotic colonization impacted the ways we feel about our work and any treatment plans with clients? Are you coming from a wellness or medical model? Indigenous ways of mental health incorporate a wellness perspective, wherein the totality of one's experience is included as part of the treatment. The following case exemplifies sharing cultural knowledge in the form of disclosure as a tool for a decolonial therapeutic approach. Native American culture and language will be used to illustrate the impact culturally relevant therapy interventions can have on clients.

Tommy was 16 years old when we started working together. At the time, I was a first-year marriage and family therapist intern, gathering hours working with high school students in the San Francisco Bay Area. Tommy was referred to counseling because his history teacher began to notice a marked decline in his attendance and grades. I was asked to work with Tommy because the counseling coordinator believed we would be a good fit because of our shared cultural background. I identify as Native American (Poarch Creek) and White. Tommy identifies as Native American (Navajo) and South East Asian. Through our work, I would also learn that Tommy and I also shared a minority gender and sexuality status. Due to the school-based setting of our work, Tommy would often have 20 or 30 minutes for a session, as opposed to a standard 50-minute session. The following para-phrased exchange reflects an early session in our work, as we were continuing to build and establish trust. I remember this particular session as being brief. Tommy was late for his appointment because he had to take a quiz the first half of our scheduled time. In this session, Indigenous language was used as an intervention to help reflect upon sexuality.

Tommy: I saw the poster for the powwow, the one you told me about. Looks nice. I want to know more about Two-Spirit.
  (Tommy says all of this first thing when he steps into my office, before he sits down.)
Roger: Thanks. The graphic artist is a really cool Two-Spirit friend. I put the posters around campus yesterday. (I pause and allow for both of us to take our seats. He continues standing. I seek to normalize his inquiry without pressuring him to conform to standard psychotherapy formali-ties.) *Two-Spirit* is a contemporary term that Native folks use to describe people outside of gender binaries and those who are do not identify as heterosexual. (I sit down and take a sip of tea. I offer him a cup. He shakes his hand to dismiss the offer.)

He sat down and threw his backpack on the ground, a behavior I had seen him do before when he had something he wanted to talk about. I saw his brow furrow and he pulled his cheeks inward and his lips rested in a turned-up pucker. His feet danced as he sat slumped in the worn-out loveseat in my office (which was also used as a dressing room for the theater department). I could tell that he was holding his breath. I held space for a few moments until I saw him shift in his seat again. I let out a loud long exhale. He looked up at me and we locked eyes for just a moment. I could tell he was fighting back tears.

Roger: I notice you have what looks like tears in your eyes. (His head is turned slightly to me. He wipes his nose with the sleeve of his faded NVTS hoodie and takes the fidget toy I kept on a small table. He flicks at the spinner while continuing to avert my attention.)
Tommy: Are you Two-Spirit? (He asks in way that felt like a nervous laugh.)

I reflect upon Duran's (2006) work and the importance of Native people trusting the therapist. I also remember an article I read during my graduate course studies wherein Prenn (2009) states, disclosure "is neither good nor bad; it is the quickest way to have an experience between two people" (p. 89).

Roger: Yes, I am. I am Two-Spirit. (I pause here for just a moment and con-template what I am going to say next.) I am Two-Spirit and I am proud.

I share with him the word that is being used in the Mvskoke language to describe Two-Spirit people, *Ennvrkvpv* (pronounced eh-nuth-ka-buh), which loosely translates to "in the middle." I also share this is the word *Mvskoke* (Creek) people use for Wednesday, which creates of moment of shared laughter between us. I share that because of colonization, my people (Poarch Creek) have lost a lot of our culture, including language, and how this has impacted the way sexuality has been perceived in my tribal community. Tommy has already shared in a prior session that he knows very little of his Diné language. I recognize this as an opportunity to make an intervention emphasizing his Native culture and language.

Roger: Did you know Navajo people have a word for those who experience gender and sexual orientation variance? (His eyes widen and a smile spreads across his face.) *Nádleehi* (pronounced nah-gleh-heh), I tell him. He is silent again for a few moments.

Tommy: I think that's what I am. I think I'm *Nádleehi*. (He starts to cry and smile and once again uses his hoodie to wipe his nose. He shares for a few minutes about his feelings and attractions to some of his friends. We process what it will be like to go back to his classes after his share. As it is close to our session ending, Tommy begins to place the fidget toy back on my desk.)

Roger: Want to keep it? Big day for you today. Made the ancestors proud again.

He flashes his big smile and puts the toy in his pocket. Here, I am acknowledging the work that Tommy did today, his step forward into *becoming* (Byrd, 2015) who he is. We often speak of making the ancestors proud. He has shared this as meaningful to him and reminds him of something he used to do when he was younger.

Tommy: *Ahéhee'*. (I know this word to mean thank you in Diné. He grabs his backpack and heads towards the door.) I'm going to call my grandma tonight. Haven't spoken to her in a few months. I'm going to ask her about *Nádleehi*, see if she knows anymore. *Ahéhee'*.

Prior to this session, Tommy hadn't talked about his sexuality. Though I had shared he was welcome to discuss questions or concern he had around the topic, it had not been addressed. After that session, Tommy would bring topics around sexuality and his Native identity whenever he had an appointment. I would learn that his grandmother was very supportive, and he eventually shared his identity with other family and friends. He began to study his Diné language and is currently pursuing an undergraduate degree with a double major in American Indian studies and computer science. Though our clinical work has ended many years ago, I continue to see Tommy at the BAAITS powwow,[2] where for the past three years he has attended with his partner.

Case 2: Sovereign Eco-Erotics

Barker (2017) states that "nature is sex, sex is nature, and we are nature" (p. 233). This idea of nature and eroticism as one aligns with the Indigenous value of interconnectedness. It also centers the importance of connection with the land. The following case exemplifies the use of Indigenous knowledge and a Two-Spirit value of mending the hoop as a treatment modality for erectile challenges and sexual performance anxiety.

Jay identifies as a 38-year-old Two-Spirit urban Indian.[3] He has only travelled to his tribal homelands in his early childhood. He struggles with his identity as a Native person, often feeling conflicted about portrayals of Native people in media and the use of Native imagery as sport mascots. He had been told by his medical doctor that the erectile concerns were psychological and was referred to a therapist for help dealing with the pressures he experiences while engaging in sexual acts with others. Jay reports he is able to maintain strong erections while engaging in solo sex and only struggles when he is having partnered sex. The following paraphrased exchanges reflect several sessions that centered on using the Medicine Wheel as guidance in our work. Prior to beginning these sessions, Jay and I explored any meanings he had associated with the Medicine Wheel.[4] We discussed how exploring the various quadrants and the significance they hold (physical, mental/intellectual, emotional, and spiritual) could be a benefit in our work and allow the exploration of erotic survivance.

Roger: (I have a whiteboard in my office. Prior to the session, I had already drawn a medicine wheel representing the four quadrants and labeled each quadrant as either the words Body, Feel, Think, Inquiry. See Figure 12.1.) We started to talk about your body last week. We spoke about this quadrant being representational of the body as well as land. What did you feel after our session last week?

Jay: It made a lot of sense to me, this idea that my sexuality is tied to the land. That my sense of self-worth and connection can come from the land. It makes sense, feels right. What do I do with it?

Roger: I'm remembering the story you told me about your camping trip to Tahoe last summer. (In a prior session, Jay shared a story about masturbating in the woods alone at night and how powerful it made him feel. He said no one from his group noticed he had left, "trickster energy[5]" he called it.) Remember how that moment made you feel? (Jay responds by cracking a joke and saying it felt "hella good." I give him a smile in return, acknowledging the importance of humor in our work.) I remember you saying you felt powerful, "trickster energy." (He nods his head in agreement. I point to the quadrant on the board labeled Body.) Tell me about how your body felt when you were connected to the land erotically. (His eyes widened a moment and he took a sharp inhalation.)

Jay: I hadn't thought about it in terms of sex. (He says with a what I read as a confused look on his face.)

Roger: What I am talking about is your erotic connection to the land, which doesn't have to be considered a sexual connection. (We had previously spoken about the erotic and the ways colonization has impacted our sense of connection to our own bodies and spirit and land.)

Jay: Walking alone out there, in the woods, at night, most people would be afraid. I loved it. I felt a sense of peace, like a deep knowing, a deep sense of belonging. That's why I felt powerful. I wasn't horny. I wanted to express this feeling of power within.

Roger: Wow, that sounds amazing. Some folks call that eco-eroticism, a kind of erotic liberation that is tied to one's connection with land. (His eyes widened once again, and he let out a little laugh.)

Jay: And so you think that I was experiencing an eco-erotic moment, or what? (His eyes remained fixed on me, he leaned forward in anticipation for what I would say.)

Roger: I think you had a moment of connection with the land and it created a sense of pleasure; this pleasure was then celebrated through masturbation, orgasm, and ejaculation. (He sits back in the chair, begins to run his fingers through his hair, and takes a deep inhalation.)

Jay: So that's the answer. Every time I want to have sex with someone, in order for my dick to get hard I have to go out into the woods? (He laughs at his own suggestion then again leans forward. He turns his gaze downward and averts my eyes. I suggest we take a deep breath together; he joins. We go through an exchange of three inhalations and exhalations, concentrating on making the exhalations longer to return to a greater sense of balance in the moment.)

Roger: Let's turn back to the wheel. We could put the ED in the quadrant marked "Body." We could also put disconnection from homeland, place, and land here. Reclaiming your relationship to the land, nature, home, whatever you want to call it seems important to you. I imagine that if you allowed yourself more time to connect with yourself in nature, you may be able to take some of that positive energy and connect with others, maybe even sexually.

We talked about the possibility of Jay engaging in weekly solo nature dates, to see if this shifts his perception of his self, his body, and his connection to the erotic. He also practiced somatic-based exercises focused on sensing into his pelvic floor through slow gentle tense and relax engagement with his muscles. As our work progressed over the next months, Jay would often express how rewarding connecting to nature and to the land had been for him. He shared a sense of wholeness when he is in nature and noticed decreases in his anxiety and depression symptoms. He also shared that his sex life had improved, and his erectile challenges were happening less often. He noted the difference between "hook-up sex" and connected sex with a person he trusted. At the conclusion of our work, which lasted eight months, Jay was using the Medicine Wheel to help understand and process his relationship to self, community, ancestors, and culture. Connecting with nature and engagement with his sexuality were parts of his erotic survivance and helped change his narrative. When we last spoke, he shared he was spending the weekend in Tahoe with his new boyfriend. He shared he couldn't wait to show him his favorite spot in the woods, his laughter once again filling the room, granting me comfort in knowing Indigenous knowledge and methodology can lead to healing experiences across many mental and physical health areas.

For non-Indigenous clinicians who would like to use Medicine Wheel methodologies in their work, it is imperative that you let your clients know where this knowledge comes from. Speak to the Indigenous wisdom that created the practice of using the Medicine Wheel to better understand ourselves and our experiences.

Counseling Strategies—Mending the Hoop

Two-Spirit perspectives on sex therapy are situated in the ideas of balance and liberation. A Two-Spirit perspective is reflective of a quote often credited to Maori activist, Lila Watson, "If you have come here to help me you are wasting your time, but if you have come because your liberation is bound up with mine, then let us work together" (n.d.). A Two-Spirit perspective is inclusive of maintaining relations with "land, language, people, ancestors, animals, stories, knowledge, medicine, culture, and spiritual environment" (Linklater, 2016, p. 27). A Two-Spirit perspective is also centered in helping clients develop a "strong cultural identity" (Linklater, p. 142). Duran (2006) states, "If we inflict a system that is based only on cognition, as in the logocentric Euro American tradition, we are committing hegemony on a patient who believes otherwise" (p. 20). Two-Spirit sex therapy and sex education models should include the concept of mending the hoop, a reference to the medicine wheel that was "damaged when Indian societies began to no longer incorporate sexuality and gender differences into their cultural practices and identities" (Gilley, 2006, p. 167). For Two-Spirit people who seek counseling, the concept of oppression should be a welcome area of conversation because oppression does not only impact marginalized communities, but it impacts individuals within those communities whose voices are already abandoned or forgotten. Further, "It is important to understand the influence of oppression on that person's experience and to assess the extent to which the process of acculturation has affected or continues to affect cultural identity [because] it is important to be sensitive to how [Two-Spirit people] express their identities and to the meanings that they attribute to various dimensions of their identities" (Garrett and Barrett, 2003, p. 135). Raymore (2018) advocates for "culture as prevention" when considering working with Two-Spirit clients and issues relating to HIV/AIDS and sexual health. I apply the lens of decolonizing sexuality with all of my clients, incorporating a BOLD ADDRESSING[6] model (Hays, 2001; Kuhn, 2018). I believe it is important that sex therapists and sexuality educators become curious and engage with sexual sovereignty and erotic survivance.

Lessons Learned—A Remembrance

The deleterious impacts of erotic colonization continue. Providing sex therapy and sexuality education through a decolonial lens challenges the dominant perspectives on sexuality that are often harmful and traumatizing for BIPOC clients. By centering Indigenous wisdom, values, spirituality, and connection to community in my work, I have learned the importance of incorporating all aspects of a client's lived experience into the therapy process. Through the work with the client's shared in this chapter, I have learned interventions based on Indigenous knowledge and culture can be transformative in the clinical work. There is also a remembrance that I experience. Working with and centering Indigenous knowledge is a direct connection to my ancestors. This connection reminds me of the deep peace that comes from returning to Indigenous ways as sources of healing.

Critical Reflections for Clinicians

- What is your relationship to erotic colonization? How has your work been impacted, especially for those who hold professional licenses or are affiliated with professional organizations, by having to adhere to laws and policies that perpetuate oppression?
- How can your clinical and/or pedagogical perspective be influenced by sexual sovereignty and erotic survivance?
- How do you honor Indigenous wisdom and occupied territory in your practice and work?

Suggested Reading and Resources

Duran, E. (2006). *Healing the soul wound. Counseling with American Indians and other native peoples.* Multicultural Foundations of Psychology and Counseling Series. New York: Teachers College Press. Columbia University.

Linklater, R. (2016). *Decolonizing trauma work: Indigenous stories and strategies.* Vancouver, BC: Langara College.

Tuck, E., & Yang, K. (2012). Decolonization is not a metaphor. *Decolonization: Indigeneity, Education & Society, 1*(1), 1–40.

Wibur, M., Keene, A., & Tall Bear, K. (n.d.). Retrieved from www.allmyrelationspodcast.com/podcast/episode/468a0a6b/ep-5-decolonizing-sex

Conclusion

Roscoe (1996) states, "When it comes to the history of Native Americans we can no longer cling to a pre-Foucauldian idea of power flowing in only one direction and always from the top down, for we will invariably end up characterizing American Indians as passive recipients of White conquest and culture" (p. 218). Foucault's (1978) idea of power and sex are relevant because he believes that "to say that sex is not repressed, or rather that the relationship between sex and power is not characterized by repression, is to risk falling into a sterile paradox" (p. 117). Not including sexuality in the discussion around decolonization would result in a similar sterile paradox and perpetuate erotic colonization. Across North America, Native people continue to have struggles including addiction, education, health, HIV/AIDS, poverty, and the continued trauma of colonization. Yet, despite these adversities, Native people, including Two-Spirit people continue to fight for improved quality of life and recognition that they are still here, still part of a vibrant and rich culture that believes in environmental, sexual, and social justice. These issues impact sexual health and vitality of Native people and should be included when working with Two-Spirit people and communities.

In order for there to be equity in the fields of sex education and sex therapy, Indigenous values and perspectives must be included. This will require a decolonial framework that can be applied to interventions, diagnostic procedures, and educational content. There is great wisdom to be learned from Indigenous epistemologies towards sexuality. By recognizing the fluidity of Native sexuality, sex therapists and educators can expand upon their own understandings of how their positionality may be impacting their epistemology (Takacs, 2003).

The sexuality field should also recognize for Native communities, prior to first-contact gender and sexual orientation variance were normative. This is reflected in the motto of the former Denver Two-Spirit Society: "Homophobia is not Indigenous to these lands; acceptance and diversity is" (n.d.).

Notes

1. The author of this chapter identifies as Two-Spirit and is an enrolled member of the Poarch Band of Creek Indians, a sovereign nation in the state Alabama located in the southeast United States.
2. The author of this chapter is an organizer for the BAAITS powwow.
3. *Urban Indian* is a phrase that is used to describe Native people who were either born and raised in urban environments or have relocated there from rural or reservation communities.
4. The Medicine Wheel is used by many Indigenous communities, and each quadrant may represent a different perspective, depending on tribal culture. Readers may also note a sense of familiarity with using Medicine Wheel concepts as this has been noted as a source of inspiration in the work of Dr. Gina Ogden (4D Method, 2018).
5. "Trickster energy" is a reference to stories in various Native American cultures wherein some kind of tricks, intelligence, or medicine are used to achieve a particular goal.
6. Pamela Hays created the ADDRESSING model after working with Alaska Natives and recognizing her need to deepen her cultural perspective. The acronym stands for: age, disability (life-long), disability (acquired), religion, ethnicity (race), socioeconomic status, sexuality, nation of origin, and gender. In my lectures with counseling psychology graduate students I added the BOLD acronym to include the body, occupation, lifestyle, and desires of the client(s).

References

Balsam, K. F., Huang, B. H., Fieland, K. C., Simoni, J. M., & Walters, K. L. (2004). Culture, trauma, and wellness: A comparison of heterosexual and lesbian, gay, bisexual, and two-spirit Native Americans. *Cultural Diversity and Ethnic Minority Psychology*, 287–301.

Barker, J. (Ed.). (2017). Getting dirty: The eco-eroticism of women in Indigenous oral literatures. In M. K. Nelson (Author), *Critically sovereign: Indigenous gender, sexuality, and feminist studies* (pp. 229–260). Durham, NC: Duke University Press.

Byrd, C. M. (2015). The associations of intergroup interactions and school racial socialization with academic motivation. *The Journal of Educational Research*, *108*(1), 10–21.

Constantinides, D. M., Sennott, S. L., & Chandler, D. (2019). *Sex therapy with erotically marginalized clients: Nine principles of clinical support*. New York: Routledge, Taylor & Francis Group.

Duran, E. (2006). *Healing the soul wound. Counseling with American Indians and other native peoples*. Multicultural Foundations of Psychology and Counseling Series. New York: Teachers College Press. Columbia University.

Foucault, M. (1978). *The history of sexuality*. New York, Vintage Books.

Garrett, M., & Barret, B. (2003). Two spirit: Counseling native American gay, lesbian, and bisexual people. *Journal of Multicultural Counseling and Development*, 131–142.

Gilley, B. (2006). *Becoming two-spirit gay identity and social acceptance in Indian country*. Lincoln: University of Nebraska Press.

Hays, P. A. (2001). *Addressing cultural complexities in practice: A framework for clinicians and counselors*. Washington, DC: American Psychological Association.

Kuhn, R. (2018, September 11). *Positionality and epistemology* (Lecture presented at California Institute of Integral Studies), San Francisco.

Linklater, R. (2016). *Decolonizing trauma work: Indigenous stories and strategies*. Vancouver, BC: Langara College.

Prenn, N. (2009). I second that emotion! On self-disclosure and its metaprocessing. In A. Bloomgarden & R. B. Mennuti (Eds.), *Psychotherapist revealed: Therapists speak about self-disclosure in psychotherapy*. New York: Routledge Press.

Raymore, S. (2018). Artist Statement. Retrieved September 20, 2021, from https://sheldonraymore.com/about

Roscoe, W. (1996). *The Zuni man-woman*. Albuquerque, NM: University of New Mexico Press.

Smith, L. T. (1999). *Decolonizing methodologies. Research and Indigenous peoples*. London, UK: Zed Books (and Otago University Press).

Takacs, D. (2003). How does your positionality bias your epistemology? *Thought & Action,* 27. Retrieved from http://repository.uchastings.edu/faculty_scholarship/1264

Vizenor, G. (2008). *Survivance. Narratives of native presence*. Lincoln, NE: University of Nebraska Press.

Wibur, M., Keene, A., & Tall Bear, K. (n.d.). Retrieved from www.allmyrelationspodcast.com/podcast/episode/468a0a6b/ep-5-decolonizing-sex

Wilson, W. A., & Yellow Bird, M. (Eds.). (2005). *For indigenous eyes only: A decolonization handbook*. Santa Fe: School of American Research.

13

HOLY SEX

Using Narrative Therapy and Mindfulness to Address Church Hurt and Embrace the Erotic

De-Andrea Blaylock-Johnson

Key Terms

church hurt: the pain individuals may experience that has been inflicted upon them by their religious institutions

Religious Trauma Syndrome (RTS): the condition experienced by people who are struggling with leaving an authoritarian, dogmatic religion and coping with the damage of indoctrination

Black Existential Theory: the philosophical discourse that tackles issues surrounding Black existence and critiques oppression; Unlike European existentialism, Black existentialism is rooted in the collective experience of People of Color and eschews individuation.

Church hurt is a term that is often used in Black religious circles to refer to the pain inflicted by houses of worship and other religious institutions. It can show up in many ways, but the result is often a separation from not only a specific place of worship, but a distancing from faith as a whole. Church hurt can be compared to Religious Trauma Syndrome in that although it is not an official diagnosis in the DSM 5, it can mimic symptoms of multiple mental health diagnoses. Religion has the power to influence many areas of our lives, specifically our views on and experiences of our sexuality. Because of this power, those who have experienced church hurt often also experience dysphoria, as it relates to understanding their own sexualities and having the freedom to express them. However, when able to reclaim and re-author their stories by using aspects of narrative therapy and mindfulness, individuals have the unique opportunity to define their own truths, even within Christian contexts, and fully embrace their erotic selves without shame.

DOI: 10.4324/9781003034063-14

Religious Trauma Syndrome (RTS) is a phrase first coined by psychologist Marlene Winell. She defines RTS as "the condition experienced by people who are struggling with leaving an authoritarian, dogmatic religion and coping with the damage of indoctrination" (Winell, 2020). She explains religious teachings that are particularly restrictive can severely impact cognitive, emotional, social, and cultural aspects of one's life and, in turn, can be terroristic and toxic. Terrorism can be described as using force or violence (or even the threat of violence) to intimidate and control. Although RTS is not listed in the DSM 5, it can mirror the symptoms of Post-Traumatic Stress Disorder, Major Depressive Disorder, Major Anxiety Disorder, and many other illnesses. Some religions, namely Christianity, use the threat of damnation and eternal separation from God to control sexuality. Because of this, people often repress their sexual desires for this fear of damnation and do not feel empowered to freely express themselves, often equating any type of sexuality outside of cisgender, heterosexual, monogamous marriage as deviant, flawed, and outside the will of God.

Although there is growing interest in Religious Trauma Syndrome, most information and resources are tailored towards those seeking to escape the White evangelical movement. There are conferences for those recovering from religion in hopes of finding community amongst those who are in similar situations. Conversely, there does not seem to be an equal amount of support for People of Color, specifically Black folks, who seek to maintain a connection to their Christian faith while recovering from church hurt and negative religious teachings. Part of this lack is the American church's inability to truly grapple with the myth of White supremacy and how it has influenced not only the spread of Christianity, but the shame that permeates the faith as it relates to sexuality and furthermore, Black sexuality. Kelly Brown Douglas explains that "Western Christianity's dominant approach to sexuality has contributed to White culture's ability to challenge Black people's humanity by impugning their sexuality" (Douglas, 1999). Additionally, "It is necessary for White society to control Black people's sexuality, meaning their bodies and reproductive capacities, so as to control them as a people. It is also necessary to impugn Black sexuality in order to suggest that Black people are inferior beings" (Douglas, 1999). By othering the sexuality of Black people, Western Christianity perpetuates the myth of White supremacy and further separates God's people from the gift of sexuality and sensual experiences.

It's important to understand that the separation of spirit from sexuality occurred during the early spread of Christianity with the influence of Greek ideas, specifically Platonic and neo-Platonic thought.

*A*ccording to Platonism the real world of value and beauty was that which could be perceived only by the soul. This world was conceived as timeless, changeless, and immaterial. The body and its senses could not *grasp such a world. To appreciate this world, therefore, one had to essentially deny bodily pleasures and activities, including sexual activity, and strive for a more contemplative, ascetic life.*

(Douglas, 1999)

Stoic philosophy of Rome further influenced Christianity by viewing sex as corrupt when it emerged from a place of passion. Since Christianity was formed as this Greco-Roman thought permeated the region of its creation, it adopted and integrated these ideas. Conversely, pre-Christian Hebrew life embraced sexuality as a gift from God and an integral part of the human experience, not a source of separation from the Divine.

In *Embodiment: An Approach to Sexuality and Christian Theology*, James Nelson explains:

The alienation of spirit from body, of reason from emotions, of "higher life" from "fleshly life" found both impetus and expression in the subordination of women. Men assumed to themselves superiority in reason and spirit and thus believed themselves destined to lead both civil and religious communities.

(Nelson, 1978)

This speaks to the idea of being the progenitor of modern Christian thought, which supports the myth of White supremacy and denigrates any types of connection to sexuality since it is seen as connected with femininity.

In *The Uses of the Erotic*, Audre Lorde describes the erotic as:

A resource within each of us that lies in a deeply female and spiritual plane, firmly rooted in the power of our unexpressed or unrecognized feeling. In order to perpetuate itself, every oppression must corrupt or distort those various sources of power within the culture of the oppressed that can provide energy for change.

(Lorde, 1984)

Her speech and (later) published essay assert that, for women, this has meant the suppression of the erotic is considered a source of power. However, it can be applied to Blacks in America as well. There is an idea that suppressing the erotic brings a closer proximity to Whiteness which, in turn, brings a certain level of safety. If you dress a certain way, conduct business a certain way, speak a certain way, and even have sex a certain way, you'll be accepted by a society that prioritizes and categorizes Whiteness as a standard to achieve. However, that proximity to Whiteness does not shield you from the damnation perpetuated by the myth of White supremacy and its effects.

Mindfulness has its beginnings in ancient meditation practices. However, Jon Kabat-Zinn popularized the modern-day understanding of it after founding the Stress Reduction Clinic at the University of Massachusetts Medical School in the late 1970s. Lori Brotto, however, explored ways in which to incorporate mindfulness into sex therapy to help women cultivate desire. Mindfulness is one tool that can help reintegrate mind and body, even though it seems the foundations of Western Christianity seek to perpetuate their separation. Additionally, there is power in telling your story. Narrative therapy provides a conduit and vehicle through which storytelling can be healing. In this chapter, we'll examine how by embracing the erotic and tapping into that source of power, Black Christians can reclaim sensuality and sexuality that is uniquely our own and still honors God by reintegrating spirit and sexuality and authoring our own stories.

Case 1: Jada

At 42 years old, Jada is a very recently divorced Black mother of three girls who has decided to explore her sexuality. She was born and raised in the church and is very active in her faith community. She currently attends a non-denominational church and serves as a trustee and a member of the choir. While married, she attempted to be a good, Christian wife by doing what she thought was the right thing according to her beliefs. She had sex with her husband whenever he demanded and sat through regular critiques of her performance, which he provided immediately after their intimate experiences. She had also neglected her own pleasure.

Although she did not have very many sexual experiences before those with her husband, she expected sex to come naturally and be easy after they got married. However, she never felt free to fully explore her desires or even experience pleasure. Solo sex was something she did not do because it was taboo; good girls don't do that. Besides, she believed you should deny your flesh, abstain from all expressions of sexuality, and focus on worshipping God. Unfortunately, the myth that sex will be magical after saving it for marriage did not prove to be true, and Jada was in a relationship with less-than-enjoyable sex. She began to lose desire. Additionally, a medical condition impacted her ability to self-lubricate, and the use of lubricants was frowned upon by her husband. She was enduring painful sex because she felt it was her wifely duty to make sure her husband was satisfied.

She remained faithful to their agreement of monogamy although her husband did not. She contracted several sexually transmitted infections from him, and he both denied having sex with other partners and blamed her for not meeting his sexual needs.

After deciding to separate from her husband, she did engage in solo sex to "get over the hump." When she started dating again and decided to become intimate with an attentive partner, her desire for sexual intimacy increased as did other noticeable signs of arousal. However, one thing remained elusive: orgasms.

When asked about her specific goals for sex therapy, Jada got straight to the point. "I've never had an orgasm, and I need to know if something is wrong with me." Also, she's not sure if she wants to abstain from having sex with her current partner.

Case 2: Les

Les is a 32-year-old same-gender-loving Black woman whose gender expression is masculine of center, much to the discontent of her mother. She explains that as recently as two years ago, her mother insisted she wear a dress to a family member's birthday party. She was incredibly uncomfortable the entire time but went along with her mother's wishes to avoid conflict. Les grew up attending a non-denominational church with her parents. However, her father joined the Church of Latter Day Saints when she was 13 years old. Although he did not insist the family follow him, Les noticed some changes in the way her family talked about God. She didn't come out to her family until she graduated from college and, with more conservative views shared by both religious traditions of her parents, she wasn't sure how she'd be accepted. What she learned was they would always love and accept her as their daughter, but she continued to feel damned by their religious communities.

She was diagnosed with depression and anxiety while in high school by a psychiatrist and is currently taking Escitalopram. Although she feels medication management has been helpful in dealing with anxiety, she has been experiencing sexual side effects, specifically delayed lubrication and overall decreased libido. She's just not as interested in sex as she used to be, although initiating had always been a challenge.

She's been in a monogamous relationship with her partner for almost five years but is considering making some changes. Her partner has been dishonest with money since the beginning of their relationship, although she only became aware of this after recently checking her credit report. Her partner opened a credit card in her name two years ago without her knowledge, and this uncovered more issues for them.

"I think I'm just an anxious person," Les said during the first session. "But I really want to learn different ways to deal with it. And I feel like I should be at least wanting to have sex. Right now, I'm just not ever interested. And church. I want to find a good church home."

Even though Les and Jada are facing very different challenges, both women are exploring the ways in which their Christian beliefs greatly impact their sexuality, be it expression of sexuality or finding a church that would be affirming and not just accepting. They are working on challenging some deeply held beliefs that may no longer serve them and deciding to write their own stories moving forward.

Insights and Guiding Principles for Therapy

Narrative therapy is based on the idea that through therapy, "the truth of experience . . . [is not] discovered, [it is] created" (Nichols & Schwartz, 2004). Therefore, the goal of therapy is not to learn facts, but to examine the deeper meaning that clients have attributed to their experiences. In using this model, therapists take the idea that problems arise because clients internalize self-defeating views and feel as though they have to perform as if the world is watching them. According to Wylie (1994), individuals internalize the demands of varying norms and ultimately become judges of themselves, "[policing] their own lives." Because of this, therapists encourage clients to externalize their problems, shifting from viewing themselves as the problems and beginning to see themselves as separate entities.

Narrative therapy tends to reject views of normalcy, specifically rejecting the characterization of overarching views of "normal" behavior. Furthermore, "when the stories people tell themselves lead to construe their experience in unhelpful ways, they tend to get bogged down with problems" (Nichols & Schwartz, 2004). These problem-saturated stories only perpetuate negative behaviors. As long as these stories exist and are not altered or fixed, the problematic behavior or belief will ensue. However, those using narrative therapy techniques do not focus on the behavior, but on the way in which clients narrate their experiences. Because the problems are externalized, therapists look outside towards cultural norms and ideas as possible causes to problem-saturated stories.

There are certain conditions for change in behavior, which include the act of deconstructing narratives. White (1992) explains that clients are encouraged to explore their "[private] stories and knowledge that guide their lives and speak to them of their identity." Externalizing is the first step, which is where therapists emphasize the fact that clients are not the problems themselves, but that they are dealing or working with problems. After externalizing these conversations, clients then encounter a landscape of action and consciousness questions (or relative influence questions) that lead them to further deconstruct their problem-saturated stories. Other techniques include assertive power over the problem, reading between the lines of the problem story, and reinforcing the new story. In rewriting the story, clients are not simply identifying the positive aspects, but this process engages clients in exploring hidden meanings the therapist may not be able to decipher.

One aspect of narrative therapy is existentialism, which examines the idea that reality is socially constructed, can be influenced by language and cultural context, and that there is no objective reality or absolute truth. In Christianity, however, one of the guiding beliefs is that Jesus is *the* truth, meaning there can be no objection to this idea for believers. Because of this incongruence, it can seem challenging to use this model of therapy for those with a deeply held belief of what *the* truth is. However, it can be helpful to explore the ideas of Africana Critical Theory or Black Existential Philosophy for Black clients. Lewis Gordon, an American philosopher, explains that although European existentialism is "'predicated on the uniqueness of the individual as well as on a universalist conception of humans and their obligation to self,' Africana critical theory or Black existential philosophy is predicated on the liberation of all Black people in the world from oppression (Bassey, 2007)." The White concept of self is overwhelmingly independent. However, the Black concept of self includes community and the idea of a collective experience. With this in perspective, Black clients can interrogate their deeply held beliefs without threatening their idea of truth as it relates to faith, but they can understand that examining or objectifying truth does not have to involve dismantling the foundation of their religion. It can include assembling their own ideas about how their beliefs about sexuality came to be and moving forward with creating stories for themselves that make sense.

Mindfulness provides an opportunity to be fully connected to our physical selves. Although early Christian texts were influenced to separate the mind and body, being fully connected to our body and emotions connects us to a sense of power. The Bible itself explains that we are temples of the Holy Spirit; that the Divine resides within each of us. In reintegrating mind, body, and Spirit, we are able to tap into that Holy Ghost Power and truly experience life as whole persons through God, even in sex. With the varied messages about sex outside of monogamous heterosexual marriage being sinful, spectatoring or being outside of the body during sex can be a normal occurrence when your sexual experiences don't mirror the model. However, learning to be fully present to explore pleasure and tap into the erotic can provide a space and conduit for healing.

Case Application

Jada

Jada's initial focus of therapy was her inability to have orgasms. Although she had been married for over 10 years and had sexual partners before that, she explained she did not have orgasms. I asked her of her definition of an orgasm and she explained that although she sometimes enjoyed sex, "nothing comes out. It will feel good, but I don't have that big finish." While using a vulva puppet to reference anatomy, I explained that "during orgasms, there are involuntary muscle contractions of the vagina that may occur after stimulation of the vulva or any other area of the body. There is also a release of 'feel good' chemicals in the brain such as dopamine and oxytocin which can contribute to feelings of closeness and joy. Female ejaculation is a separate phenomenon, but sometimes simultaneous event. Some people with vulvas may experience the expulsion of liquid from the urethra during stimulation while others may not." I also explained that it is not urine, although some scientific tests show the presence of urine in the fluid.

After hearing this, a look of confusion, then relief washed over her. "Well, I think I've had that. All this time, I thought that cuming meant that I had to have something come out of me. I think I may have had an orgasm."

Here, simply providing clear and concise information was beneficial. Jada had not been exposed to comprehensive sexuality education and never had "the talk" with her mother. She was piecing together a definition of orgasm from porn (which she did not often consume) and rare conversations about sex with friends. After being provided with this information, Jada was able to appropriately evaluate her past experiences and was open to further exploration, specifically her ideas about having sex with her new partner.

"I've always been worried about how I was performing since my husband was giving me a scoresheet afterwards, just felt inadequate. He'd say things like, 'Your mama didn't teach you anything about being a woman. What kind of woman don't know how to give head?' But with my boyfriend, I laid it out for him. I told him I'm not that sexually experienced. I may not be the best at new positions. And you know what he said? He said we can learn together. But what really doesn't make sense to me is that I can have sex with this man, my ex, who is emotionally abusive and gave me chlamydia while I was pregnant with our daughter. That's perfectly okay in the eyes of God, but if I decide to have sex with this man who respects me and is patient and kind and is willing to provide for me, it's a sin? That just don't make sense to me. And then I feel convicted when I go to church. I feel like I can't worship God because I had sex with a man I'm not married to."

We began to explore the stories Jada was telling herself about herself and her experiences. In deconstructing the idea of a "good girl," she was able to examine how holding onto this ideal perpetuated feelings of inadequacy. We also discussed how her personal theology influenced her ideas about sexuality. However, in learning she could create her own personal ethic, Jada was able to become open to new ways of understanding her faith and how healthy sexual expression does not have to be antithetical to it.

Earlier in treatment, Jada explained that she was open to bibliotherapy, but would prefer short articles as opposed to books. She explained that with her career as a hospital administrator, she just didn't have a lot of time to spare. She was directed to examine various articles by Candice Benbow, a Black feminist Christian theologian and essayist whose work centers the experiences of Black women and invites them to embrace themselves as good creations. After reading several of her articles, Jada was able to move past externalizing problems and move into asserting power over her problems by encountering consciousness questions.

Les

A big part of working with Les was helping her to change her language about herself. She would often refer to herself as an anxious person. However, in externalizing the problem she was able to move to say she experiences anxiety, not that she is anxious. Also, one of her concerns was her ability to be present while having both partnered and solo sexual experiences.

"It's like I'm having an outer body experience. I'm there, but I'm stuck in my head. It's easy to focus on her pleasure, but I don't feel comfortable with her touching my chest or putting all her attention on me. I'm not able to really enjoy it." I then asked her to talk about times where she felt connected to her body.

As a hobby, Les is a boxing instructor and works out regularly outside of classes. She explains that, "when I'm moving, I'm focused. I have to be, as you say, 'in my body' to make sure I'm properly demonstrating the moves so that I and my students avoid injury. I'm paying attention to specific movements, so I'm all in." I asked, "What do you think helps keep you present? What reminds you to stay connected to your body?" "I'm actually just enjoying myself," Les replied. "I'm feeling the sweat on my forehead, the tension of my body, and I think just focusing on the different movements is what keeps me in the moment."

"When people think of mindfulness or meditation," I explained, "people often think of yoga or sitting still in a lotus position, working to clear your mind. However, mindfulness is not about emptying your mind or abandoning our to-do lists. It's about applying the idea of present-moment focus to all areas of our life, even sexuality. The way you are able to focus on the movements of your body during boxing can be applied to sex and can help with staying connected with your body."

We then discussed ways to recreate this feeling of connectedness in sexual situations. Les shared she was more comfortable with masturbation than with partnered sex and would feel comfortable with exercises that included solo sex.

In session, we completed a mindful eating exercise using my favorite brand of gummy bears. In this exercise, we were careful to honor all the senses and allow for reflection for each (sight, smell, touch, sound, and taste). Les was able to discuss how she noticed when she initially put the gummy bear in her mouth, she noticed she began salivating, even before biting into it. We later talked about how that was related to the mind-body connection, how her mind was preparing her body to help with digestion. We also talked about how arousal works in this way, and Les was able to make connections between mindful eating and mindful masturbation.

Strategies and Highlights

Throughout treatment, both clients were assigned a series of homework assignments, specifically Yass or Nah, a worksheet created and published by Rafaella Fiallo and Dalychia Saah, social workers and sexuality educators who are the brilliant minds behind Afrosexology. When asked, neither Jada nor Les were able to clearly identify specific sexual acts they enjoyed, explaining they never gave themselves space to explore their desires but always worked to fulfill those of their partners. However, this worksheet provided an opportunity for them to clearly identify things they may like to try solo or with a partner. Another helpful resource from Afrosexology that was assigned to Jada was the *Solo Sex Workbook*. This workbook takes individuals through a variety of exercises that assists them in examining their deeply held ideas and beliefs about sexuality and rewriting their own sexual ethic. Exercises in the workbook actually assist clients in rewriting their own stories about past experiences and describing pleasure they would like to explore.

Specific techniques used from narrative therapy include:

- Externalization of the problem
- Deconstructing the problem
- Examining unique outcomes
- Existentialism through the lens of Africana Critical Theory or Black Existential Thought

Mindful masturbation was suggested and completed as home assignments to help clients better connect with their bodies and begin to focus on their own pleasure. Other mindfulness exercises were completed in session, such as the mindful eating earlier described and mindful breathing.

Additionally, clients were invited to think critically about how their beliefs about sexuality were informed by their faith communities and were given a safe space in which to interrogate those ideas. Since both clients identify as Christians, we were able to incorporate scriptural study in sessions, and clients were invited to look at the Bible as both the inspired word of God and a work written within a certain cultural context.

Lessons Learned by the Author

One of the biggest lessons I learned was how straightforward certain aspects of narrative therapy were integrated into practice. The core techniques of externalizing the problem and deconstructing larger problems into smaller issues helped clients to clearly identify their self-defined goals. However, the challenge was presented with the idea of existentialism for Christians. In viewing this technique through the lens of Black Existential Philosophy or

Africana Critical Theory, this helped to make that aspect more approachable for Christians who hold one specific truth that is not debatable. Additionally, in reframing mindfulness as something that does not have to be a still meditation, clients found it more approachable and were more apt to include these practices. Also, examples of individuals doing the hard work of interrogating their beliefs normalized this process for clients.

Critical Questions for Readers to Consider

1.   What are ways in which conventional models of therapy can be made applicable for People of Color, specifically Blacks in America?
2.   How can constructing new narratives about religious beliefs support clients in their healing journey?
3.   How can therapists create space for Black Christians to interrogate ideas about sexuality and embrace Audre Lorde's ideas about embracing the erotic?

Suggested Readings and Additional Resources

- Afrosexology.com
- CandiceBenbow.com
- *The Deep Yes: The Lost Art of True Receiving* by Dr. Rosalyn Dischiavo
- *What is Narrative Therapy: An Easy to Read Introduction* by Alice Morgan
- *Existentia Africana: Understanding Aficana Existential Thought* by Lewis R. Gordon
- *The Cross and The Lynching Tree* by James Cone
- *Liberating Sexuality: Justice Between the Sheets* by Miguel A. De La Torre
- *Pure: Inside the Evangelical Movement That Shamed A Generation of Young Women and How I Broke Free* by Linda Kay Klein

References

Bassey, Magnus O. (2007). What is Africana critical theory or Black existential philosophy? *Journal of Black Studies, 37*(6), 914–935.
Lorde, A. (1984). *Sister outsider*. Berkeley, CA: The Crossing Press.
Nelson, J. B. (1978). *Embodiment: An approach to sexuality and Christian theology*. Minneapolis, MN: Ausburg Publishing House.
Nichols, M., & Schwartz, R. (2004). *Family therapy concepts and methods* (6th ed.). Boston, MA: Allyn and Bacon.
White, M. (1992). Deconstruction and therapy. *Dulwich Centre Newsletter*, No. 3.
Winell, M. (2020). *Religious trauma syndrome*. Retrieved from http://journeyfree.org/rts/
Wylie, M. S. (1994). Policing our lives. *Family Therapy Networker, 18*(6), 49.

14

QUEERING "STRAIGHT" BLACK RELATIONSHIPS

Navigating Sexual Behavior and Relationships with Black Heterosexual Individuals and Couples in the Southern United States

Marla Renee Stewart

Key Terms

Gender Role Strain (GRS): "GRS encompasses psychological distress associated with failing to meet masculine ideals, difficulty enacting and maintaining normative masculine expression, and negative experience with the masculine socialization process" (Fields et al., 2015). I also apply this to the feminine ideals, expression, and socialization, as well.

Religious Trauma Syndrome (RTS): As defined by Winell, "RTS [Religious Trauma Syndrome] is a function of both the chronic abuses of harmful religion and the impact of severing one's connection with one's faith."

non-monogamy: Dating multiple people or having multiple serious relationships happening at the same period of time.

polyamory: A sexual orientation that emphasizes having multiple loving relationships.

BDSM: A sexual orientation that emphasizes power exchange amongst sexual and/or non-sexual partners.

kink: A sexual or non-sexual behavior that involves using sexual energy to do a behavior that has not been normalized to the individual.

Introduction

The Southeastern part of the United States, popularly known as the Bible Belt, has been a breeding ground for various repressions around sexual identity and behavior. When it comes to navigating sexuality, the South has been

DOI: 10.4324/9781003034063-15

notorious for shaming and stigmatizing people based on their sexual orientation, sexual identity, and/or sexual behavior. This is commonly rooted in religious trauma from family upbringing, as well as identity tropes, such as the "Southern Belle" and the "Southern Gentleman," which cause identity strain and tension.

In this chapter, I aim to do three things:

- Examine sexual identities and behavior with Black individuals and couples, especially as it relates to femininity and masculinity
- Educate counselors, therapists, coaches, and sex educators around the nuances of Black sexualities in the South
- Give practical techniques to help release religious and/or identity tension

As a sexologist, a sex coach, and a sex educator, I have seen many Black clients who have struggled with their identities, which ultimately affects their communication and behavior patterns. This includes, but is not limited to anal sex, kinky sex, bisexual identities, and diverse (or alternative) relationship styles. Using Intersectionality and Queer theoretical frameworks have enabled my success with working with clients who are not used to being understood, usually because of their heterosexual and patriarchal privilege, and I use these frameworks to open the dialogue that would otherwise be silenced. The practical lessons that I learned are highly useful and could be used effectively by therapists, counselors, and coaches when they approach Black individuals and couples.

Background

Working in the South, I've had the opportunity to coach many clients who have come to me because of my particular expertise in non-monogamy/polyamory, communication, and sex skills mastery. Most individuals who come and see me are trying to understand themselves and have a better connection to their desire, or they are couples who are trying to get to the bottom of their sex life that has fizzled out and needs resuscitation. The reasons are varied—ranging from past sexual trauma to opening up their relationship—and being able to address these have made me a stronger coach and educator.

The South has a reputation for niceties and tradition, and Black people are "returning" to the South to experience these things, along with economic opportunities that are not as feasible in the more expensive West and North (Woodward, 1996). In addition, in urban centers where Blacks are either the majority or a large portion of the population, it's easier to find a greater range of identities in the realm of all the Blackness in these communities. However, the pervasive identity tropes of the Southern Belle and the Southern Gentleman are salient, and the behaviors that go with those identities are highly favored.

The Southern Belle is a woman who embraces the domestic sphere and embodies femininity, delicacy, gentility, hospitality, beauty, simplicity, and submissiveness, as well as welcomes the role of "nurturing mother, dutiful wife, and social moral pillar" (Brown, 2000). The complement to that is the Southern Gentleman, who oversees the economic survival and protection of the family, as well as follows suit to chivalry and class with an embodied masculinity. Black women and Black men submitting to this identity trope essentially buy in to the White patriarchal societal standard, which may or may not be beneficial for them and their families.

Having these Southern gendered and stereotyped ideologies can cause Gender Role Strain (GRS). Fields et al. (2015) explain that "GRS encompasses psychological distress associated with failing to meet masculine ideals (discrepancy strain),[1] difficulty enacting and maintaining normative masculine expression (dysfunction strain),[2] and negative experience with the masculine socialization process (trauma strain)."[3] We can also apply this to the feminine, where there is distress associated with failing to meet feminine ideals, difficulty enacting and maintaining normative feminine expression, and negative experiences with the feminine socialization process.

In addition to the GRS, religious trauma is rampant in the South. Marlene Winell states that "RTS [Religious Trauma Syndrome] is a function of both the chronic abuses of harmful religion and the impact of severing one's connection with one's faith."[4] While some of my clients have a complete disconnection with their faith, some people's faith still remains intact as they struggle with religious tension from their own thoughts and behaviors and religious doctrine. Navigating this can be really difficult, especially if the ties to the religion are tight and there is still an element of subscription to their religious stronghold.

It's also possible that we can also see these kind of strains on a person's identity through a person's deviance, which, in sociology is named as an action or behavior that contradicts societal norms, whether formal or informal. I'll be referring to deviance as "non-conformity" as it pertains to heteronormative patriarchal societal standards in the South. Non-conformity in this chapter applies to bisexualities and behaviors around bisexuality and heteroflexibility for cisgender women, anal sex for heterosexual cisgender men, non-monogamy (including infidelity and open relating) and/or polyamorous relating, and kinky behavior as it is associated with BDSM.

A Brief Note on the Theories

Intersectionality and Queer theory are the two frameworks that shape my work. The main concept of Intersectionality, coined by Kimberle Crenshaw in 1989, is that race is the first and foremost attribute that is signified to people. This theory posits that categorical identities (i.e., non-monogamous/ polyamorous, kinky, etc.) and/or demographics (i.e., race, sex, age, class, ability, gender, education, occupation, etc.) work dialogically to shape people's life experiences. Sandoval (2000) states that in *ourselves* and in *our* bodies and identities, *we* are both the oppressor and the oppressed, which is salient throughout my times with my clients.

Queer theory tends to construct and deconstruct, destabilize and stabilize definitions that are problematic to people who are non-normative, and therefore, oppressed by a variety of social institutions. My clients' experiences exemplify Queer theory. While destabilizing essentialist notions of what a person is supposed to do sexually, they are stabilizing their sexual acts as durable parts of their sexuality. At the same time, they are visible as People of Color, and because of this, they destabilize the notion of being kinky and non-monogamous/polyamorous (because studies reinforce that participants who mostly engage in these communities are white). Concurrently, they stabilize the hypersexual moniker ascribed to kinky and non-monogamous/polyamorous communities, not because they are hypersexual or sexually immoral, but because of society's lack of knowledge about the variation of Black sexualities and communities.

Integrative Strategy

Because I am a sexologist and a sex coach, my approach is a combination of sex therapy, somatic therapy, and comprehensive sexuality education. Although I'm not a psychotherapist, I do make connections and talk through sexual functions, sexual feelings, and intimacy with individuals and couples, which is quite similar to the actions of sex therapists. With regards to somatic therapy, I use breathwork, vocal work, movement, touch, and massage. The comprehensive sexuality education that I use includes giving young people and adults knowledge about sex and sexuality, reflecting on what a healthy attitude looks like, developing their personal awareness and sex skills, and helping them recognize their life and sexual values so that they can make healthy and appropriate choices for their sex lives. My own personal practical curriculum that I've formulated over the years is a reflection of these strategies and aforementioned theoretical approaches. Because it is an integrative approach, it has allowed me to see the issues from different angles, as well as to problem-solve the issues quickly to enrich the relationships of individuals with themselves and for couples with themselves *and* with each other.

Introduction of Cases

Case 1: Eva and Damien

Eva, 37, and Damien, 32, were friends for five years before they began their on-and-off relationship for one and half years. For the past three months, they were going to talk therapy once a week to figure out more about themselves and about each other. Eva is a very successful performance artist and vocal actor with two young teenage boys. She owns her own house and she's self-sufficient all around. Damien is younger than Eva, unemployed, and occasionally makes money as a video gamer by acquiring social media followers. He moved into Eva's house with her two children and is usually in the bedroom rarely interacting with the children. Eva and Damien both have health problems. Eva has some thyroid issues for which she takes medication, and she also has some reproductive issues because she was born with two uteruses. Damien has daily aches and pains due to Sickle Cell and takes pain and anxiety medications. They are in a monogamous relationship where Eva is encouraged to experiment with other women through their occasional swinging and threesomes. However, at this time, their sex life is currently non-existent.

Eva's goals:

- A better relationship and sex life with Damien
- To build up her sexual confidence and self-esteem
- To be more comfortable about her sexual attraction to women

Damien's goals:

- To learn more about himself
- To find new ways to love and express his desire with Eva

They are particularly struggling with their sexual life because Damien sees Eva "like a man" and feels like she lacks sexual experiences, especially as it pertains to sex with other women. Eva self-proclaims that she has a lot of masculine energy and that she has trouble balancing her feminine and masculine energy, despite Damien invoking his masculinity and dominance in the bedroom.

After our first few sessions together, it was evident that they had a mental connection, but their sexual connection faded after six months because they were bored with one another. They wanted more of an organic connection, but after those sessions, they realized that their sex life had to be more calculated in order to drive that "organic" connection for the future. In addition, I also realized there was a lot of restraint in their communication, so I decided it would be best to temporarily suspend the couples' sessions and get to know them individually.

In my first individual session with Eva, I learned that she actually desires to be in a monogamous relationship, but she knows that Damien will be turned on if she has sex with other women on her own time and then tells him the details about it. She feels like she's on a constant quest to turn him on, and the more that he indicates that he's bored, the more her self-esteem is negatively impacted. Raised in the South, she's determined to adhere to the Southern Belle identity trope but is finding an incredible amount of GRS regarding her role as a "dutiful wife" (despite not being married) and not fulfilling her duty to please her partner accordingly. Her stress level with regards to keeping Damien happy makes her anxious and feeling like a failure.

In my first individual session with Damien, he expressed that he'd rather have an open relationship so that he can explore who he is and date more people, but that he doesn't want to lose Eva. He expressed that he was originally attracted to her because she was confident, self-sufficient, and a great performer; he was also impressed with her Verizon cell phone and American Express credit card. (He claimed that "Black people don't have those," so he was impressed by the status that those items had for him.) At the same time, he was also turned off by her having two kids with two different fathers; he'd prefer to have one father for all kids (including his thoughts of future kids with her). He stated, "I don't have time to spend and build with kids that aren't mine," feeding into the Southern Gentleman trope of not protecting a family that isn't his, while giving examples of how she is a weak mother. Even with the differences in their values, he felt like she was good for his future, but he was not happy in the present.

Application of the Integrative Strategy

Right away, I felt the need to tackle Eva's confidence. One of my strategies is to identify the things that a person wants to change about themselves by reframing their negative characteristics, re-anchoring their somatic feelings, and then equalizing and boosting other positive qualities about themselves, including their sexual self. Within this exercise, you have to identify the positive aspects to those negative characteristics (which is often the hardest part of this exercise) and then you have to identify the counter aspects to those negative characteristics (which is another way of identifying the opposite of those characteristics). This is all done using positive affirmations that are present-tense. Bonus points if the affirmations evoke emotion and involve a justification.

In my practice, some people break open and affirm things that they have (sexually) repressed, which in Black cisgender women sometimes looks like crying and in Black cisgender men sometimes looks like anxiety and questioning of their own identity. While doing this exercise with Eva, she made a realization that she actually enjoyed women and wasn't just doing it to please her partner. Many memories came back to her as she cried and voiced how she had to repress her feelings for women because it was not welcome in the South, so she did her best to try and shut those feelings out. We talked in detail about those feelings and decided that she should journal about what other feelings and behaviors she might be repressing due to her socialization.

With Damien, I felt it was best to name all of his values around relationship styles, children, finances, and sex life. These tend to be the things that break relationships apart, so I felt it was best to understand where he stood on these issues so that he could make the best possible decision for himself and for this relationship. We talked about each of these things in our sessions together, and he was encouraged to journal outside of our sessions about how he wanted his future to look, as well as how he intends to have a relationship with Eva in the future.

Because they were separate, I encouraged them to be more integrated in each other's lives, which included Damien spending more time with the children and helping with their discipline. I also encouraged open dialogue to talk about their sexual experiences, emotional and physical, outside of the relationship to see what kind of boundaries were going to be best for them. By the time our sessions concluded, Eva had restored most of her confidence, Damien assumed a parental role and became employed, their sex life picked up, and they even bought a house together to establish a partnership that worked for them.

Case 2: Tracy and Robert

Tracy, 33, and Robert, 31, came to me after knowing each other for ten years and being married two months. They are both Muslim and raised in the South. Tracy is an activist and criminal defense lawyer who loves fanfiction, and Robert is a restaurant manager. His brother is crashing on the couch for a while, and his sister and his sister's boyfriend are staying with them in the house, which causes them to spend most of their time in the bedroom. Tracy finds penis-vagina sex painful and uncomfortable, and she feels that she needs to relax. She was sexually assaulted ten years ago, right before knowing Robert and is not sure whether or not it is affecting her ability to have sex with him.

Their goals:

- Get to a place where they can enthusiastically make love at least two times a week
- Attain a better sexual connection and genuinely understand each other's feelings, fears, and physical limitations
- Be more open and grow together sexually with open communication and mutual respect
- Enhance their sex skills

Tracy and Robert's religious views caused some tension in the relationship (one week before the wedding, Robert converted to Islam). While Robert was laxer when it came to their religion, Tracy often would be stricter around religious dogma.

Tracy is extremely turned on by Robert, often comparing him to Malcom X. She is also turned on by his anger and when he yells at her. Robert is turned on by Tracy's body and loves to hear her past stories of when she's been with other men in extreme detail. Her taking control sexually is something that turns them both on, but they are unsure how to approach their sexual life in this manner, since they had been taught that the man should be the lead and that the woman should be there to follow.

Application of Integrative Strategy

In the first couple of sessions, I asked them questions so that they could define their sexual relationship identity. This model of work is adapted from Dr. Ian Kerner in his book, *Sex Detox* (2008). I found that modifying some of the questions to get to the root of how they want their ideal sex life to look like helps couples get an idea of what they see in their sexual future with each other. Having them answer the questions together allows them to have conversation and compromise on what feels good to them. For couples who are not good at communication, this is a great first step to help them realize that they need to talk about what they want in order to start a more sexually satisfying relationship. I coupled this with homework of daily appreciations and increased affection, which includes kisses upon entering and leaving a space, kisses whenever you pass by your partner, and a one-minute hug every day to help increase the dopamine and oxytocin in each other.

To accomplish their goal of having sex at least twice a week, we needed to work on penis-vagina sex. Tracy says that Robert's penis is very big and sex is often painful. Instead of diving right into sex, I helped them learn more about themselves with seduction and foreplay. We went over their Seduction Learning Style© from *The Ultimate Guide to Seduction & Foreplay* (Stewart & O'Reilly, 2020), combined that with their Love Language˚ (Chapman, 2014), and then figured out which erotic activities they would like to try and which ones turned them on and had them share these with one another (from a non-exhaustive list that I created). After understanding these things, they each individually came up with a seduction plan for how they can turn on each other. With the combination of some comprehensive sex education around Tracy's vagina and helping Robert understand her body more, we were able to make some major headway with less painful vaginal penetration and move into more pleasure and eventually better orgasms for Tracy.

Through our talk sessions, we learned that Tracy was extremely turned on by power and dominance. Since she loved fanfiction, I tapped into this by asking her what characters she sees herself and her husband playing. We then explored this fantasy, and she was encouraged to write her own personal fanfiction where she embodied Marie (Rogue) and fantasized Robert as Logan (Wolverine) of the X-men. Her homework was to embody the powerful character that she had imagined and to dominate the sexual interaction. They were extremely satisfied and even ventured into pegging[5] as a way to explore more of their sexuality and pleasure zones in their respective bodies. They really loved this part of the work and it was assigned occasionally throughout our time working together.

Although, we tackled many issues in the nine months together, there are still some issues that need to be addressed that came up in the work, including shame and guilt with the anal sex (from Tracy, not Robert) and embracing more role play in their sexual interaction. Unfortunately, since the COVID-19 pandemic had a negative effect on their household, including more people moving in and Robert being unemployed, they had to pause their work with me in order to stay within their budget constraints.

Strategies Used

- Building Sexual Confidence Exercise (Stewart & O'Reilly, 2020)
- Breaking down values, with regards to major social institutional factors
- Sexual Relationship Identity (Kerner, 2009)
- Seduction Learning Style© (Stewart & O'Reilly, 2020) and seduction and foreplay strategies
- The 5 Love Languages® (Chapman, 2014)
- Erotic activity sheet
- Integration of client's hobbies into their sex lives
- Sex education around vaginal anatomy and pleasure and sexual assets

Lessons Learned

With these two cases, I learned that the Southern tropes that cause GRS are deeply ingrained and need quite some time to analyze and break down the many aspects of where the guilt and shame are coming from. Using these strategies to unlearn these ideas that are stunting their sexual growth is necessary to move forward to see progress in their lives. With the integration of the various strategies, using their imagination and fantasies were ways for these clients to get away from the Southern tropes, suspend their GRS, as well as a way to escape persistent religious dogma. I learned that once they have used these strategies, their self-confidence went up and they were better able to communicate effectively, engage more intently with their partner, and become more satisfied with their sex life.

Critical Questions for Readers to Consider

1. What are some other ways that you can combat GRS with people who are/have been deeply committed to a community identity or an identity trope that is harmful?
2. The intersections of Blackness and sexuality vary depending on geography, so if you are working locally, what are the ways that you are researching Black sexualities in your communities?
3. Do you think queer people in the South will benefit from these strategies if they subscribe to these identity tropes? Why or why not?

Suggested Readings

- Richardson, R. (2007). *Black masculinity and the U. S. South: From uncle Tom to Gangsta*. Athens: University of Georgia Press.
- Russell, T. (2008, March). The color of discipline: Civil rights and Black sexuality. *American Quarterly, 60*(1), 101–128.

Notes

1. Psychological strain that results when one fails to meet external or internalized masculine expectations or manhood ideals.
2. Psychological strain or other negative consequences that result from maintaining normative masculine expectations. Although these expectations or male characteristics may be viewed as desirable, they can have negative side effects on the men themselves and those close to them.
3. Psychological strain resulting from experiencing the masculine socialization process, particularly during childhood, adolescence, and early adulthood.
4. https://journeyfree.org/rts/
5. Pegging is when a woman anally penetrates a man while wearing a strap-on. Typically the individuals are cisgender, but this is not always the case.

References

Brown, A. G. (2000). The women left behind: Transformation of the southern belle, 1840–1880. *The Historian, 62*(4), 759–778.

Chapman, G. (2014). *The 5 love languages: The secret to love that lasts*. Chicago: Moody Publishers.

Fields, E., Bogart, L. M., Smith, K. C., Malebranche, D. J., Ellen, J., & Schuster, M. A. (2015). 'I always felt I had to prove my manhood': Homosexuality, masculinity, gender role strain, and HIV risk among young black men who have sex with men. *American Journal of Public Health, Research and Practice, 105*(1), 122–131.

Kerner, I. (2008). *Sex detox: Recharge desire. revitalize intimacy. Rejuvenate your love life*. New York: HarperCollins e-books.

Sandoval, C. (2000). *Methodology of the oppressed*. Minneapolis, MN: University of Minnesota Press.

Stewart, M. R., & O'Reilly, J. (2020). *The Ultimate Guide to Seduction & Foreplay: Techniques and Strategies for Mind-Blowing Sex*. Jersey City, NJ: Cleis Press.

Woodward, C. (1996). Look away, look away. *Journal of Southern History, 59*, 489–504.

15

BLACK POLYAMORY

Exploring the Complexities of
Race and Sexual Freedom

Ericka Burns

Background

Polyamory challenges cultural and social norms since many people are taught that only two people can have an emotional attachment and/or sexual relationship. This ideology and practice opposes social norms and is a counternarrative and revolt against the ideas of what a healthy relationship should look like. Polyamory is presented as a form of sexual freedom that can be expressed by any person (Easton & Hardy, 2017). However, for Black people, that freedom does not come as easily. Poly spaces are still mostly White and even though Black people are invited to poly events, there are still some who must face being the only Black person in the room (Sheff & Hammers, 2011). Navigating White poly spaces is nothing new for Black people, but when discussing sexual freedom, Black people may want a break from code switching. Code switching is how people navigate all forms of communication in different social settings; for example, using your "White voice" at work (McWilliams, 2018, para 4). Code switching is a survival tactic Black people use in White spaces especially.

When introducing Black people to polyamory, there are major factors to keep in mind. First, sex educators and therapists must acknowledge that Black sexuality has been viewed as hypersexual (Wyatt, 1997; Collins, 1990; Collins, 2004). Being poly attempts to relinquish control over societal norms; however, according to Mireille Miller-Young the author of *A Taste for Brown Sugar: Black Women in Pornography*,

*B*lack gender and sexual outsiders—sex workers, queers, gender *nonconformists, and others—offer a lens through which to view how*

DOI: 10.4324/9781003034063-16

racial power is always bound to gender and sexuality, and how those
persisting under these intersecting oppressions labor to negotiate and
shape the forces of race, gender, and sexuality in their lives.

(p. 28)

Those who embrace polyamory may be considered as sexual outsiders. Sexuality therapists and educators may need to have additional training that takes into account some of the stereotypes and myths surrounding Black sexuality and its impact on how clients (and therapists) perceive themselves during therapy or educational observation. Therapists and educators have to be able to observe and understand the power dynamics of race, gender, and sexuality in order to provide better insight on how to negotiate spaces that are predominantly White as well as how to be comfortable in spaces that may be exclusive to Black and Brown members of the poly community.

The second factor to consider is that there is a divide between Black and White poly communities (Easton & Hardy, 2017). Kevin Patterson, the author of *Love's not Colorblind: Race and Representation in Polyamorous and Other Alternative Communities*, discusses how race is a factor in poly spaces and that there are some White people who do not see that Black people and other People of Color "could have different experiences . . . in mostly-white polyamorous spaces" (2018, p. 30). Patterson discusses how when searching online or on social media, those who lead the discussion on polyamory are White scholars and that includes books and resources about polyamory. Patterson asked a question that I have been asking for years: "But where are the people of color?" (2018, p. 45) Patterson continues to state,

If the topic is about love and acceptance, why is the scope of representa-
tion so limited? Why are so few respected names using their influence
to raise the voices of marginalized people? And more importantly, why are
we hesitant to address this in the same loud-and-proud manner that we
address one-penis policies?

(Patterson, 2018, p. 45)

Due to the lack of representation in research and educational resources, how can Black people feel safe and supported? Ron Young, cofounder of an international support group called Black & Poly, stated that "Polyamory may be many things to many people, but, as a [B]lack man, I see it as an opportunity to break free from the chains that have bound us for so many years, by empowering us to shed the way we've done things in the past and embrace true freedom for *all* through loving with intention and compassion" (para 6, nd). Sexual freedom should not just be for White people; freedom belongs to all.

Educative Approach: Comprehensive Sexuality Education

Comprehensive sexuality education allows for students to learn more about their body and sexual health, all while creating a space to discuss their values and beliefs around sex, relationships, and other health-related issues. One challenge that emerges, depending on the state, school district, family beliefs, and/or lack medically accurate information, is that many students do not get the opportunity to learn about their sexual health. As a sex educator, I have two jobs: (1) provide youth with information without shame while creating a supportive environment, and (2) fill in the gaps of adults who missed these lessons. I am often pulled aside or messaged by adults of varying ages about sexual health issues because they were not taught about it in school. When it pertains to poly relationships, this is no different. Many people are asking the same questions I received in high schools and colleges:

- How do I protect myself?
- How do I communicate my needs to my partner(s)?
- How can I express my sexual desires without feeling shame?

I have worked with Mark and Felicia for over a year and these were some of their initial concerns with me. Felicia brought up the idea to Mark about opening their relationship, and now she wants a stable triad with another woman. Communication has been a huge factor in their relationship since they initially met through online dating. Mark and Felicia are both open communicators and completely supportive of each other's sexual and emotional desires. Since they are new to the poly world, it was important for me to provide them both with resources that are specific to their needs, such as finding an online community they can be a part of and navigating finding a partner who would best support their growing family.

Case: Mark and Felicia

Mark is a 28-year-old Black and Mexican, heterosexual, cisgender man. He is married to a woman, Felicia, and they are in polyamorous relationship with each other. Felicia is a 26-year-old Black, bi-romantic, bisexual, cisgender woman. This is both Mark's and Felicia's first poly relationship, and they are currently navigating this new adventure with each other. Felicia expressed a desire to eventually have an additional partner and both agreed that this will support their growing household since they have two children and one on the way.

Originally, their understanding of a poly relationship was about them focusing on their relationship as the "main" or "primary" relationship while they dated and had sex with other people who they met via online dating. Their relationship with each other provided the emotional support they needed, while their other partners were purely physical and sexual. As time went on, Felicia was more interested in having a more stable partner to support both Mark's and Felicia's emotional needs, not just the physical needs. Felicia has stated, "No more unicorns!" Currently, they both have girlfriends, and they are assessing whether their partners are willing to join their growing family. They are prioritizing their time with each other, and each person can schedule dates with their girlfriends as long as it does not conflict with their time with their family. Felicia feels that having a triad would provide help with their family; however, they have yet to meet a partner who they are willing to bring around their children. Home dynamics such as childcare, living arrangements, and financial support have yet to be discussed thoroughly with their respective partners until everyone is comfortable.

Discussion Points

The following are some of the main concerns of Mark and Felicia that will be addressed:

- Bringing another partner to their relationship
- Co-parenting with a third partner
- Potentially having children with third partner
- Cohabitating as a triad with children

Coaching Strategies

1. Meeting people where they are.

    - Acknowledge the anxieties of meeting new people while being introverted and address the issues pertaining to race and belonging.

2. Provide resources to support client needs.

    - Rather than general advice that dismisses race, gender, and sexuality, it is important to provide support systems that will meet the needs of their relationships.

Case Application: Black and Poly Dating

Mark: I think that [being mixed] as far as preferences . . . people may have some advantages to some degree as far as people who are looking to talk to them. . . . Though I am Black and Mexican, I identify as being more Black because there's a culture around me. I feel that there are some aspects of my life that are different than those who are completely Black.

Counselor: Can you explain what advantages you are talking about?

Mark: I feel like as far as people's attractiveness, people tend to be attracted to lighter [complexions]. I would be considered "light-skinned" . . . and I think that for some people who [say they] would not "date Black guys," they wouldn't have a problem dating me because I don't necessarily look Black. I am lighter-skinned, I look more Hispanic, though you can see that I am mixed.

Colorism does play a part in dating and in everyday life. Colorism is discrimination based on the color or shade of someone's skin, and this is seen in interracial and intraracial dynamics. Colorism's history links back to slavery and colonialism that particularly affect "Africa, Asia, and the Americas" (Townsend, Neilands, Thomas, & Jackson, 2010, p. 274). Lighter complexions with features closer to Whiteness elevated someone's social status amongst Black Americans (Wallace et al., 2011; Townsend et al., 2010). However, in the 21st century, these stereotypes still continue. Social media, especially Black Twitter and Instagram, have used "Team Light Skin" and "Team Dark Skin" to describe the characteristics of Black people. Those of lighter complexions are seen as stuck up and appearing to be above everyone else, while men of lighter complexions are thought to have more "feminine" qualities such as being more emotional compared to men of a darker complexion who are seen to be more tough and "manly." Mark is noticing these differences as he navigates online dating. Online dating does provide a way to "swipe" past someone based on their looks without personal interaction; however, I am sure people still notice who may or may not be interested in participating in a sexual or romantic relationship.

Counselor: Have [you and Felicia] ever been to any meet-ups for poly folx, or anything like that?

Mark: We've wanted to [attend parties] however . . . we aren't very social as is. So, it seems like a lot of work and for us to put a lot of effort to talk, be social, and I do not want the feeling to be fake. They may think that because we are at this party that we are outgoing people and I am definitely not. I prefer a one-on-one interaction.

Counselor: If you do decide to go to a party, do you have any concerns about being tokenized or being the only Black people there, how would you feel about being in those spaces?

Mark: I don't worry about being a token because I do not think I fit the norm of being an African American adult male. I have always been very different. I would feel that I was outcasted than being the token. . . . I feel that people wouldn't necessarily want to talk to me because I feel I would be the second-rate pick if it were me and other White people. I wouldn't feel that I would fit in, and I wouldn't feel the "token-ness" of it all.

Counselor: From what I am hearing, it appears that online dating feels safer and more comfortable than being in a large social setting.

Coaching Strategies

1. Meet People Where They Are

For those who seek another partner for their relationship, there are several factors to consider. First, race is an important factor that cannot be ignored. When Mark and I discussed specific race preferences, he stated that it did not matter to him; however, he did notice that mostly non-Black women reach out to him online and, aside from his wife, he does not experience too many Black women who are interested in dating him. His experience with women who "don't date Black guys" but will date someone who has a lighter complexion is not a new phenomenon since, historically, lighter complexions are deemed more desirable than darker complexions. Even though Mark stated that he does not have a racial preference, he noticed who was and was not considering him as a potential partner.

Second, being poly does not always equate to being a social person. Mark made a point about appearing as "fake" if he attended a poly party or meetup since it was not true to who he is. He has expressed some anxiety around attending because he does not want to feel like a "second-rate pick" and no matter the setting, from picking teams for dodgeball to poly meetups, no one wants to feel that way. Though it may feel unfortunate, it is the reality of Black people who enjoy expressing their sexuality in ways that are not socially accepted, and it is important to be aware of a person's safety and well-being. As an introverted couple, they primarily use dating apps to find partners. I introduced them to the Black & Poly online dating website so that they can create a joint account for themselves and specifically choose the best poly configuration that is best for them. The best social interaction for this couple would be online modalities in order for them to take their time meeting and getting to know someone new.

2. Provide Resources to Support Client Needs

When sexuality coaches and educators suggest meeting people in a larger social setting (e.g., night clubs or parties), this can trigger social anxieties including anxiety pertaining to race, initiating and maintaining communication, or uncertainty about how to negotiate intimacy. Mark stated that dating apps work best for him to avoid those feelings, which is a way for him to remain safe while dating. Felicia is a bit more social but prefers dating apps to provide a better opportunity to get to know someone before meeting them in person. Felicia is not against going to a poly meet-up, but she is still learning about these spaces and would like to take things slow. This is their first poly relationship, so it is best to go at a pace that feels comfortable for the both of them. I wanted to provide resources that cater to their needs of continuing to meet people online and learning about Black and poly experiences:

- Black & Poly—online dating resource for Black poly individuals and partnered-relationships
- Black Poly Nation—Instagram and Facebook group for in-person or online meetups
- *Love's not Color Blind: Race and Representation in Polyamorous and Other Alternative Communities* by Kevin Patterson

Love's not Color Blind by Kevin Patterson was recommended because this book is a rare find where a Black man specifically addresses concerns, fears, and anxieties of being Black and poly.

Case Application: Loving a Black Woman

Counselor: How do you define your experience being poly and Black?

Felicia: As a Black woman . . . there is common knowledge that being Black already has its downsides. Being a Black woman . . . everything that I've known growing up, if I were to describe a Black woman off the top of my head the first thing I think is angry, overly proud, that's what's been engrained in me through my life through the negative things I hear about Black women. But I also hear that we are powerful, we are strong, we are beautiful, and we love hard. I think that is a huge pro in being a lesbian or bisexual or a woman loving another woman, that when [Black women] love, we love hard and I can only imagine what it would be like . . . but I am excited to love another woman like that.

Counselor: Wow. It is powerful that despite what you hear about Black women, you are still interested in loving a Black woman. Sounds like by loving a Black woman, you are healing yourself from the negativity that you hear as well.

Coaching Strategies

1. *Meet People Where They Are*

Felicia is not the only Black woman who has heard multiple negative messages about themselves. Black women have been controlled by race and gender politics since slavery, thus creating harmful stereotypes about Black women (Wyatt, 1997; Collins, 1990; Collins, 2004). What was profound was how Felicia praised how Black women love strong and is excited to be in a relationship with a Black woman in order to share the commonalities of being strong and powerful together. Black women's desirability has always been in question (Miller-Young, 2014; Avery et al., 2021).

Before meeting Mark, Felicia was a single Black mother of two children, which is often deemed undesirable based on racist stereotypes to shame Black women (Avery et al., 2021). Not only is Felicia facing stereotypes of being a "Jezebel" or "undesirable," she is breaking barriers and establishing a relationship where she is supported by her partner to ensure that her needs are met. When Felicia talked with Mark about adding another partner to their relationship, he was completely open to it. He feels that it will be an opportunity to support Felicia's sexual needs, all while supporting their growing family. According to Easton and Hardy (2017), marriage is no longer needed as a means of survival; rather, "we marry in pursuit of comfort, security, sex, intimacy, and emotional connection," and it appears that Mark and Felicia's relationship supports this (p. 11). Healing Black women starts by supporting what is best for them despite societal norms. This does not dismiss the realities of how their extended families may feel or how their religion affects them; rather, this is a starting point to support, heal, and affirm Black women's desires.

2.   Provide Resources to Support Client Needs

I wanted to find resources that are supportive of Black women's sexuality and that have a grasp of the cultural foundations and context that impact sexual decision-making and functioning. The following are recommendations that center Black women and pleasure:

- *Black. Queer. Southern. Women.: An oral history* by E. Patrick Johnson— This is a beautiful oral history of women and their experiences exploring their sexuality. Recommending this book hopefully will allow Felicia to see Black women and their sexuality outside of those stereotypes that she was used to hearing.
- *Pleasure Activism* by adrienne maree brown—Pleasure is a right, and accessing pleasure as a Black woman is a revolutionary act.
- UrbanXPlay—Supportive Black kink and poly community
- Poly Patterson—Provides some insight on more dynamics of a Black and poly relationship
- Black and Poly Nation—Provides supportive events, information, and educational resources for poly folx

Lessons Learned by the Author

Polyamory challenges traditional relationships as we know it. Being Black and poly creates a freedom that couples are tapping into without shame and with support from their partners. As professionals, we can create spaces that support sexual freedom among Black men and women, rather than perpetuating damaging stereotypes. What was not discussed with Mark and Felicia was the use of social media because they do not use social media as often, but there are online support groups such as the Black & Poly Facebook group or the #BlackandPoly hashtag that is useful for Instagram and Twitter users. Even these online resources are limiting because, depending on your location, one may need to travel to find others who are Black and poly. As they both start to become more comfortable with introducing a third partner to their family, I will continue to work with them to assist with that transition. This transition might not be easy for their extended family since being poly challenges many people's moral beliefs that may have been developed by religious beliefs and/or upbringing (Easton & Hardy, 2017). Working with this couple has taught me that there is still more work to be done to expand the amount of accessible resources. However, as more Black people start to explore their sexuality and challenge heteronormative values, we can truly start to liberate Black sexual pleasure.

Critical Questions for Readers to Consider

When working with poly Black folx, please consider the following:

- Discuss expectations of being in a poly relationship and the type of poly dynamic that is best for them as individuals and/or for their relationship(s).
- Talk about how their racial identity might impact sexual experiences and partner selection.
- Address the anxieties of meeting new people in unfamiliar spaces, including White spaces.
- Discuss values, expectations, and roles of family members and how that can support or hinder sexual and relational experiences.
- Develop communication skills around issues of sexual and emotional needs.

References

Avery, L. R., Stanton, A. G., Ward, L. M., Cole, E. R., Trinh, S. L., & Jerald, M. C. (2021). "Pretty hurts": Acceptance of hegemonic feminine beauty ideals and reduced sexual well-being among Black women. *Body Image*, 38, 181–190.

Collins, P. H. (1990). *Black feminist thought: Knowledge, consciousness, and the politics of empowerment.* New York: Routledge.

Collins, P. H. (2004). *Black sexual politics: African Americans, gender, and the new racism.* New York: Routledge.

Easton, D., & Hardy, J. W. (2017). *The ethical slut, third edition: A practical guide to polyamory, open relationships and other freedoms in sex and love.* Emeryville: Greenery Press.

McWilliams, A. (2018). *Sorry to bother you, Black Americans and the power and peril of code-switching.* Retrieved from www.theguardian.com/film/2018/jul/25/sorry-to-bother-you-white-voice-code-switching

Miller-Young, M. (2014). *A taste for brown sugar: Black women in pornography.* London: Duke University Press.

Moultrie, M. (2018). Putting a ring on it: Black women, Black churches, and coerced monogamy. *Black Theology: An International Journal, 16*(3), 231–247. doi: 10.1080/14769948.2018.1492304

Patterson, K. (2018). *Love's not colorblind: Race and representation in polyamorous and their alternative communities.* Portland, OR: Thronetree Press.

Roberts, D. (2018). *Killing the black body.* New York: Vintage Books.

Sheff, E., & Hammers, C. (2011). The privilege of perversities: Race, class and education among polyamorists and kinksters. *Psychology & Sexuality, 2*(3), 198–223. doi: 10.1080/19419899.2010.537674

Townsend, T. G., Neilands, T. B., Thomas, A. J., & Jackson, T. R. (2010). I'm no Jezebel; I am young, gifted, and Black: Identity, sexuality, and black girls. *Psychology of Women Quarterly, 34*(3), 273–285. doi: 10.1111/j.1471-6402.2010.01574.x

Wallace, S. A., Townsend, T. G., Glasgow, Y. M., & Ojie, M. J. (2011). Gold diggers, video vixens, and jezebels: Stereotype images and substance use among urban African American girls. *Journal of Women's Health, 20*(9), 1315–1324.

Wyatt, G. E. (1997). *Stolen women: Reclaiming our sexuality, taking back our lives.* New York: John Wiley & Sons, Inc.

16

WOMEN OF ASIAN DIASPORA AND BDSM

Understanding Layers of Identity Impacting Kink Exploration and One Practical Strategy

Midori

Key Terms

internalized racial tropes: Racial tropes are stereotyped narrative of behavior ascribed to individuals who are from, or are assumed by others to be from, certain racial, ethnic, or cultural groups. These are repeated in the greater community in media and daily social interactions. BIPOC people, as being part of the greater community, are as likely to believe in these, consciously or subconsciously. These beliefs may be held about other racialized groups or about their own people and groups.

gender performance: A person's behavior and expectations formed by cultural or community norms based on expectations of masculinity and femininity. This plays out in gender roles in families, workplace, romantic and sexual relationships, and other realms of life. A person can experience varying degrees of stress and strain when their own desires, wants, and drives don't align with these gendered expectations.

sex positive self-actualization: A process of seeking and striving towards a more authentic state of self, which includes a compassionate and humanistic embracing of one's erotic and sexual evolution.

Introduction

This chapter considers the impact of intersectionality of identities, layers of gender performance expectations, internalization of racialized sexual tropes, and BDSM role stereotyping for women of Asian heritage in the US as they explore sexual and erotic satisfaction in kink. We will consider a method

DOI: 10.4324/9781003034063-17

using an intentional linguistic shift and a pragmatic model for individuals and their partners to better assess and explain their desires and engage in more fulfilling play. While we consider a specific population here, the investigation of layers of multiple role expectations, the limitations they cause, and strategy shared can be effective with other multicultural and BIPOC peoples.

As a sexuality educator, I facilitate small-group, multi-day workshops on BDSM, erotic dominance play, and empowerment for women and feminine-of-center people. In this supportive group environment they discuss their assumptions around BDSM desires and unpack the assets and liabilities they bring to their erotic lives. I work with them through extensive pre-workshop writing and reading assignments, group exercises, workbooks, and one-on-one office hours. Many of them continue to work with me in private coaching sessions with objectives going beyond sex and BDSM.

Background

Demographics and the Asian Diaspora

Tallying intake forms from 2018 to 2019 roughly 18% of those who attended my workshops at the ForteFemme Women's Dominance Weekend Intensiveare Asian or Asian-mixed heritage. Comparatively while this is higher than the general Asian-American population of 5.7% (US Census Bureau, 2020), the erotic milieu, the overall presence of those with Asian heritage in the BDSM social sphere is likely smaller than the general population. I base this on first-hand observation, but more importantly on the subjective reporting of my Asian heritage students. I prioritize their perception here. How they see themselves represented or not contributes to how they understand and internalize behavioral norms for kink play and kink-centered socializing.

The umbrella term of *Asian* refers to a vastly diverse population. According to US Office of Management and Budget and the US Census Bureau, "*Asian* refers to a person having origins in any of the original peoples of the Far East, Southeast Asia, or the Indian subcontinent, including, for example, Cambodia, China, India, Japan, Korea, Malaysia, Pakistan, the Philippine Islands, Thailand, and Vietnam." This extends to Hmong, Laotian, Cambodian, and further national or ethnic groups. Depending on the individual, people of Pacific Island heritage may self-identify or be perceived by others as Asian. This is well over 20 countries, hundreds of languages, and a vast array of histories, political and religious backgrounds, and economic and education status (Pew Research Center, 2021).

The Asian diaspora includes people who may not identify with externally imposed "race" or their ancestral heritage and who can be easily misidentified by others. For example, CT, a 48-year-old bisexual cis female American woman was born to a Filipino father of Chinese ancestry and a White mother. CT identifies as a Filipina. She reports that many identify her as Chinese, though she does not. The Asian diaspora in the 19th century created populations of Chinese heritage people in Chile and Japanese heritage in Brazil who may identify as Latinx. South Asians in Africa are another example. BF, a 45-year-old gay cis male, a naturalized Canadian citizen living in Chicago, is from South Africa and is read as Black, but he identifies as Asian-Canadian and aligns himself with his Indian heritage.

In the US, nearly 74% of the adult Asian population were born in other countries (Pew Research Center, 2021). The historical forces of the Asian diaspora is reflected in the number of generations in each ethnic group that are born in the US. For example, Japanese people began arriving in the US in the 19th century, and today only 27% are foreign born, while recent refugee arrivals, such as the Bhutanese, are nearly all foreign-born today. Of the foreign-born, some came over as children with their families, maintaining linguistic and cultural practices to their cultures of origin. Others emigrate as adults, maintaining or abandoning cultural practices. Many still were adopted, such as the Korean adoptees after the Korean War, as infants into predominantly White American families and socialized into the cultures of their adoptive families. LK, a 42-year-old queer cis female from Texas was adopted from Korea as a child into an Italian American family. She is most comfortable identifying as an Italian American Texan but recently is identifying with and learning about her Korean heritage. She started her introduction by saying, "I'm not a typical Asian." To which I enquired, "What do you think is a typical Asian?"

From the Families and Cultures of Origin

With this vast diversity also comes a wide variance in gender, relationship, and sexual expectations that people carry over from, and internalize from, their families of origin.

EM, a 65-year-old bisexual cis female is a fifth-generation Japanese American. While her family maintained linguistic and social connection to Japanese communities in San Francisco, they were integrated into the middle class social norms of the Bay Area. She felt at ease in dating and partnering with White partners, taking the leadership role in family decisions, and eventually seeking out queer poly relationships and being fully out to her family about non-traditional relationships and kink. She feels her identity and sexuality is accepted by her family.

On the other hand, RS, a 40-year-old Indian American woman from a Brahmin caste family, is the first of her family to be born in the US. After dating several White men in her twenties, she experienced discomfort and disappointment. Eventually she sought out a monogamous marriage partner through an Indian matchmaker to a man of the same caste but different linguistic group. They have chosen a family life that's fairly traditional to her family's culture. Her family is overtly homophobic, but other than that she feels her wants and her family's expectations of her gender role to be in alignment.

Alternatively, MK, a 50-year-old queer cis female immigrant from Japan who came over as a young adult, questioned much of her cultural expectations of gender performance and explores BDSM in a predominantly White social circle. She feels misunderstood and in opposition with her family's expectations of her social and sexual role.

Several of my students have reported that their Asian families consider sex positive self-actualization and sexual affinity-based socializing to be a "White thing." As such they have not mentioned their interest in BDSM to them.

The Stereotypes

Despite this rich diversity of the Asian diaspora, the majority of Americans are unaware of this complex reality. Instead, people are lumped together under a single label of "Asian" and its accompanying stereotypes. The Asian heritage individual themselves may be inured to this simplification, internalizing stereotypes and racist ideas of the population they live in.

These stereotypes extend into expectations of tropes of sexual behaviors. Here are some common stereotypes that have come up for my students:

- Asian women are submissive.
- Asian women are dragon ladies.
- Asian men are submissives and bottoms.
- Asians are compliant or pliable.
- Asian men are asexual, passionless.
- Asian = feminine or effeminate.
- Asians are quiet and smart.
- Asians don't make trouble or object.

Common Source and Strategy for Learning About Kink and BDSM

People today gain information, knowledge, and skill about BDSM through combination of various sources. The followings are some common pathways:

- Partners
- Posts in dating and hook-up websites
- Porn
- Social media

- Blogs and podcasts
- Romance novels and other fiction
- Munches—in-person social gatherings
- In-person play events
- Classes, virtual and in-person
- Online articles
- Instructional books
- Sex workers, including but not limited to professional dominants

Most of these sources rarely have Asian representation, if any. When they do, most of these sources repeat or perpetuate stereotypes in various ways. Some BDSM porn capitalizes and furthers harmful stereotypes and race/color fetishization. Even sources that are conscientious and responsible generally represent BDSM through the lens of White bias. Tropes about Asian women's sexuality and kink behaviors are widespread and deeply engrained.

If we consider only the factors listed here, as there are more, a woman of Asian diaspora in the US must contend with these following pressures as she accesses her BDSM fantasies and actually explores play. That is, if she is able to recognize her own desires through these layers (Figure 16.1). Some will internalize the stereotypes and assumptions, which may lead to internalized racism or shame. Some will deny or reject BDSM as an erotic option to reduce the negative stress from these factors. Some may settle for less-than-fulfilling sexual activities as an internal compromise.

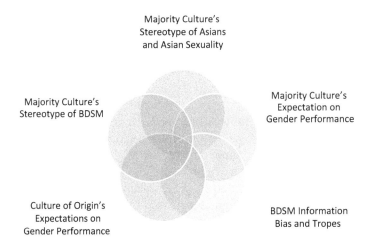

Figure 16.1 Layers of Internalized Behavioral Expectations, Gender Performances, and Racial Tropes—A simplified diagram.

When working with women of the Asian diaspora and BDSM:

- It is important to gain compassionate understanding of the client's complex narrative of identity within the Asian diaspora and how this impacts their sexual identity.
- Encourage curiosity towards discovery of genuine satisfaction and joy by disentangling from pressures, stereotypes, and tropes.

Strategy of Shifting Pleasure Framework Through Languaging:

We begin by examining the assumptions the client has around the commonly used BDSM terms. I have listed the terms below. Then we investigate what the client believes that the BDSM communities and general public assumes around these terms.

- Dominant
- Submissive
- Sadist
- Masochist
- Top
- Bottom
- Switch
- Master/slave

The purpose of this is to address a very common issue for my students. They, and their partners, assume the commonly used BDSM terms have universal or standardized definitions. This, in combination with internalized racism and stereotyping can lead to miscommunications or failure to accurately identify and explain one's own desires and expectations clearly. The outcome may be experiences ranging from suboptimal sexual pleasures to consent violations.

Also clinicians and clients may be working using muddled notions layered with assumptions and stereotyped behavioral expectations, blocking effective progress.

I re-introduce these terms with reframed definitions around "appetites," or recreation-seeking behavior to create a desired temporary change of state. This has the effect of removing the notion of one having to have permanent attachment to any particular kind of play or race or gender-adhered roles. In my work, this method has been received with relief and active use. This is a practical and judgment-neutral framework. Many of my students have actively incorporated the information here with great success, clarifying communication, enhancing mutual satisfaction, reducing misunderstandings, de-colonizing, and de-stigmatizing consensual pleasure-seeking.

Clarifying Terms

Dominant: A shorthand to mean that at the moment the person is likely to experience sensual, sexual, systemic arousal, and/or change of state through the temporary redistribution of authority, hierarchy or control towards them. I use the analogy of Lead-Follow in paired dancing.

Submissive: A shorthand to mean that at the moment the person is likely to experience sensual, sexual, systemic arousal, and/or change of state through the temporary redistribution of authority, hierarchy or control away from them.

Sadist: A shorthand to mean that at the moment the person is likely to inflict or direct the sensual, sexual, systemic arousal, and/or change of state through creating intense sensation in another. Intense sensation is subjective and does not require it to be pain.

Masochist: A shorthand to mean that at the moment the person is likely to experience sensual, sexual, systemic arousal, and/or change of state through creating intense sensation in another.

Top: An umbrella term, originally used by gay men about the person penetrating. Quickly it was absorbed into gay Leather culture to mean the person doing actions on another. Shortly thereafter it was generalized to a broader base of kink practitioners.

Top may indicate the person sexually penetrating, the person interested in redistribution of authority towards them, or person creating intense sensation. Use and intention varies widely between individuals, social circles, demographics, generation, and geography. Because of the ambiguity of meaning, we should consider "top" or "to top" as a beginning of a conversation.

Bottom: An umbrella term, originally used by gay men about the person being penetrated. Quickly it was absorbed into gay Leather culture to mean the person receiving another's action. Shortly thereafter it was generalized to a broader base of kink practitioners.

Bottom may indicate the person sexually being penetrated, the person interested in redistribution of authority away from them, or person receiving intense sensation. Use and intention varies widely between individuals, social circles, demographics, generation, and geography. Because of the ambiguity of meaning, we should consider "bottom" or "to bottom" as a beginning of a conversation.

Switch: Rather than adhering to a binary model, take into consideration the previous terms. Someone who switches taps into a broader a la carte menu of desires.

Not all of their interests are present at all times to all people.

I often use the term "Box Jumper" in conjunction with the Appetite Grid.

Master/slave: Structure of relationship between people of consented, opted-in, authority-distributed decision-making. This framework exists to identify a unique bond. Terms of relating are used to streamline decision making, to enhance a sense of belonging, to express and cherish one another. The objective of this structure in itself is not to create change of states through play, though play can happen (or not happen) within the relationship. M/s (master/slave) Relationship or D/s (dominant/submissive) Relationships are often confused with M/s Play or D/s Play. Language of master and slave is often very problematic to many, especially but not limited to BIPOC people. I often use the example of "Thing 1 and Thing 2" to decouple from the very real and terrible reality of enslaved or trafficked peoples.

Thought Squirrels: Conscious or subconscious mental chatter of all sorts. This is the antithesis of mindfulness. I find people grasp this concept and phrase instantaneously. Acknowledgement that we all have "thought squirrels" tends to reduce blame and focuses the attention on active solutions to "squirrel-be-gone."

The humor of this term makes this effective and significantly less intimidating than "practicing mindfulness," which can be perceived as a "White person activity" by many BIPOC people.

Active Appetite Statements, Not Identity Labels

The terms (*dominant, submissive, sadist, masochist, top, bottom and switch*) are all about transitory appetites. I emphasize that these are not concrete or constant personality traits, nor are they consistent across context and the arc of one's life and relationships.

Successful BDSM scenes, like hunger and a good meal, are likely to resolve in reduced or dissipated desires.

I encourage people to "speak in verbs, not nouns." Examples:

Instead of "I am a dominant:"

- "I want to dominate you tonight."
- "I hunger for your submission."
- "Let me dominate the hell out of you!"

Instead of "I am a bottom:"

- "Let me bottom to you today."
- "Bottoming to you turns me on like crazy!"

Using these active terms, I've created a table called Midori's Appetite Grid (Table 16.2) and presented it at the 2018 American Association of Sexuality

Table 16.2 The Appetite Grid—From my class "Best Kink Advice Nobody Told You."

		Control		
		Neutral	*Dominance*	*Submission*
Sensation	Neutral	Vanilla	Dominance Sensation Neutral	Submission Sensation Neutral
	Sadism	Egalitarian Sadism	Dominance Sadism	Submission Sadism
	Masochism	Egalitarian Masochism	Dominance Masochism	Submission Masochism

Educators National Conference to help clinicians and educators support their clients identify their desires in the moment. This is understood to be temporary and for the purpose of fun and joy. This basic table may be used in many nuanced ways to examine discordant desires while in the moment, unspoken expectations, scene shifts in mid-play, multiple partner scenes, and shifts of desires over time. We practice naming our BDSM desires in the moment, separate from cultural or stereotyped expectations.

Case Study: SC

SC, a 43-year-old first-generation Taiwanese-American cis woman from San Francisco was raised with traditionally Chinese gender role expectations by her immigrant parents. She was told by her parents that she should not be so "bossy" or no one will want to marry her. She was taught to be calm, kind, and nurturing, and she was admonished for being physically competitive with her younger brother. As the oldest child she was expected to be responsible and successful in academics. Her Californian socialization, however, gave her feminist ideals in her girlhood and early teens, which conflicted directly with values her parents raised her with. She discovered the alt-sex and BDSM communities, where she experimented with various aspects topping and bottoming. She encountered many men who assumed that she would be submissive to them due to her ethnicity. She was drawn more towards being "bossy" and delighted in discovering that her joy in dominance was considered desirable by many.

She found it extremely challenging to understand what she wanted, and she felt she often failed to negotiate successfully. She also experienced confusion and disappointment that she didn't seem to reconcile her general kindness with her sadistic desires, and potential partners' expectations of her style of dominance.

We used the Appetite Grid intensively in a series of drills during the class, and also as ongoing assignment over a period of two weeks, to identify desires, desire shifts, and intensity.

She was able to successfully assess her wants and to convey them effectively to partners. She also gained greater confidence in identifying potential partners who were imposing racist stereotypes on her in approaching her for play.

Counseling Strategies for Consideration

Here are some potential cues for engaging counseling strategies:

- When the client begins to speak using common labels listed earlier, take that as an opportunity to unpack what they mean and their expectations around these roles and labels.
- Are they feeling stress or pressures to perform or experiencing expectations that echo common racial tropes listed earlier?
- Do they equate sexual roles with their gender roles in everyday life?

Lessons Learned

An important lesson I learned is the complexity of layers of identities that Asian diasporic women live with and the barrier that this creates in accessing their authentic desires or fantasies.

I am seeing more clearly the potential harm of the culture of polite silence on part of Asian women. Asian diasporic people are often seen as "model minorities," believed to be academically, economically, and socially successful. Many of them come from cultural or familial background that shames discussion of sexuality or seeking mental health support. Several cultures elevate the idea of silent suffering as a virtue. Japanese call this *Gaman*. I realized that these factors combine to make it very challenging for the women to seek help.

I've found that there aren't much writing, resources, or discussion on Asian diasporic women and their sexuality. This reality doesn't help clinicians in their work with their clients. It is my hope that more nuanced discussion and research will emerge as we move forward.

In the meantime, following are my thoughts on how clinicians may help address sexual wellness and sex-positive self-actualization for their clients. As clinicians work with Asian heritage women exploring BDSM or kink these are some points to consider:

- Complex factors of cultures, family, stereotypes of race and gender contribute to Asian heritage women limiting their exploration of BDSM.
- What assumptions about Asian heritage people and women has the clinician been exposed to or internalized?
- Partners and therapists may also be making assumptions of their sexuality because of these tropes. This can complicate their communication with their partners and their therapists.

- Acknowledging and listening to the complexity of the client's intersectionality by the therapist will greatly improve the therapeutic process.
- Simple but powerful reframing of language of BDSM, accompanied by the Appetite Grid tool, may rapidly decrease stress and empower the person.

Suggested Readings

Hardy, J., & Easton, D. (2003). *The new topping book* (2nd ed.). Emeryville: Greenery Press.

Hardy, J., & Easton, D. (2015). *The new bottoming book* (2nd ed.). Emeryville: Greenery Press.

Henkin, W. (1996, 2015). *Consensual Sadomasochism.* Los Angeles: Daedalus Publishing.

Midori (2005). *Wild side sex: The book of kink.* Los Angeles: Daedalus Publishing.

Taormina, T. (Ed.). (2012). *Ultimate guide to kink: BDSM, role play and the erotic edge.* Jersey City: Cleis Press.

References

Budiman, A. & Ruiz, N. G. (2021, April 29). *Key facts about Asian American, a diverse and growing population.* Washington, DC: The Pew Research Center. Retrieved from https://www.pewresearch.org/fact-tank/2021/04/29/key-facts-about-asian-americans/.

Midori. (2018, June). *Midori's appetite grid.* Workshop presented at the American Association of Sexuality Educators, Counselors and Therapists 2018 Annual Conference. Denver, CO.

United States Census Bureau. (2020, April 30). *Asian and Pacific Islander population of the United States.* Retrieved from https://www.census.gov/library/visualizations/2020/demo/aian-population.html.

INDEX

Page locators in **bold** indicate a table
Page locators in *italics* indicate a figure

Black woman: defined124, 132; loving/
relating to 203–204
Bond, Susan B 127
bottom/bottoming (sexual position) 210,
212, 213–214, 215
box jumper/jumping 110, 111, 213
Boyd-Franklin, Nancy 52
Brotto, Lori 179

Canada: gay communities, working with
76, 82; indigenous population
3, 35
Carrillo, Héctor 94, 97
Cass, Vivienne C 79
Cauldwell, David O113
chattel slavery 53, 124, 201, 203
Chinese GL (gay/lesbian): identity
awareness, developing 78, 83; identity
validation 88; intergenerational
differences 89; therapeutic alliance,
establishing 84–85
Chinese LGBTQ+: discrimination against
83, 89; mental health issues 77, 84
church hurt 176–177
cisgender 10, 18, 31, 80, 117, 130, 144, 192
clinical supervision, practice of 8–9, 11
code switching 32, 197
collectivist culture 76
Collins, Patricia Hill 124–125
coming out process: disclosure of sexual
identity 76, 80–82; stages of 79–80
consensual non-monogamy 136, 144
(CNM)
couple and family therapy (CFT) 9–10,
14–15
Crenshaw, Kimberlé Williams 4, 8, 189
cultural humility: concept of, lifelong 85;
defined as 35, 49, 76; practice of 36, 40

de Shazer, Steve 17
DeGruy, Joy 52
Dell, Don M 27
Dhamoon, Rita Kaur 8
discrimination: colorism 201; minority
status 76, 95; racial 15, 32, 52–55,
135; sexual 10, 83; sexual health and
wellness 4, 8, 47
diversity: appreciation of 5, 173, 210;
gender, transgender 114; training 30;
underrepresentation of 2
diversity, equity and inclusion (DEI) 30
dominance 191, 194, 208, 215, **215**
dominant 127, 212–213, 214

dual minority status 76
Duran, Eduardo 167, 171

Easton, Dossie 204
educators: empathy toward settlers 40;
role of1–3, 5–7, 36, 39; sexuality,
resources for 133
Epston, David 17
Espín, Oliva 94, 96
ethnosexuality 135, 138, 141–142, 144,
147

Ferber, Abby L53
Fields, Erroll (et al) 189
Foucault, Michel 173
Franklin, Anderson J 52
Freud, Sigmund 112–113

gender: colonized gender 118–119,
121; dysphoria 109–110, 112, **121**;
euphoria 110, 116–117, 120, **121**;
gender expression 109–111, 119, **121**,
166, 180; gender non-conforming
109–110; gendered expectations
118–119, **121**
gender identity: defined as 109–110, 112;
disclosing 76; process; disorder 114;
rejecting 82; spirtuality and 45; see also
coming out
gender labels: 2SLGBTQQIA 35, 36,
39; gay 77, 80–82, 86, 144; gender-
queer 10, 15, 111; lesbian 77, 79, 203;
LGBTQI 164; trans/transgender 109;
Two-Spirit 109
gender performance: expectations 207,
210, *211*
gender role strain 187, 189
Gendlin, Eugene T 70
Greenlee, Alecia 26

Halberstam, Judith 115
Hamer, Forrest M 27, 29
Hardy, Janet W 204
Harvey-Braun, Doug 44
Haskell, M 125
Hays, Pamela 174n6
hetero supremacy, theory of 10, 17–18
heterosexism, addressing 9, 84
heterosexual: identity 26, 31, 56, 65, 80,
112, 188–189, 199; non-heterosexual
identity 79–80, 167; relationships 11,
14, 36; stereotyping 4, 19, 54,
177, 182